BRITTEN'S CENTURY

Britten's Century

Celebrating 100 Years of Benjamin Britten

EDITED BY
MARK BOSTRIDGE

INTRODUCED BY
NICHOLAS KENYON

BLOOMSBURY
LONDON • NEW DELHI • NEW YORK • SYDNEY

First published in Great Britain 2013

This collection and editorial material copyright © Mark Bostridge, 2013

Copyright in individual chapters is held by the contributors.

The moral right of the author has been asserted

No part of this book may be used or reproduced in any manner
whatsoever without written permission from the Publisher except in the
case of brief quotations embodied in critical articles or reviews. Every
reasonable effort has been made to trace copyright holders of material
reproduced in this book, but if any have been inadvertently overlooked
the Publishers would be glad to hear from them.

A Continuum book

Bloomsbury Publishing Plc
50 Bedford Square
London WC1B 3DP

www.bloomsbury.com

Bloomsbury Publishing, London, New Delhi, New York and Sydney

A CIP record for this book is available from the British Library.

ISBN 978-1-4411-7790-2
10 9 8 7 6 5 4 3 2 1

Typeset by Fakenham Prepress Solutions, Fakenham, Norfolk NR21 8NN

Printed and bound in Great Britain by CPI Group (UK) Ltd, Croydon,
CRO 4YY

Contents

Editor's Note

My thanks to the Britten-Pears Foundation for their support of this project. In particular, I'd like to express my gratitude to Richard Jarman, the Foundation's General Director, and to Ghislaine Kenyon, one of its trustees, for all their kind assistance.

Information concerning the worldwide celebrations of the Centenary of Britten's birth in 2013 may be found on the Foundation's website: www.britten100.org/home.

At Bloomsbury, thanks are due to Nicola Rusk, Joel Simons and Robin Baird-Smith.

M. A. B.

Introduction
The Outsider and the Insider

Nicholas Kenyon

I never knew Benjamin Britten. I never met him, I never saw him
conduct or perform live. Yes, I sang his music, and loved it; yes, I
heard his music, and marvelled, but I had no contact at all with
him as a person. This would be supremely unimportant, were it not
for the turmoil of claimed closeness and controversial relationships
(or non-relationships) which lie at the heart of so much testimony
about him. Britten is one of those supreme creative figures who
exert a quasi-magical personal attraction: as Michael Tippett said
when he died, 'I think that all of us who were close to Ben had
for him something dangerously close to love.' Through all the
elements of his life – his writings, his interviews, his conducting,
his car-driving, his walking on the beach, his festival planning
and his piano-playing – you sense a magnetic personality which
affected all those who came into contact with him. As a result,
throughout his life and after, people have wanted to own him.
Colin Matthews recalls how so many recollections of Britten are
'burnished' through being repeated constantly over time – which
may be the fate of any great figure, but this goes further. In another
context (writing about Mozart) Maynard Solomon has described
biography as 'a contest for possession', and how true that is in the
case of Britten. There is something equally Mozartian in the way
we feel we can touch Britten the man through the vividness of his
communication, both musical and verbal; but how much was deliberately unrevealed, and in the end repressed?

As Paul Kildea's opening chapter vividly describes, reflecting on
the biographies that have preceded his own, Britten's reputation has

been continuously contested – by his executors, his 'corpses', his colleagues, his performers, by modernists and anti-modernists, and more recently by gay studies. It is entirely natural that those who felt most touched and transformed by contact with the composer should argue the case for their view of him. But a century after his birth, we perhaps need to stand back. This book assembles a collection of testimonies, ranging from those who worked most closely with Britten to those who in a newer generation are reacting to his music, and those who offer new perspectives on his work. Together they offer a certainly partial but hopefully stimulating perspective on the creative years of Britten's century.

When, at the BBC Proms in 1997, we invited Philip Brett to give a broadcast lecture as part of a Britten weekend (or as he put it, typically apologizing for being too establishment, 'appearing under the auspices of *the* Proms Lecture funded by *the* BBC') it was already over two decades into his ground-breaking writing on the influence of Britten's sexuality on his work. He had started from where Hans Keller had begun, in showing the impact of Britten's homosexuality on *Peter Grimes* (an 'enormous creative advantage', Keller had called it), but developing this thought to articulate a much broader concept of Britten's 'difference'. Though the influence of Britten's sexuality had been widely debated in the decades after his death, the line of argument that Brett advanced was not even by then a comfortable one for some who believed that Britten's homosexuality was essentially peripheral to his artistic achievement. Brett argued that it was central, and shortly after, his view of Britten was accepted into the citadel of recognized musicology, *Grove's Dictionary of Music and Musicians,* in the form of a new entry on the composer. That fine article (oddly marred by a gender misprint in its opening section!) should have led, as Kildea explains, to a new full-length biography that was cut short by Brett's own untimely death.

A key figure in maintaining and interpreting the reputation of Britten after his death has been his executor, chronicler, publisher and friend Donald Mitchell. In retrospect it seems entirely right and generous that, as the single person to whom we owe most for our detailed knowledge of and understanding of Britten's life, Mitchell in the end backed away from the prospect of writing a full biography of the composer. He embraced and promoted the most comprehensive documentation, but in spite of Britten's request to him, left an overall re-interpretation to others. Mitchell initially reacted strongly against Humphrey Carpenter's freshly re-thought and lively biography (1992), which, as Kildea points out, used a second-hand report of an early traumatic incident as the basis on which to construct an entire theory of Britten's personality. Brett tried to point out (in a review of the earlier volumes of Britten letters) that Mitchell, who 'has a great deal invested in Britten's stature', should see the question of Britten's homosexuality not as primarily a sexual issue but as an issue with 'broader cultural and societal implications'. This was a key to understanding the composer, which led us to the heart of one issue which recurs through this book of essays: was Britten an insider or an outsider? Did he consider himself to be one or the other, yearning to be accepted into the middle classes while retaining a lifestyle that was reviled by many of that class, or maintaining an external pose while accepting the trappings of the establishment? Did he attempt to influence or construct his identity, or did he simply create his music and let others decide?

Brett's seminal lecture, reprinted here in the spoken form in which he gave it, and his subsequent *Grove* article, contain one of the most thought-provoking sentences that has been written about the composer, expressed with typically concise eloquence: *'Britten's artistic effort was an attempt to disrupt the centre that it occupied with the marginality it expressed.'* This is certainly not a formulation that the composer would have recognised, with his repeated claims to be of use to people, to serve the community. 'It is quite a good thing to please people', he said, and thus proposed a rather cosier view of his place in society. The broad concept of 'difference' is one that Brett articulated in his other primary area of study, that of early music. He wrote a generation ago that the historical performance movement 'has given us a sense of difference, a sense that by exercising our imaginations we may, instead of reinforcing our own sense of ourselves by assimilating works unthinkingly to our mode of performing and perceiving, learn to know what something different might mean and how we might ultimately delight in it.' That has a very close resonance with the story of Britten, because what has happened since it was written is that Britten's music (just like the performance practices of the early music movement), having started as a resolutely non-central, critical feature of our musical life, has actually become central to it. As a result, in both areas, the centre has moved.

Perhaps a quarter of a century on from Brett's original lecture, we could reformulate that thought just slightly and say that Britten *transformed the centre that he came to occupy with the marginality which was so productive for him*: trying to capture the sense that Britten's experience as an outsider (and let us not forget, for much of his life an illegal outsider), was a crucial and positive part of his creative stimulus. He did not noisily disrupt the centre (as for instance, during this period of classical music, it could be argued that first the modernists and then the minimalists did); he worked from within to gain increasing acceptance, so that by the time of the *War Requiem* he was seen as encapsulating a national mood and a broad appeal. He was an initially awkward social outsider, who sought middle-class acceptability and warm contact with royalty, as long as it did not restrict his creative freedom. So Britten's place at the centre of our musical life was earned through hugely increasing and broadening the range of what was accepted at that centre, without betraying the source and inspiration of that in his own difference. That can be seen too in Britten's avoidance of conventional forms in his output: there is no long string of symphonies or concertos in his output, and even 'opera' was reinvented in the church parables. Instead he created new forms for young people's music-making, highly individual scorings, unusual and innovative approaches to text. It is one of many paradoxes that Britten did not 'compromise' in order to reach people; he never wrote down to his audience. Yet on the other hand his music does crave to be accepted through what Brett called its 'desperately inviting surface'.

It is revealing that in his diaries, now scrupulously selected and edited by John Evans (*Journeying Boy: The Diaries of the Young Benjamin Britten 1928–1938*, Faber), Britten is so fascinated by and interested in performance. You might expect a composer to be interested above all in works: new pieces, rival composers, classic discoveries, scores to be explored – and the young Britten does comment repeatedly on these from *The Rite of Spring* on. His discovery of Mahler can be traced to radio listening in this period. But in his fascinating accounts of what he heard on the radio, scarcely an entry passes without a comment on whether or not the music he heard was well performed. 'I am v disappointed with orchestra; marvellous playing but ensemble bad' ... 'bad slips on part of orch.' ... 'played with fire & spirit but rather inaccurate' (1931)...' the performance was only a Kensington drawing room apology for the wild, sensuous & beautiful music'.... 'Performance was scandalous. Super refinement – without style and taste – string playing as dead as nails' (1935). Throughout his life the composer continued to be obsessive about performance, especially how his own works were to be performed – Edward Gardner is fascinating here on the daunting degree of detail in Britten's performance indications, in which he tries to specify so closely what he means as to potentially leave the performer too little scope for freedom.

The importance that Britten gave to how music, his own and others, actually sounded, and his wish to control it, provides one key motivation for why he devoted so much time and effort to the major and demanding undertaking of the Aldeburgh Festival. The mythic origins of the Festival lie in Peter Pears's oft-quoted line 'Why not make our own festival? A modest festival with a few concerts given by friends.' But that is only half the story: given by friends, *for* friends: the essential appeal was to those who shared the interests and enthusiasms of Britten and Pears. To what extent these overlapped with the needs and tastes of the local community is at the very least an open question. Unlike some composers who are relatively unconcerned about how their works are treated once they have been written, Britten wanted as much creative control as possible over how his works were performed by the musicians he chose, in the circumstances he wanted, and thus to ensure that they were well received by an audience that was as sympathetic and understanding as possible. The experience of collaborating with Glyndebourne on *Lucretia* had not been a happy one, and the later ghastly experience of Covent Garden premiering *Gloriana* for the Coronation, vividly recalled by Lord Harewood, was a watershed in Britten's attitude to the wider world. He wanted his work to travel around the world, but he wanted to be sure it was created in the way he conceived it.

Yes, Britten wanted his music to be useful to people, but like most great creative artists, he wanted to be useful to people *on his own terms*. Performers and administrators served his ends – hence they came and went, even those with long and devoted service, with alarming unceremoniousness, in one day and out the next. (Even as key a performer as Janet Baker reveals in her account here that she deliberately did not 'get too close to the flame'.) 'A few friends' were not beyond being sacrificed by Britten to the needs of the work in hand. That was unavoidable if the work came first, and it always did. Later on, that original Pears thought about the Festival would be reimagined and reformulated as a key part of the Britten persona, both in his famous Aspen Award speech (1964) and his acceptance of the freedom of the Borough of Aldeburgh (1962). 'I believe, you see, that an artist should be part of his community, should work for it, with it and be used by it.' But to characterize the key purpose of the Festival as a service to the community is a little disingenuous. If the community liked it, so much the better, but it was at root a service to the performance of his own music (and the music he loved) in the best way possible. We should probably not take as too typical the witnesses Tony Palmer captured for his fine 1967 film *Benjamin Britten and His Festival*, but they do stick in the mind: the first rather tweedy, the second a fisherman on the beach giving their reactions to local involvement in the Festival: 'Well there's a hard core, they just go away…one goes to Aberdeen, he reckons that's far enough, another one who's reputed to get a case of whisky, lock the door and doesn't answer it till it's all finished.' 'Benjamin Britten is a very nice man, he'll stop on the beach and have a word with you. But it'd be a laugh on the beach if I tell the fishermen I've been to the opera…'

We should probably take as a truer articulation of Britten's purpose the more nuanced line he took with Lord Harewood in a 1960 radio interview: 'There are enough people who like the things that we like.' He refers to the character and size of the buildings: 'the shape of the festival… is very much dictated by the town itself, the buildings, the size of those buildings, and the quality of those buildings.' Then in the Aspen speech this is developed: 'I believe in roots, in associations, in backgrounds, in personal relationships…I write music now, in Aldeburgh, for people living there and further afield, indeed for anyone who cares to play it or listen to it.' That is very deftly put: the roots and associations are to do with his, Britten's, relationship to the place, and the result is for 'anyone who cares…to listen.' Rather, like many great impresarios, Britten led taste through his own decisive views and his own superb performances.

I do not mean to imply that the Aldeburgh Festival has been anything but a tremendous artistic achievement for most of its years, and a great force for musical good. Its agenda links directly into thinking about Britten's 'difference'. It was outside the centre of musical life when it was founded, and could thus be a perfect example of the word Kenneth Clark invented, a 'micropolitan' culture, at one remove from and in tacit criticism of what was going on in the metropolitan mainstream. When the Aldeburgh Festival started, in London the post-war Proms were in the ascendant, with a populist agenda under Malcolm Sargent that became ever more pronounced in the 1950s with constant annual reiterations of Beethoven, Brahms and Tchaikovsky symphonies. By contrast, in the whole period up to Britten's death the Aldeburgh Festival did not include a single symphony by Beethoven, Brahms, Tchaikovsky or Sibelius – and not just because of the size of the Jubilee Hall (where the festival was based until the opening of Snape in 1967), since Britten did do Schubert and Mozart, and when he wanted to perform Mahler's *Fourth Symphony* he did so in Orford Church (see also my Hesse Memorial Lecture 2007 'Metropolitan, micropolitan, cosmopolitan', and Rosamund Strode, *Aldeburgh: Music of Forty Festivals*).

The Aldeburgh Festival became distinctive by building around Britten's works a shapely collection of marvellous music which both illuminated and contextualized his work and helped to reshape the concept of the Western canon: Purcell and Dowland songs, Mozart piano concertos, Bach cantatas, Schubert lieder, the series of medieval and renaissance music that Imogen Holst brought to Aldeburgh Church. Over the first forty festivals, there were about 132 works by Britten, 136 by Bach, 136 by Mozart, 138 by Schubert, 112 by Purcell: a highly characterized musical cosmos. Then there was other contemporary music, where the record is more ambiguous. In the early years there was innocuous new music by friends and colleagues, and later the Society for the Promotion of New Music brought music by Richard Rodney Bennett, Susan Bradshaw, Cornelius Cardew, Hugh Wood, Maxwell Davies and Harrison Birtwistle in their early days. Britten certainly encouraged its inclusion, though he tended not to involve himself in its performance, though Pears occasionally did. One of the main achievements of all this repertory was to enable us to understand Britten's own music better: a worthy but, again, a not unselfish aim.

This suggests another way of considering Britten's status as an insider or an outsider, and that is his position in relation to tradition. This is tellingly raised in one of the most sympathetic interviews he gave to Donald Mitchell in 1968, when Mitchell asked him whether he was burdened by the 'great burden of tradition behind you'. Britten replies 'I'm *supported* by it Donald, I couldn't be alone. I couldn't work alone. I can only work really because of the tradition that I am conscious of behind me. ...I feel as close to Dowland, let's say...as I do to my youngest contemporary.' That view places Britten very close to T. S. Eliot, another key twentieth-century figure who consciously placed himself in a line of tradition, and viewed every new work that was written as modifying the picture of the past and future. But how interestingly Britten's way of expressing that place is characterized by his choice of composer. He said he cited Dowland just because Mitchell and he had just been discussing his music, but the example means that he was appealing to a very different tradition – dependent not on immediate predecessors like Elgar and Vaughan Williams but on distant ancestors like Purcell and Dowland, challenging many conventional notions of Englishness.

For Britten, belonging to a developing strand of tradition seems almost a moral position, but it does not need to be a continuously developing tradition which grows out of what immediately preceded it. In the same interview Britten identifies John Tavener as a composer who with 'many others like him, adore the past and build on the past', but he then criticizes in no uncertain terms (anonymously but identifiably) Harrison Birtwistle whose music-theatre piece *Punch and Judy* had been performed at Aldeburgh at the time Britten had been performing Mozart. 'I know it was probably because of the tightness of time, and the absorption in his own job, but it seemed to me very strange that he didn't want to go and see how Mozart solved *his* problems.' Birtwistle might well have acknowledged some different precursors to his tradition of music drama (probably not Mozart) but what is revealing here is that Britten's stated reason for not responding to Birtwistle's work is its lack of connection to tradition, not what it sounded like...

For those of us who listen to Birtwistle with as much engagement as we do to Britten, and to composers Britten could not feel close to like Beethoven and Brahms with as much enjoyment as to him, no such choice needs to be made. We can accept Britten as a unique voice in the music of the twentieth-century. The status of its supposed conservatism or its relation to the European mainstream is irrelevant. You would not need to hear more than the 16-year-old Britten's *Hymn to the Virgin,* or the later *Hymn to St Cecilia*, to know that it was produced by a genius, or equally to hear in the late works *Phaedra, A time there was...* and the Third Quartet a spare distillation and concentration of a lifetime's experience: an experience often concealed, hidden, but powering the most intense expressiveness in its bare shards of music. It is a common thread lurking somewhere in our musical psyche, as true of Elgar as it was of Britten, that emotional repression in whatever form is an enormously creative force, and indeed articulating that rather than overcoming it is a key strand in musical 'Englishness'.

The periodically vicious assaults on Britten's reputation as a composer seem to be in abeyance; they coloured even his obituaries (which were described by Hans Keller in 1976 as 'a macabre orgy of the bankruptcy of music criticism'). On YouTube you can still come across the period-piece denunciation by the critic Tom Sutcliffe in the TV programme *J'Accuse* (1990): 'Much of what he wrote in the sycophantic closed world of Aldeburgh was academic and loveless, spiritually dead long before he was buried there in 1976', with much about his emotional pulse growing weaker. That has been comprehensively disproved by the increasing impact of his late works, especially *Death in Venice*. Then there has been the new attack from the unexpected source of a former artistic director of the Aldeburgh Festival, the composer Thomas Adès, in several sustained pages of vitriol in interview with Tom Service (*Thomas Adès: Full of Noises: Conversations with Tom Service*, Faber 2012) over-dramatizing the perfectly acceptable observation that Adès writes very different operas from those of Britten.

It is a final paradox that the start of Britten's Centenary year has been launched not with a productive debate about the worth of his music, but with an essentially fruitless (because unresolvable) argument about the cause of his death, arising out of Kildea's new biography. Does it really matter? We can reflect instead that in the 'test of time' that is conventionally applied to the greatness of artworks of the past, the public has spoken decisively and Britten's works are now thoroughly embedded in the musical and especially the operatic repertory. This has certainly been helped by the fact that the musical world has moved away from the extremes of the post-war era to a more inclusive stance, but it is still too simplistic to say that Britten's instinct for success put him on some 'winning side'. By sticking to its principles, by charting a single line of beauty, his work has demonstrated an undeniable integrity. In the Centenary year there will be an extraordinary range of worldwide performances, and through his exceptionally well-managed legacy, a reassertion of his central, humane place as one of the greatest composers this country has produced.

January 2013

PART ONE

BRITTEN – THE MAN

Britten's Biographers

Paul Kildea

'Biography lends to death a new terror', said Oscar Wilde. Though did he really? It sounds like him, and the sentence has been reproduced in countless anthologies under his name, each anthologist stepping gingerly around the problem of the missing source. But the line does not, as might reasonably be presumed, come from Wilde's 'The Critic as Artist' (1891), a dialogue between two aesthetes on modern literature, criticism and biography. 'They are the pest of the age, nothing more and nothing less. Every great man nowadays has his disciples, and it is always Judas who writes the biography.'[i] Nor does it appear in *De Profundis*, Wilde's long explanatory and reconciliatory letter to Alfred Douglas written in prison three years before his death, his mind focused on how history would treat him. Nor is it part of Lord Henry's alluring, aphorism-filled conversation with Dorian Gray. ('Death and vulgarity are the only two facts in the nineteenth century that one cannot explain away.'[ii]) Yet still we accept that he must have said it to someone somewhere, even though forty years ago Monty Python proved how easy it is to put such words in Wilde's mouth. ('Your Majesty is like a dose of clap. Before you arrive is pleasure, and after is a pain in the dong.'[iii])

Whether it was his line or not, Wilde had little to fear from his biographers, although in such censorial times it is understandable he felt otherwise. A close friend and ex-lover, Robert Ross, was his literary executor, tracking down and buying back the rights to Wilde's works, which had been sold off at the time of his bankruptcy, and treating him in print with respect. Other friends wrote reminiscences, his son produced memoirs, his grandson the correspondence. And then in 1988 Richard Ellmann published an authoritative and sensitive biography independent of Wilde's family or friends, scooping a Pulitzer along the way. It remains the definitive work on Wilde, if such things can be said to exist.

Virginia Woolf would have thought the Wilde line suspect. Biographers are tied by facts, their task straightforward, she said. 'When and where did the real man live; how did he look; did he wear laced boots or elastic-sided; who were his aunts, and his friends; how did he blow his nose; whom did he love, and how; and when he came to die did he die in his bed like a Christian, or ...'[iv] Biography was a mere craft to Woolf, and those who write it are charged with sorting truth from Wildean apocrypha. Criticizing her friend Lytton Strachey's biography of Queen Elizabeth I, the sketchy details of her life inked in with Strachey's pen, she wrote, 'The Queen thus moves in an ambiguous world, between fact and fiction, neither embodied nor disembodied. There is a sense of vacancy and effort, of a tragedy that has no crisis, of characters that meet but do not clash.'[v]

Britten's biographers have pitched their tents anywhere between the ground marked out by Woolf on one hand and Strachey on the other. (Wilde's and Elizabeth's problems are not Britten's: his life is extremely well documented.) His first was Eric Walter White who soon after the première of *Peter Grimes* wrote *Benjamin Britten: eine Skizze von Leben und Werk*, commissioned by a Swiss publisher and released in November 1948, Boosey & Hawkes publishing the English original at the same time. White was appointed Assistant Secretary to the Council for the Encouragement of Music and the Arts in the same year Britten and Pears returned from America (1942) and here their paths crossed: the two musicians toured England under the Council's aegis, performing in canteens and concert halls, on Steinways and barrelhouse pianos, lifting the morale of war-weary subjects as they went.

White was knowledgeable, passionate and courteous to his subject, his interest and training in English literature shaping his narrative. 'These little essays on the operas lay no claims to offer musical analyses in depth,' he wrote in 1983 in the preface to an updated and expanded edition. 'Their aim has been simply to try to answer some of the more obvious questions an astute listener is likely to ask.'[vi] The biographical details are well told, Britten having co-operated on an area then undocumented. There are a few errors: Britten acquires 'a converted windmill', whereas he paid for the hard graft of renovating the mill; for the *Grimes* libretto 'he had thought of asking Christopher Isherwood; but after his return to England, it was clear that the choice would have to fall on someone who was living in England,' whereas Isherwood turned him down; 'Britten's work as concert pianist and accompanist since his return from America had helped to familiarize him with the music of Purcell,' whereas he was an American discovery.[vii] Nothing major, but it suggests that though Britten saw the text 'and commented on it in draft,' he did so hurriedly.[viii]

White almost certainly knew the exact nature of Britten's relationship with Pears, but he characterizes it neutrally: 'Britten was accompanied on this voyage by his friend Peter Pears ...'[ix] (The code at the time was 'very dear friend' or some subtle variant, which White ignores.) He glosses over the failure of *Gloriana*, largely dismisses the Guthrie–Moisewitsch production of *Grimes* at Covent Garden in 1947, preferring the cumbersome original showing at Sadler's Wells, cutely stressing that, after all, a realistic setting was 'specified in Montagu Slater's libretto'.[x] When quoting Hans Keller on Britten's pacifism ('by dint of character, musical history and environment, he has become a *musical* pacifist too') he leaves out the meaty, controversial first part of Keller's assessment: 'What distinguishes Britten's musical personality is the violent repressive counter-force against his sadism.'[xi] He writes of Britten's 'sense of humour (or should one say his sense of proportion?); his brisk fancy and ambivalent imagination; his fondness for children,' before crying off pursuing these character traits in any depth.[xii] For all its style and original observations, it was very much an in-house work.

The book in which Keller made his comment was published in 1952. It was no biography, as its clinical title established (*Benjamin Britten: a Commentary on his works from a group of specialists*), but it contains an insightful short sketch of Britten by his friend the Earl of Harewood. 'As a composer, he came to maturity in America: there can be little doubt that the works he wrote there show, not perhaps a new, but at least a more consistent sensitivity and depth.'[xiii] Harewood further wrote that Britten's professionalism 'evolved in the teeth of opposition from every tenet of birth, upbringing and environment, and it had to contend not only with the Englishman's innate lack of seriousness in his attitude towards the arts, but also with the determined amateurism fostered in the public schools, and supported by every form of pressure, social and moral, at their command.'[xiv] Amid dissections of the works there are jigsaw-piece descriptions of the man, such as Paul Hamburger on Britten's pianism: 'He plays a Mozart concerto (alas, only one or two a year) not merely as if he had written it, but as if he had written it last night.'[xv] But it is necessarily an episodic book, one which aggravated critics for being too admiring of its subject and which Britten came to resent, telling Imogen Holst it was like schoolboys dissecting a rabbit in the science lab.

Holst took the hint in her own biography, published in 1966 (revised and expanded four years later), which is a well-written but studiedly un-intimate portrait from such a good musician so close to Britten. Her diaries, published posthumously in 2007, are another matter, full of acute observations and a sympathetic understanding of Britten as man and musician:

> Then he talked about rehearsals – I'd been trying to persuade him to play for the Hugo Wolf [concert] in spite of having too much to do – and he said what he could do was to do a very little rehearsing and then just mesmerize them into doing it properly. 'That's probably what I'm meant for,' – 'I'm no good at rehearsing, I just get bored and irritated. I can rehearse with Peter till the cows come home: and I can rehearse with Joan [Cross]. But not other people.'[xvi]

Alas, there are not many such glimpses into life in Crag House, subsequently the Red House, in Holst's biography. Peter Pears is 'his friend', a description in keeping with England still a year from passing the Sexual Offences Act 1967. There is the slightest hint of the hostility Holst felt towards Pears – a mixture of jealousy and the conviction Pears's treatment of his partner was frequently shabby – but it passes as suddenly as it arrives. 'Peter Pears joins us at week-ends and bank holidays, whenever he is free from his London concerts or his foreign tours …'[xvii] But despite its popularity at the time, it was a wasted opportunity, partly because Holst was no doubt worried about writing anything more revealing lest her own feelings towards Britten were betrayed.

Holst was writing in more discreet times (and for a young readership). A year after her book first appeared, however, biography as a genre changed forever. Michael Holroyd released *Lytton Strachey*, a revealing and hugely stimulating romp through Bloomsbury, which Raymond Mortimer in his review perceptively called 'the first post-Wolfenden biography'. The Bloomsbury gang was mostly aghast at Holroyd's indiscretion, which made Wilde's reputed terror seem small beer indeed, though one member, Frances Partridge, picked up the historical paradox: 'I'm more than faintly surprised at their [the homosexuals'] secretiveness just when their position seems to be about to be legally ratified.'[xviii] Nancy Mitford's sentiments – 'Rather wonderful & terrible how *all* that can now be said' – were shared by many outside Bloomsbury's fortified walls.[xiv] Holroyd received hate mail and public admonition (Auden thought the book should never have been written), and there was a gnashing of teeth in the *Spectator* about likely biographical subjects burning their correspondence or being discreet in their journals ('the private records of our times, perhaps the most articulate in history, will be paradoxically sparse unless we impose on ourselves some sort of limitation on what is to be published and when'), but there was no putting the genie back in the bottle.[xx]

Yet what occurred in literary biography did not necessarily translate into musical biography. Literary biographers and critics do their training from a young age by reading, learning about style through absorption and conversation. Serious musicians do their training practising an instrument, spending their spare time in adolescence alone, playing not reading, going on to a conservatorium to study an often narrow vocational degree. This lends the genre a different backdrop, and music biographers end up either writing perceptively (if often technically) about the music or stylishly about the life and historical context, but rarely both. It is a generalization, but we end up as analysts, not storytellers. There are brilliant exceptions – Richard Taruskin's muscular writing on Stravinsky and Russia; Stephen Walsh on the same composer; Arnold Whittall taking a single thread and stitching from it a marvellous if small tapestry – but music biography is a strangely unformed beast, hostage to musicology's lack of interest in the genre for most of the twentieth century or to specialists' inability to engage with modern biographical practice and opportunities (Norman Del Mar on Strauss, for example). It is what Joseph Kerman had in mind when in 1985 he wrote, 'We do not have musical Arnolds or Eliots, Blackmurs or Kermodes, Ruskins or Schapiros. In the circumstances it is idle to complain or lament that critical thought in music lags conceptually far behind that in the other arts. In fact, nearly all musical thinkers travel at a respectful distance behind the latest chariots (or bandwagons) of intellectual life in general.'[xxi]

Michael Kennedy was different. A journalist, editor and critic, Kennedy saw woods where other music writers found only trees. His 1981 biography followed Philip Brett's ground-breaking article on Britten and *Grimes* (1977) and Tony Palmer's film *A Time*

There Was (1980), and appeared the same year as Christopher Headington's short monograph (1981), which left him free to talk about Britten's sexuality.[xxii] This Kennedy did sympathetically. 'There should perhaps be no more prejudice against homosexuality than against someone's being left-handed, but there is.'

> As for the effect of his homosexuality on his music, we have the reference by so close a friend and colleague as Hans Keller to 'the enormous creative advantage of Britten's homosexuality: however little Britten may have been alive to the fact, his psycho-sexual organization placed him in the privileged position of discovering and musically defining new truths which, otherwise, might not have been accessible to him at all.'[xxiii]

Kennedy does not attempt to place Britten in a wider political or artistic context, and having divided the book into two parts – life then works – he gets through the narrative at quite a lick. But he is careful about the episodes he relates, employing a sceptical newspaperman's eye, writing of Britten's periods of insecurity, quoting from bad reviews as well as good. By including W. J. Turner's coruscating review of *Lucretia* in the *Spectator* ('rotten with insincerity and pretentiousness', Turner then owning up to 'reluctant admiration for so much musical cleverness whose purpose remains neither intelligible nor sensible ... I was bored'), he paved the way for his own critique.[xxiv] The flaw in *Lucretia* to Kennedy is 'the comparative failure to involve the audience in Lucretia's tragedy':

> Except at the very end, she is an unapproachable symbol rather than creature of flesh and blood ... One observes her fate with a detachment unthinkable in the case of Grimes. It is an essay in evocative sonorities rather than as a stage drama that The Rape of Lucretia *commands profound admiration.*'[xxv]

Though Kennedy does not extrapolate from this remark a broader observation about Britten's trouble creating successful female characters, it demonstrates his perceptiveness.

At the end of his life Britten entrusted his publisher at Faber Music, Donald Mitchell, with the task of writing his official biography.

> I had originally discussed with Britten the character of the book that I would write about him, in response to his invitation, in the summer preceding his death in December 1976. We talked

at length one afternoon sitting in the garden of the Red House,
and that same night I drew up an outline scheme which he
approved next morning.[xxvi]

'I want you to tell the truth about Peter and me,' Britten said.[xxvii]
Moreover, Mitchell was to remember that the biography 'isn't the
story of one man. It's the life of the two of us.'[xxviii] Mitchell began
work on the book but different things got in the way, not least
Pears suggesting Mitchell first publish Britten's correspondence.
Even before Pears's intervention 'it had already begun forcefully to
strike me that Britten's letters and diaries together formed a source
that could provide a comprehensive documentation of his life and
works *in his own words*... When complete, this series of volumes
might be said to contain the autobiography that Britten himself
would never have written.'[xxix] There was a little more to it than this.
Mitchell's close friendship with Britten made him reluctant to take
on the role of biographer in those post-Holroyd times. He made
noises to the contrary ('It is a book I still intend to write'), though
Donald always gave the impression he was happiest documenting
Britten's life and commenting intelligently on his music, but leaving
other issues well alone. He remained contemptuous of those who
tried to explain his life through his music, wanting, as Britten did,
the music to speak for itself. 'I certainly saw this [biography] at the
time as an integration of "life" and "work", though not quite in the
sense that fashionable biography is pursued today.'[xxx] Donald had
no truck with his old friend Hans Keller's views on how Britten's
homosexuality influenced his music.

He had no truck either with playwright Paul Godfrey, who
in 1990 wrote *Once in a While the Odd Thing Happens* for the
Cottesloe at the National Theatre. The title was lifted from the
operetta *Paul Bunyan* but here was to signify the slow-blossoming
relationship between Britten and Pears. 'Of course I wish Paul
Godfrey the best of luck with his drama, but I find it very hard to
match his conception of Britten and Pears with what I know of
them,' Mitchell told a journalist. 'Really, I think it might have been
prudent to wait until more material was available.'[xxxi] Godfrey,
having been warned not to trust the version of Britten's life given
him by his principal source, Beth Britten, took his dispute with
Mitchell and the composer's estate to the press. 'Every major artist
attracts Salieri figures, and Benjamin Britten was no exception.'[xxxii]
Mitchell was to be caretaker of the Britten story, he seemed to say.

Mitchell was later much kinder about the play ('But this was a work serious in intent and ambition, seriously researched and rooted in the main in fact, not fantasy'), which junks chronology and fact at key points: Britten and Pears first kiss after Britten's serious illness in 1940, whereas they had become lovers the previous year; Auden at one point turns up in US Army uniform, whereas he failed the medical test following the draft.[xxxiii] It nonetheless captures the emergence of a more independent and confident composer, out from Auden's shadow. And as Mitchell himself has noted, Britten told him in the last years of his life when working on revisions to *Bunyan* the odd thing to happen to him was Pears; Godfrey's use of the line as his title could not have been more apposite.

As the letters project grew in scale, Mitchell handed over the task of a single-volume biography to Humphrey Carpenter who had none of Mitchell's reluctance on matters sexual. He had written good biographies of Auden and the 'Brideshead generation' in which (same-) sexuality is necessarily given a good run. Carpenter was also an amateur jazz musician, a keen exponent of the music the Brideshead generation danced to at society parties in London. (Appropriately, his band, made up of Oxford dons and publishers, was called Vile Bodies.) He had more form as a literary critic than a music critic, which saw him throughout the book walking stubbornly on the thin ice of musical semiotics (C major = purity, et cetera). He could construct a good narrative, however, and he interviewed everybody who knew Britten, some telling their story for the first time, others going over old ground. (Colin Matthews has said how those close to Britten have 'burnished memories' of him – a phrase he borrowed from surviving soldiers of the First World War – since they are asked so often the same questions about him, codifying their answers over time.)

Carpenter wasn't always a particularly sceptical interviewer: he took many stories at face value even when he was unable to corroborate them, tellingly in his use of unpublished notes by an embittered Eric Crozier, written in 1966 when Crozier's friendship with Britten was over, furious at being excised from his former friend's life in Holst's biography. The notes are of their time, discoursing on whether Pears 'was or was not a homosexual by nature' and the like. 'No doubt is possible, however, in Britten's own case. He told me he had been raped by a master at his school, as if his sexual deviation had stemmed from that one incident – but nobody who knew him well could doubt that he was inherently and undeniably homosexual.'ˣˣˣⁱᵛ Carpenter did ask others about the story, though none other than a friend of Britten's from the 1940s thought it true. Carpenter interpreted his findings:

> *It seems unlikely that, if Britten did experience sexual abuse as a child, it would have been enough by itself to make him homosexual. Present day psychiatric opinion regards it as impossible to identify a simple set of causes for homosexuality. There can apparently be many factors, including an exceptionally close relationship with the mother, but possibly also a genetic disposition, so that Joan Cross may be right that Britten was 'born homosexual'.*ˣˣˣᵛ

Only a heterosexual could write this, although by 1992 possibly shouldn't have.

If Carpenter had stopped with this one trial balloon all would have been fine, but he was convinced that the alleged incident was the key to the adult Britten's attraction to pre-adolescent boys, and this hijacked his entire approach to his subject. He interviewed a long line of middle-aged men who had known Britten when they were eleven or twelve, only to discover he treated them courteously and with full probity. This did not deter him. Critics before Carpenter had often commented on the theme of innocence destroyed in Britten's work, helped along by one line in *The Turn of the Screw* that Myfanwy Piper clumsily borrowed from Yeats: 'The ceremony of innocence is drowned.' Biographers hadn't emphasized it, and Britten himself thought it a ridiculous generalization. Yet Carpenter enmeshed this idea as the prism through which to view Britten and his work.

Carpenter created a Britten for the twenty-first century: cranky, cruel, sexually repressed, childlike, disloyal to his friends, forever revisiting a single theme in his works. Overnight the book changed the way people thought of him, which is of course what good biography should do. But Alan Britten, the composer's nephew, was hardly alone in not recognizing the portrait Carpenter sketched. It was far from Mitchell's one-paragraph description of his friend in 1971, a throwback to biography before Holroyd, which goes some way to explain Mitchell's annoyance with Carpenter's book:

> *Those who are close to his art know that at the centre of his music there is an intensely solitary and private spirit, a troubled,*

*sometimes even despairing visionary, an artist much haunted by
nocturnal imagery, by sleep, by presentiments of mortality, a
creator preternaturally aware of the destructive appetite (the
ever hungry beast in the jungle) that feeds on innocence, virtue
and grace. All this is, as it were, a B. B. contained within the
B. B. who is the eminently practical, rational man, the most
professional of colleagues and also the kindest and most
generous of friends.*[xxxvi]

Some of the works on Britten published after Carpenter have
corrected his depiction, others (like Bennett) have perpetuated it.
In 2006 John Bridcut wrote a subtle and revealing study of Britten's
relationship with young people, based on his documentary film
Britten's Children. It catalogues the gleeful naked bathing at
midnight with young guests at Crag House, the relationships
with pre-adolescent boys throughout his life, and the occasions
on which Britten came close to stepping beyond propriety. Bridcut
convinced Wulff Scherchen, Britten's lover in the late 1930s, to be
filmed in the Old Mill at Snape where they first consummated their
relationship, and although both subject and interviewer were coy
about the exact nature of this relationship (Scherchen had gone
on to marry and sire), it was the fullest picture of this liaison in
the literature. (Mitchell had agreed with Scherchen to exclude
the more intimate letters and greetings in the first volume of
correspondence, leaving the two men as close friends, potentially
nothing more.)

David Matthews worked with Britten in the 1960s and 1970s.
'It was the best kind of training for a young composer, and this
book is in one sense an expression of my gratitude to the man
who made it possible.'[xxxvii] His counterpoint to the prevailing
Carpenter narrative is short and relays a now familiar story,
but is nonetheless full of insight. No one since Kennedy has
written so well about Britten's music in a biography: 'All that
can be said in mild criticism of *Saint Nicolas* is that there
are a few places where the music seems to lack complete
conviction – where it has more to do with piety than with true
religious spirit.'[xxxviii] Or the end of *Phaedra*: 'above it are heard
fragments of Phaedra's song, which drift away as if blown by
a breeze.'[xxxix] Or the end of *Death in Venice*: 'It is a precarious
affirmation, but an affirmation nonetheless. And so, at the last
moment, Plato has been proved wrong: beauty and love have

led to redemption.'[xl] Frustratingly he keeps himself out of the narrative at the key moments he was actually present in it – like the occasion when David and Colin Matthews played through on piano Britten's new *String Quartet No. 3*, the long silence afterwards finally broken by Britten asking, 'Do you think it's any good?'[xli] In being so scrupulous a biographer Matthews robs us of such moments, but it is still a nice tribute to his former mentor.

At the time of his death in 2002, Philip Brett was about to embark on a full-length biography of Britten, expanding his masterful *New Grove* entry, having been awarded a Guggenheim Fellowship. Brett was a charming and brilliant man, a scholar who could write, untouched by the self-censorship or sexual cack-handedness of previous Britten biographers. It is a great loss that the man who steered the conversation about Britten in such a new and original direction in the years following his death never wrote the book. But his sad, early death left the opportunity open for another biographer to take on the task, which I did late in the decade. I'm writing this chapter a week after finishing the biography, in the calm, anti-climactic period of copyediting, copyeditor queries, typesetting, photographs, galleys and indexing. I'm too close to it to know whether it's any good, unsure of whether I've avoided the pitfalls of music biography I describe above, and still some months from knowing its critical fortunes. But I think I've been true to my determination to place Britten in a much broader historical context than previous biographers. 'It is doing him no more courtesy than that now extended Arthur Miller, or (perhaps more aptly) the homosexual Tennessee Williams – the former two years younger than Britten, the latter two years older,' as I write in the early pages of my book.

'Whatever you do, don't make it cradle-to-grave,' Hermione Lee advised me when I was thinking about undertaking the book, weary after finishing her superb biography of Edith Wharton. I didn't take her advice, because the story of Britten is the story of the emergence of a strong, confident musical England and needs to be told in detail, using the extraordinary documentation assembled by Mitchell, Reed, Cooke, Carpenter and others as my starting point. Britten himself would no doubt disapprove. 'One of the most disturbing features of this time is that so many people seem to prefer to read about art rather than to experience it.'[xlii] But he would say that, wouldn't he?

Notes

[i]   Oscar Wilde, 'The Critic as Artist', *Intentions*, Josephine M. Guy ed., *The Complete Works of Oscar Wilde*, vol. 4 (Oxford: Oxford University Press, 2007), p. 126.

[ii] Wilde, *The Picture of Dorian Gray*, Richard Ellmann ed., *The Picture of Dorian Gray and Other Writings by Oscar Wilde* (New York: Bantam Books, 1982), p. 183.

[iii] 'The Oscar Wilde Sketch', *Monty Python's Flying Circus*, ep. 39 (18 January 1973).

[iv] Virginia Woolf, 'The Art of Biography', *Collected Essays*, vol. 4 (London: Hogarth Press, 1967), p. 227.

[v]   Ibid., p. 225.

[vi] Eric Walter White, *Benjamin Britten: His Life and Operas* Second Edition (London: Faber & Faber, 1983), p. 16.

[vii] Eric Walter White, *Benjamin Britten: A Sketch of his Life and Works* Second Edition (London: Boosey & Hawkes, 1954), pp. 28, 45, 53.

[viii] Ibid., p. viii.

[ix] Ibid., p. 30.

[x]   Ibid., p. 59.

[xi] Hans Keller, 'The Musical Character', Hans Keller and Donald Mitchell (eds), *Benjamin Britten: a Commentary on his works from a group of specialists* (London: Rockliff, 1952), p. 350.

[xii] White (1954), op. cit., pp. 81–2.

[xiii] The Earl of Harewood, 'The Man', Keller and Mitchell (eds), op. cit., p. 4.

[xiv] Ibid., p. 6.

[xv] Paul Hamburger, 'The Pianist', ibid., p. 315.

[xvi] Holst diary, 24 Oct. 1952. Chris Grogan ed., *Imogen Holst: A Life in Music* revised edition (Woodbridge: Boydell Press, 2010), p. 201.

[xvii] Imogen Holst, *Britten* second edition (London: Faber & Faber, 1970), p. 50.

[xviii] Michael Holroyd, *Lytton Strachey* (London: Vintage, 1995), p. xxii.

[xix] Ibid., p. xxvi.

[xx] Ibid., p. xxiv.

[xxi] Joseph Kerman, *Musicology* (London: Fontana, 1985), p. 17.

[xxii] Headington, a composer, had a good eye for comedy. 'One evening Christopher Isherwood and Basil Wright, dining with Britten, said to each other when he was out of the room: "Well, have we convinced Ben he's queer, or haven't we?"' *Britten* (London: Eyre Methuen, 1981), p. 35.

[xxiii] Michael Kennedy, *Britten* (Guildford: J. M. Dent & Sons, 1981), pp. 122, 123.

[xxiv] Ibid., p. 49.

[xxv] Ibid., p. 183.

xxvi   Donald Mitchell and Philip Reed (eds), *Letters from a Life: Selected Letters and Diaries of Benjamin Britten* Volume One 1923–39 (London: Faber & Faber, 1992), pp. 55–6.

xxvii Ibid., p. 56.

xxviii Ibid., p. 59.

xxix   Ibid., pp. 56–7.

xxx   Donald Mitchell, Philip Reed and Mervyn Cooke (eds), *Letters from a Life: Selected Letters of Benjamin Britten* Volume Three 1946–51 (London: Faber & Faber, 2004), p. 3.

xxxi   Andrew Linklater, 'Once Britten, twice shy', *The Age* [1990].

xxxii Ibid.

xxxiii Mitchell, Reed and Cooke (eds), op. cit., p. 7.

xxxiv Humphrey Carpenter, *Benjamin Britten: A Biography* (London: Faber & Faber, 1992), p. 20.

xxxv   Ibid., p. 22.

xxxvi Donald Mitchell, 'Britten and Pears: A Double Portrait', Mervyn Cooke ed., *Cradles of the New: Writings on Music 1951–1991* (London: Faber & Faber, 1995), pp. 488–9.

xxxvii David Matthews, *Britten* (London: Haus Publishing, 2003), p. viii.

xxxviii Ibid., p. 95.

xxxix Ibid., p. 152.

xl   Ibid., p. 147.

xli   'Do you': David Matthews interviewed by Oliver, 1997, BPL.

xlii   Britten, 'On *Pravda*, Art and Criticism' (1963), Paul Kildea ed., *Britten on Music* (Oxford: Oxford University Press, 2008), p. 236.

The Britten Century

Philip Brett

I have deliberately chosen to talk today about a fiction, the Britten Era. To reduce British musical history from the mid-1940s to the mid-1970s to a single expression of this kind is misleading or plain wrong on a number of counts. It would for instance ignore the second wave of the folk-music movement that started in 1950s. Even more notably it would omit the British contribution to what was arguably the most important musical development of the postwar years: if the roots of rock-'n'-roll are embedded in the much-looked-down-upon northern part of England; and rock music since has been much indebted to the inventiveness, vitality or sheer bravado of the British contingent within it.

In the world of art music with which I am concerned today, there has been a notable tendency in Britain since the late nineteenth-century to focus upon a single figure representative of national musical pride. As my friend Elizabeth Wood reminds me, there has been a kind of relationship between the leading composer of the day and his British public that might be characterized as serial monogamy. The reputation of Sir Edward Elgar, she feels, queered the pitch for Ethel Smyth, whose biography she is completing. There have been grumblings of late that Ralph Vaughan Williams, generous to a fault in his dealings with other musicians of all kinds, nevertheless caused the occlusion of some notable contemporaries of his own. A feature of this singling out has been a comple-mentary doubling which has either bolstered the prestige of the central figure or provided a safety valve for dissenting connoisseurs: Stanford and Parry, Elgar and Delius, Vaughan Williams and Holst, and finally Britten and Tippett, perhaps the last of these pairs before the onset of pluralism and postmodernism made further such constructions impossible. The challenge for the professional composer within reach of the post of head boy in this earlier situation, then, has been how to work the school rules in favour of his candidacy. This Britten set out to do.

It surely helped in Britten's case that he decided to become a composer of opera. Not only was it a genre in which for one reason or another British composers had not managed to make an impact on the standard repertory, but it also encouraged thought about self-presentation. Of course, operas have to be about something. Britten never wanted to hide behind a cloud of abstract modernism or avant-garde ideas, and would have agreed with one of his librettists, Montagu Slater, in excoriating 'that monster, the work of pure art "unmixed," as Mr. Eliot has put it somewhere, "with irrelevant considerations"'.

It is one thing to reject the autonomous modernist view of art, of course, another to find stories that connect to a group beyond one's immediate friends and associates. The library shelves of opera houses are thickly populated with operas once performed and then discarded not because of any necessarily crippling defect in either musical or dramatic technique – well-known operas, after all, abound in these – but because they have very little to say to anyone in the audience. *Paul Bunyan* (1941) was a classic false start, a patronizing attempt to evoke the spirit of a nation not his own by W. H. Auden in which Britten was a somewhat dazzled accomplice – he was quite vague about the exact nature of the title role's manifestation and staging only six months before it opened.

Finding in an imported copy of *The Listener* a radio talk by E. M. Forster on the poetry of George Crabbe barely two months after the staging of *Paul Bunyan* in 1941 was a turning point. In Crabbe's poem *The Borough*, and more precisely in its story of the ruffian Peter Grimes, Britten and his partner Peter Pears found that 'something to say'. It was an unlikely and unpromising tale of a rough fisherman who beat and lost his apprentices, and finally went mad and died. Christopher Isherwood, the friend they first turned to as librettist, later told Donald Mitchell he was 'absolutely convinced it wouldn't work'. But they saw the potential of turning Grimes into a more sympathetic figure of 'difference', a misunderstood dreamer, and worked on their vision as they prepared to return to England in 1942. After the plot had been further transformed by the librettist they eventually chose, the Communist playwright and journalist, Montagu Slater, it worked not only stupendously well, as public response to the opening production of 1945 bears out, but also in a way that uncannily connected the private concerns of a couple of left-wing pacifist lovers to public concerns to which almost anyone could relate in the late twentieth-century.

The author Colin MacInnes confided to his private diary in the late 1940s that 'Grimes is the homosexual hero. The melancholy of the opera is the melancholy of homosexuality.' Its theme of the individual who is persecuted by the community for no other reason than his difference cried out to be interpreted in this way, but could not be publicly articulated in those days. A more remarkable and far more penetrating aspect of the allegory, however, had to do with the actual social mechanism of oppression. It is the classic condition of those who do not have access to full status in society that they themselves start believing in the low opinion they perceive others to have of them. Grimes's fate is ultimately determined not simply by his isolation but by his capitulation in this way to the Borough at the climax of Act II, scene i, a much delayed and extremely powerful cadence on to B-flat, the Borough's own key. Upon striking his friend Ellen in response to her 'We've failed!' Grimes literally takes up the offstage church congregation's 'Amen' in his 'So be it,' proceeding to the cadence with 'and God have mercy upon me,' set to a musical motive that dominates the rest of the opera. David Matthews points out that its 'curt, emphatically cadential quality seems graphically to seal Peter's fate,' and the four triadic chords that define its limits and the angry brass canon it prompts both indicate that there can be no escape once the die is cast. In this symbolic moment, therefore, Peter internalizes society's judgement of him and enters the self-destructive cycle that inevitably concludes with his suicide. In this moment, Britten may at one level have been addressing his own concerns, because in spite of a certain sangfroid about what he would have called his 'queerness' there are many signs and several testimonies which point to his not being comfortable about it.

There were other private issues the opera addressed. One was inevitably the return from the irksome freedom of the America he had never fully liked to a native land about which he was also ambivalent. Since there was a war on, and he and his friends were commonly thought to have shirked their responsibilities by emigrating, he was not likely to receive a universally warm welcome. As a conscientious objector he could have faced an unpleasant term in prison. The opera contains not one but two manhunts, the second of which is one of the most terrifying episodes in modern opera. They surely owe their intensity to Britten's own sense of foreboding and victimization, and served as some sort of catharsis. Imagining the worst is a good way of dealing with a difficult situation, and if Britten's imagination was overheated in this instance, it only served the opera and his career all the better.

If I have stressed the interrelatedness of Britten and Pears's private concerns with the larger themes of Britten's music, it is not simply a matter of my own interest in exploring the stories of other gay English musicians who went to the USA, but also to combat the pointed neglect of the topic. When I began writing about Britten more or less twenty years ago, the subject of his homosexuality had not been broached in relation to his music in any serious way. Here was a composer with sixteen operas, or opera-like works, to his credit, many of which, after *Grimes*, dealt at rather important levels with male relations, often with an obviously homoerotic text or subtext; yet the subject had been ignored as though it didn't exist. There were some good reasons for this. The Sexual Offences Act, which finally legalized homosexual acts between consenting adults in private, did not pass until 1967. All mention of homosexuality on stage was specifically forbidden until 1958, and all stage material was subject to state licence until 1968. Britten himself never mentioned the topic, and it was only in 1980, after Peter Pears had declared the nature of their relationship in a prime-time Easter Sunday television broadcast (of Tony Palmer's film *A Time There Was*), that others felt fully comfortable alluding to the fact.

There was a further and more significant barrier to any criticism that would include material elements, such as politics or sexuality. Art music, like poetry, had become in this century the repository of transcendent or universal values, which is almost tantamount to saying masculine and heterosexual values. This came about for a number of reasons, but one very strong cause in my estimation was the threat to its status by a widespread notion encapsulated by Havelock Ellis in a single sentence in his book on what he referred to as *Sexual Inversion:* 'it has been extravagantly said that all musicians are inverts.' In the aftermath of the trials of Oscar Wilde, English musicians, like other artists, cultivated images that were as distant as possible from the connection of effeminacy, aestheticism and vice that had been discerned in those traumatic events; and this cultivation of masculinity and detachment extended from their personalities to their art, and remained virtually unchallenged until quite recently.

Although the attempted separation of life and art produces protection and an honoured place for the arts, as Alan Sinfield observes, 'it is at the cost of limited influence, marginality, even irrelevance. Their protected status confines them to a reserve, like an endangered species insufficiently robust to cope with the modern world.' A particularly crucial misunderstanding about any relation that might exist between sexuality and music is that it will be or should be concerned exclusively with sexual attraction or with sexual acts, or alternatively with complex psychological scenarios arising from frustrated sexual drives rather than with social mechanisms. It is clear that not only was *Peter Grimes* intended to 'cope with the modern world' but also that any suggestive psychological or pathological elements that might detract from its primarily *social* theme of the individual's tragic internalization of community values were steadily eliminated as the work grew to fruition. All mention of a domineering father incorporated into earlier versions of the libretto, for instance, was erased. The result was a brilliant appeal, made more palpable and convincing through music, to the alienation of every member of the audience. 'In each of us there is something of a Grimes,' wrote Hans Keller, 'though most of us have outgrown or at least outwitted him sufficiently not to recognize him too consciously. But we do identify him, and ourselves with him, unconsciously.'

If it was something of a feat to get the audience to identify with an allegorical figure who could most easily be interpreted as 'the homosexual', the basest member of society, and furthermore to identify the problem not as one of the 'homosexual condition' but of society's vicious treatment of difference, the opera certainly offered members of its audience a plateful of related social concerns to ponder. It laid bare the paranoid nature of society's scapegoating someone who it feels to be threatening but is not; and asks the audience to consider how each of them might feel at being similarly and inexplicably scapegoated. It questioned the operation of violence, which, as Edmund Wilson saw clearly on his first journey to Britain after the war, including a visit to this opera, affects both sides: everyone is brutalized, not merely the aggressor and the victim. Coinciding with the birth of the welfare state in Britain, it also posed the (always unresolved) question of responsibility in the relation of individual and state in modern capitalistic democracies, and this is where the question of homosexuality becomes so central. The 'more liberal view' espoused by the welfare state's authors sees deviance in particular and criminality in general as a symptom of society's failure, and tends to want to deal with it accordingly by trying either to understand and allow for it, or, in a more problematic strategy, to control it by 'medicalizing' it. The opposing view, espoused by those who resist state control in most other spheres, insists on maintaining individual conformity and responsibility, and uses institutionalization as a means of controlling deviance.

Homosexuality is deeply embedded in modern society's idea of itself. Since the trials of Oscar Wilde, exactly a half-century earlier than the opera, the male homosexual in particular, as a notionally uniform but actually incoherent identity, had been foregrounded or represented in Anglo-American society and ideology as an internal enemy causing the dislocation of an otherwise ordered society – the McCarthy era saw an extreme manifestation of this homosexual conspiracy theory. But society is in a permanent state of dislocation stemming directly from its own blockage, its own contradictions. So the dislocation, this internal negativity, was displaced and projected onto those seen ideologically as society's enemies, among whom this 'homosexual' was particularly important because of the fragile nature and infinite difficulties surrounding the institutions of heterosexuality, marriage and the family, and also because of the importance that had accrued since its invention in modern times to sexuality itself, which had replaced religion as the ultimate window onto the soul. The immanent failure of the patriarchy is especially demonstrated by, and projected on, those who exercise its privilege as men but undermine the principles of sexual relations and patterns of domination on which patriarchal authority is founded in the modern world. I shall return to this point in my conclusion.

The other operas of the 1940s, *Albert Herring, Lucretia,* even *The Little Sweep*, maintain the emphasis on oppression and internalization in different contexts and with different parameters and results. Interestingly, all except *Lucretia* also focus on working-class environments and people – though mixed in *The Little Sweep* with middle-class children to whom those in the audience who are helping to make the opera can more easily identify. And the revelation of the hypocritical nature of authority figures is powerfully continued in the person of Lady Billows and her minions in *Albert Herring* as well as in the *Beggar's Opera* realization, where the point is forcibly made that there would be no lawyers, no policeman, clergymen and politicians if there were not thieves, rogues and whores. Peachum enunciates the lawyer's credo: 'We protect and encourage cheats, 'cos we live by them.'

Developments in Britten's own life and in British society made the continuing exploration of the oppression/liberation theme an unlikely way forward – the repressive atmosphere of the 1930s, like so much else in British life, was swept away in the aftermath of World War II. Yet, paradoxically, Britain under a socialist government seems to have been less stimulating for left-wing idealism than those earlier days. Alan Sinfield has shown how artists and writers responded negatively to the threat the welfare state presented to the notion of individuality they prized so highly as a condition of art. In Britten's case, there appears to have been an increasing conservatism and social assimilation in his public behaviour, but I do not find in his works an amelioration of his relations to the state. His adoption of Lytton Strachey's outrageous Freudian view of Queen Elizabeth I for his coronation opera, *Gloriana*, was surely an ambivalent act of homage and aggression. On the other hand, it is true that the later operas, beginning with *Billy Budd,* focus on what might be called microcosmic politics, exploring power within relations themselves. The backdrop of society does not of course vanish but is localized even further into a number of small and sometimes claustrophobic worlds – the ship, the schoolroom, the family or, in *Midsummer Night's Dream*, the wood, both literal and psychological, in which the courtiers, rustics and warring factions of fairies encounter each other.

In all these works ambivalence tends to reign. Some of it must stem from Britten's own life. In his rueful and moving tribute to Britten, John Gill notes that the partnership of Britten and Pears did not coincide with any of the classic British models. These were notable for their incorporation of a discrepancy, such as the age difference emblematic of classical pederasty, or the class difference characteristic of the relations of intellectuals like Carpenter, Forster, Ackerley and others, or the race difference nostalgically celebrated by Alan Hollinghurst in *The Swimming Pool Library*, all of which are obscurely and interestingly connected to an imperial and class-based culture such as that of Britain. Britten and Pears were not only of the same generation, class and ethnicity, but also both active and celebrated in branches of the same field, doing their bit for the balance of payments – the model of Thatcherite citizenry but for their pacifism, politics and homosexuality. But Britten's imagination was also caught up with boys, mostly young adolescents. Whether or not he ever acted upon his desires in this regard – Humphrey Carpenter examined the evidence and came to the conclusion he did not – he was clearly preoccupied to a great extent with the question of power which is posed by such relations. The odd stories he told his librettists about a schoolmaster's having raped him and his own father's desire for boys are telltale indications. But stronger evidence is contained in his music. His imagination really was focused on the plight of the weaker partner, or 'innocent,' for which he found musical expression in work after work in terms that no one else in the twentieth-century has matched. But only in *Owen Wingrave*, where the 'innocent' is arrayed against the bleak and crushing might of the patriarchal family in which the women identify with the phallic power of the father, is there possibly a clear identification of composer and victim. In *Billy Budd* and *The Turn of the Screw*, most notably, an ambiguity surrounds the figures of power, Vere and Claggart, Quint and the Governess, that allows for the contemplation of real moral dilemmas, not easy slogans. Those increasingly powerful drumbeats that underpin and undermine Vere's final epiphany in the epilogue to the opera show (along with other musical clues) that he is so hopelessly contaminated by his role in killing other men – as the leader in battle as well as the naval disciplinarian – that his putative 'salvation' must be wishful thinking.

This preoccupation with authority does not always take the same turn. The moral and tone of *The Prodigal Son* appear, for instance, to reverse the carpe diem anti-establishment attitudes of *Albert Herring* in favour of reconciliation, finally, to the law of the father, personified as all-merciful and munificent in this work in a way that suggests wish fulfilment, not like the Abraham who, in Wilfred Owen's vision incorporated in the *War Requiem*, sends his sons to destruction one by one instead of sacrificing the ram of pride. But the preoccupation with patriarchal characters of many kinds is never far distant.

Needless to say, it is impossible here to encapsulate an overview of the operas, and indeed one of their strengths, arising from their ambivalence and moral questioning, is that no two people will agree about their exact program. Critical thought will remain in dialogue about them for as long as they hold their place in the repertory. But the questions that are debated in them still seem in most instances real ones at the end of the twentieth-century: questions of identity, of the relation of the individual to society, of power within individual human relations as a reflection of societal values, the liberal view of sexuality, and the exploration of loss and desire, all presented in music of great clarity, one that balances feeling with restraint in a way that even the conservative opera audiences of our time have been able to comprehend and enjoy.

As I observed at the start, opera was not a central genre for the British music audience, which Britten could not afford to ignore in any bid for a central position. About the time of the conception of *Peter Grimes,* Britten accordingly began to define his relation to the British musical tradition more clearly. An early manifestation was the release of his aggression toward it, which is the noteworthy feature of an article entitled 'England and the Folk-Art problem' that he contributed to an American music journal in 1941. In this essay, Parry and Elgar are projected as the binary opposition haunting English composition, the one having 'stressing the amateur idea and... encouraged folk-art', the other emphasizing 'the importance of technical efficiency and [welcoming] any foreign influences that can be profitably assimilated.' Studiously avoiding any mention at all of Holst and Vaughan Williams, Britten names Walton, Lambert, Maconchy, Berkeley, Darnton, Lutyens, Rawsthorne and (with reservations) Ferguson and Rubbra as indicating that 'since 1930 the influence of Parry has largely disappeared.'

Later in the article Britten reveals his current fascination with 'the nearest approach to folk-music today': this he deems to be swing and the spiritual, which as he points out are the result of utterly diverse ingredients. The point is to throw the authenticity of folksong of any kind into question, so that 'what we call folk-music is no product of a primitive society' and that the 'whole conception of folk-song as a germ from which organized music grew may prove to be false one.' The dependence on folksong as raw material is either unsatisfactory (as in *Sacre du Printemps* – Stravinsky gets better marks for its handling in *Les Noces,* and Bartók goes unmentioned), or the sign of a need for disciple which second-rate composers cannot find in themselves. Lurking behind much of the thought is the presence of W. H. Auden, a passage from whose momentous 'New Year Letter' (1940) is quoted on the last page as an indication to composers to 'accept their loneliness and refuse all refuges, whether of tribal nationalism or airtight intellectual systems.'

Britten's few words about actual English folk tunes in this article are marked by the same ambivalence that he showed about England in a letter back to America on his return, where he celebrates the country as '*unbelievably* beautiful' and yet finds that 'the accent is horrible and there is provincialism & lack of vitality that makes one yearn for the other side.' 'The chief attractions of English folk-songs,' he writes, 'are the sweetness of the melodies, the close connection between words and music, and the quiet, uneventful charm of the atmosphere. This uneventfulness however is part of the weakness of the tunes, which seldom have any striking rhythms or memorable melodic features.' The ambivalence expressed here, reflected in so many aspects of Britten's life, did not prevent the composer from making considerable use of these melodies, either be arranging them for recital use or incorporating them in original works.

Ultimately, then, Britten made sure that he had a stake in folksong while emphasizing his independence of the 'pastoral school' by what means were available, largely the very different accompaniments he devised. In the exercise of arrangements, for instance, Britten understood clearly certain things that eluded Cecil Sharp and even Vaughan Williams, who tended always to assign to folksong an idealized, essential artistic quality that was somehow in Sharp's programme 'to exercise a purifying and regenerative effect' and produce good Englishmen. Sharp apparently believed that his own anodyne arrangements preserved, as he said, 'the emotional impression which the songs made upon me when sung by the folksingers themselves.' Such blindness to the effects of changing every single parameter of performance except the notes of the tune (themselves idealized in Sharp's transcriptions, of course) is truly breathtaking viewed from this end of the century. How much more honest was Britten's recognition that the venue changed the genre and turned these songs in effect into lieder or art song.

'Little Sir William', the second song of his first published collection, may be taken as a fair example of the process. Britten's accompaniment adopts a broad narrative march-like style for the first few stanzas and then proceeds, after an almost Waltonian chord build of thirds has disrupted the mood, to portray the dead child's voice by expressive chords, one to a bar, and by creating in the accompaniment a pathetic echo of a motif from the second phrase of the tune. The song, like many in these collections, is dramatized mildly in a manner familiar to admirers of Schubert, and since it carries no obviously model connotations it is not identifiable as a folksong at all except for its words. There is a delightful recording of Peter Pears singing it in 1946.

Folksong, as manifest for instance in sets of keyboard variations by the Elizabeth and Jacobean virginalist composers, had been an important ingredient of the pastoralists' relation to English musical history. Projecting the present onto the past, Vaughan Williams wrote of 'the great School of Tudor music... inheriting its energy and vitality from the unwritten and unrecorded art of its own countryside.' For Britten, therefore, the entire Tudor period was effectively ruled out of his official English antecedents: only Dowland the proto-Purcellian songwriter, as represented by Peter Pears' remarkable artistry, merited more than a cursory mention. The choice of Purcell was both rational and literally in tune with Britten's own aesthetic programme as a dramatic composer. Everyone tends to pinpoint a different piece to mark the beginning of Britten's involvement with Purcell. My own candidate at present is 'Let the Florid Music Praise', the first song of the Auden cycle *On This Island*, Op. II, of 1937, which exactly captures the quality of Purcell's rhetorical style. Whenever it began, it is no surprise that, folksong settings having paved the way, Purcell realizations should follow. The art of 'realization', prominent up to the 1950s, suffered total eclipse at the hands of historically informed performance, and is now mercifully extinct. Seventeenth-century song as a whole works on the principle of vocally impassioned delivery or lyrical impulse, neither of which needs much more than a firm bass and a few chords to support it. Britten's contribution constantly vies for attention with Purcell's melodies or declamatory gestures and the bifocal effect inevitably becomes distracting. Needless to say, Britten is at his best when Purcell's music is at is strangest: the title cantata *Saul and the Witch at Endor*, for instance, is simple inspired in its use of piano sonorities to re-compose the work. The character and extent of these pieces – they number forty, far greater than the demand for recital fodder might seem to require – may start us wondering whether the 'realization' process is more an act of appropriation or competition than of homage, another Oedipal episode in the composer's complicated trajectory.

With a strong relation to folksong and the past, and a special investment in the comparatively neglected genre of opera, all that remained to become the national composer of the period was a clearly defined relation to the nation's choral tradition and success within it. Britten started out early on this project with his Op. 3, *A Boy Was Born*; but the work seems conceived more for instruments than voices – it is difficult to perform in a way uncharacteristic of the rest of the composer's choral music and may have been conceived, as Peter Evans puts it, 'to break ways from the rather woolly archaisms that had made such collections as the *Oxford Book of Carols* so appealing to his fellow countrymen'. Again, a considerable change came about with the American years, in fact precisely with the journey back to the homeland on which both *A Ceremony of Carols* and *Hymn to Saint Cecilia* were composed, as though to think of England was to think of choral music. How triumphant these pieces are, combining a secure technique and exquisite sound palette, a modernistic coolness in expression with a plentiful supply of emotional intensity, a musical language distinguished at once by its distinct character as well as its restraint – all the marks of what we think of as classicism, an attribute that cannot easily be discerned in earlier British music of the century. No less successful is the cantata *Rejoice in the Lamb*, written shortly after the return and containing at its centre, framed by a Purcellian prelude and postlude and cheerful choruses and solos, a surprisingly fierce choral recitative rehearsing the theme of oppression that was about to boil over in *Peter Grimes*. A pattern was set, which could have lasted through the composer's life, of works of subsidiary importance directed not so much at the church which commissioned many of them and provided a performance venue for the others but towards a social function which appealed to the composer: he often advertised, after all, his belief in the figure of the composer as a servant of the community.

In the *War Requiem* of 1962, however, Britten suddenly seemed to become a victim of his own success simply as a result of inscribing himself into the English oratorio tradition with a major work for soloists, massed choral forces and orchestra. This work even evoked an ingenious medievalism in its device of troping the liturgical Latin text with a vernacular commentary. The historical resonance, combined with an evocation of the sublime in the form of a bombed cathedral in the heart of Britain's industrial midlands and the metaphysical in the notion of reconciliation beyond the grave, gave the piece a portentous and grandiose character which seems oddly more of the age of Elgar than that of post-World War II. Some listeners have wondered, too, whether the evocation of the end of Elgar's *Dream of Gerontius* in the A major conclusion ('*In paradisum*/Let us rest now') is sufficiently undermined by the two interruptions of boys and bells sounding the portentous augmented fourth, itself so evocative of that angst-ridden genre of the period that David Drew so wittily christened it as the 'Cheltenham Symphony'. In terms of politics, too, questions have arisen about the unilateral and unmodified application of a First World War pacifist message in a post-Second World War context as though the Holocaust were not an additional factor to be reckoned with. The integrity of Britten's homosexual politics explains a great deal here, particularly the use of fellow pacifist and homosexual Wilfred Owen's poetry as the means by which to transmit his very real anger about the fate of young men sent to their deaths by an unfeeling patriarchal system as well as his critique of empty religious forms that are in collusion with that system. And it may not be too much to suggest that a metaphorical extension of those young male bodies can be made to all innocent victims of patriarchal systems, including those who perished in the Nazi concentration camps. But the choice of a major establishment genre in which to couch these messages gives pause and leads to the connecting of several threads that I have tried to explore.

To return for a moment to the questions of folksong and realization. If one adds to the sixty-eight folksong arrangements the many folksongs and singing games, traditional or composed, in the operas, and the final *Suite on English Folk-Tunes*, Op. 90, and if one adds to that the 43 realizations and the references to historic English music (e.g., in *The Young Person's Guide to Orchestra, Gloriana* and elsewhere), it becomes clear that Britten had as great an investment in these two linked phenomena as any bona fide member of the 'pastoral school'. Furthermore, Britten's being asked to write the four sample folksong piano accompaniments for an anthology published in 1968 by Maud Karpeles, Cecil Sharp's co-researcher and successor, was surely an acknowledgement of his position as the leading English composer of the folksong movement since the death of Vaughan Williams, and therefore in some way to be accounted the latter's successor as leading national composer.

Once having distanced himself from Vaughan Williams and others, both by his 'England and the Folk-Art Problem' manifesto (discreetly published abroad and not much remarked on since) and also by the very nature of his musical response to traditional musical material, Britten was nevertheless concerned to infiltrate and dominate their chosen fields of activity on his own terms. His sponsorship of the alternative Percy Grainger and his reclamation of Holst through the incorporation of his daughter into the working household at Aldeburgh were only later touches to a plan that, looked at one way, seemed from the moment of return in 1942 to match the ideology of the 'pastoral school' item by item. The invocation of the powerful British sea myth, again on the composer's own terms, in *Peter Grimes* and *Billy Budd*, and the substitution of Aldeburgh, Suffolk and East Anglia for Hereford, Gloucestershire and the West country, a substitution formalized by the founding of the Aldeburgh Festival as the polar opposite to the Three Choirs Festival, all seem to fit the pattern, as did the co-opting of the British choral tradition along the way. 'Finding one's place in society as a composer is not a straightforward job,' wrote Britten in a speech, like Vaughan Williams's *National Music,* originally delivered to Americans, and sounding remarkably like the earlier document in tone. Perhaps, as part of returning home, Britten had even consciously understood and applied to himself Vaughan Williams's impassioned belief that younger British composers (he mentions Walton, Bliss, Lambert and Hadley) could not expel traditional music from their systems, even though they might deny what he called 'their birthright'. As has often been remarked, Britten certainly moderated his eclecticism during the very same period that the onset of folksong and Purcell arrangements occurred. Perhaps, then, he ultimately understood that, returning to his native country and exorcising certain fears in the cathartic score of *Peter Grimes*, he also needed to fulfil his role in ways that were laid out by Vaughan Williams in a gracious review of Britten's first published volume of folksong arrangements. The older composer, casting himself in the role of an 'old fogey' welcomes the 'divagations', either to right or to left, of the younger generation 'so that in the end the straight line is kept intact.' The line was kept indeed, arguably to run on through Maxwell Davies.

Intact, perhaps, but not exactly straight. For what makes the crucial difference between Britten and his predecessor as a notionally 'leading British composer' is the different way in which he pursued a social and political agenda itself far removed from the liberal socialism of Vaughan Williams. Along the lines of interwar

homosexual pacifist ideals, it puts personal relations above allegiance
to institutions; it puts the individual before society; it tends to
show institutions such as the law, the military and the church as
hypocritical, unjust or simply evil; it favours erotic relations and
exposes marriage; the patriarchal family it portrays as shallow and
oppressive; justice for the victim and the victimized are passion-
ately argued; and the difficulty of homoerotic relations is presented
as a legacy of this society. In much work that has been done on the
politics of marginality in recent years, it has been observed that
the centre needs the margin to supplement or, in other terms, to
act as a symptom of what is lacking in the centre. Thus a certain
contained use of the marginal is necessary for the maintenance of
the centre. For instance, what if Britten had been forced out of his
already transparent closet by some unthinkable event? It is hard to
believe that any public exposure of his homosexuality would have
harmed his career greatly. When Sir John Gielgud was convicted of
importuning in a Chelsea mews in 1953, I remember my mother's
phrase, 'idols with feet of clay', as we drove off to Stratford for yet
another dose of his Prospero's vocal elixir. Even Michael Jackson
does not seem to have been placed beyond the pale by his fans, and
since most humans live with a sense of the complexity of gender
and sexuality, it is quite likely that not only pop stars but also
artists of all sorts gain from projecting their sexuality as 'simulta-
neously provocative and reassuring', to borrow a phrase from Dave
Marsh quoted by Martha Nell Smith in the context of a discussion
of the 'blatant homoeroticisms' evident in Bruce Springsteen
videos. Britten surely understood this, if only intuitively, since
the unspoken non-mystery of a sexuality marked by his constant
appearance with Peter Pears in every context (a gesture hiding the
deeper complication of his sublimated pederasty) was as much part
of his image as the constant presentation of his own childhood, of
his pacifism and of his regional affiliations.

In a recent book, John Champagne discerns the two critical
responses to what he calls the Other, or the marginal. One, the
liberal humanist response, grants the Other great subjectivity
by trying to remake it in the image of the dominant or centre:
for instance, this process has been at work in white responses
to African-American music, or in the male canon's tentative
acceptance of women composers. The second valorizes or privi-
leges the Other, not by extending great subjectivity to it, but by
making a resistant and transgressive use of the very lack at the

centre which first caused the construction of the margin. The processes are of course not separate but contingent on each other.

I would like in my final remarks to argue for the effectiveness of Britten's own version of marginal politics – realizing full well as I try that my own effort to represent difference may already be irretrievably compromised by my appearing under the auspices of *the* Proms Lecture funded by *the* BBC. 'All a poet can do is to warn,' is the conclusion of the Wilfred Owen epigraph on the cover of the score of the *War Requiem*. But in order to warn, or do anything else, the poet/composer has to be heard. What North America may have taught Britten and Pears, then, was that to work for centrality at home would ultimately be more artistically and therefore politically effective than marginality abroad – as a means of articulating a message to society from that margin where Britten, at least, always imagined he lived, as countless tales of his depressions and darknesses attest. His old left friends like Slater and Auden were irritated to see him waltzing up and down church aisles on the arm of the Queen Mother; gay men like myself often have to work through a certain resentment at his exercise of privilege without disclosure; younger radicals presumably have no time for his compromised politics at all. But granted the isolated space of art music and the difficulty of any effective opposition along the lines indicated by Champagne's second opinion, especially in the pre-1967 conditions under which Britten lived and under which his social imagination was formed, one still needs to grant to Britten consistency and integrity in pursuing, sometimes to his friends' acute discomfort, a fairly incisive and certainly passionate line on the linked issues of pacifism and homosexuality in relation to subjectivity, nationality and the institutions of the capitalistic democracy under which he lived. This line he maintained in his work rather than his life, where he acted out a role of charm and compliance laced with occasional brutality. The political stance of the music is all the more remarkable because it barely exists anywhere else in art music outside avant-garde circles already too self-marginalized to offer any hope of serious intervention in the status quo. And, as a starting point, it certainly wins hands down over the tired and tiring credo of the many composers today who are openly gay but vow that homosexuality has absolutely nothing whatsoever to do with their music; or those composers – composers who just happen to be gay – who ask for homosexuality to be accepted as ordinary rather than seeing it as a site from which to disrupt present notions of subjectivity and from which to imagine different organizations of power and pleasure, as I believe Britten did.

Britten's artistic effort was an attempt to disrupt the centre that is occupied with the marginality that it expressed. In this it was comparable to Forster's achievement which, though it did not specifically alleviate the persecution of his own kind, nevertheless contributed, in the novel *A Passage to India*, as much as any uprising of colonized peoples to the eventual downfall of the British Empire. 'We are after all queer & left & conshies which is enough to put us, or make us put ourselves, outside the pale, apart from being artists as well', wrote Pears in response to a letter from Britten about 'all those other dreary HRH's, you know.' It was the achievement of the Britten era, then – and this achievement was in no way contradicted by Britten's contemporary Sir Michael Tippett – that British classical or art music became during those years indelibly queer and left and conshie. And instead of being instantly marginalized, Britten's music has travelled all over the world. There is no need to argue that in the process of its inevitable assimilation it may have had some transformative effect; it is enough to note that, for anyone inclined to explore beyond its deceptively 'conservative' and desperately inviting surface, it offers not only a rigorous critique of the past but also the vision of a differently organized reality for the future.

Fathers and Godfathers

Michael Berkeley

The sea is an unblemished blue, a mirror to the cloudless sky. The boat almost gaudy in its vibrant colours: turquoise and flaming red, for this is no clinker-built fishing smack called *Sal* but an invitation to party called *Passione*. Writing this on the Atlantic coast of Brazil looking at palm trees, a warm ocean and sandy beaches, such a far cry from the lonely marshes, bracing North Sea and the shingle at Aldeburgh, I cannot but help wonder what kind of music Benjamin Britten might have written had he been born under a southern sky, had he been embraced by the extrovert joy in life that pervades so much of South America with its lack of inhibition and overt enjoyment of the human body. No need to invoke Dionysus on Copacabana Beach!

But what we love about Britten is precisely his ability to paint in music a cruel and harsh environment. In a peculiarly British way his music reflects the turmoil of society in its depiction of nature. He articulates the conflict of living with unconventional desire in an apparently straitlaced community, one that frowned on the fragility of human indulgence. From these strictures Britten found not only base metal but also gold. Consorting with George Crabbe's muse he showed how the sea can turn from glimmering calm to ferocious turbulence in an instant, just as a community can turn on its own.

Ben was both a complex character and yet in many respects a readable and even conventional one. The son of a Lowestoft dentist, he was not privileged, as I was, to find himself in an artistic milieu. In that context the emergence of his precocious gifts is quite wondrous and utterly natural. Ever since I can remember, his love of childhood and childlike things held sway. When I was a young boy in the 1950s, Pears and Britten would motor over to our cottage at Morston on the North Norfolk coast – *Cold Blow* it was called – and my father worked out that, indeed, there was nothing between it and the North Pole. We would all clamber on board Jim Temple's launch and make our way down the creek and across the 'pit', or estuary, to picnic on Blakeney Point.

Britten and Pears would arrive at the cottage with Ben grinning at the wheel of an open-topped sports car, wearing a blue fisherman's sweater and looking extremely happy. Many years earlier it was indeed a zippy AC that my father gave Ben when they lived together in the Mill at Snape. Britten loved fast cars and fast serves – he was a tennis player of Junior Wimbledon standards and that physical co-ordination and quickness of thought served him well as conductor and pianist.

Yet even here there was a conflict. Prior to performing in public Ben would often have a stiff drink to steady the nerves. The idea of mixing nimble fingering with whisky or brandy seems extraordinary, especially in someone who knew so precisely what he wanted to achieve and how, rigorously, to get it from other musicians.

My father's close relationship with Ben in the 1930s was never hidden from us three boys but nor was it elaborated upon. Lennox was too quiet, modest and private a man to mention the nature of his attachment. What was evident, and touchingly so, was his unceasing admiration for Ben's gifts, for his effortless ability to get down onto the page what he heard in his head and with such deftness that it comes back off the page with economy and clarity. Looking at a Britten score I am constantly amazed at how few notes there are and how, as a result, the ones that are there speak with such authority.

That ability to communicate through music, that unwavering focus, meant that Ben inhabited his own world and that the niceties of social intercourse could be an unwelcome distraction from the only thing that really mattered. It was as though he knew that time was not endless and that there was an imperative to get his ideas into manuscript.

Reading Mozart's letters it sometimes seems astonishing that a mind that could produce some of the most profound and perceptive insights into what it is to be human could also have such an inane and childishly retarded obsession with bottoms and farting. It's as though having written *Soave Sia Il Vento*, Mozart then chucks a stink bomb into the orchestra pit.

Ben was not, of course, so strikingly schizophrenic, but he did have a Mozartian facility as a musician and he was socially

awkward. It seems that profoundly gifted people compensate for
the development of one part of the brain by restraining growth in
another. Asperger children can tell you what day of the week your
birthday will be in five years time but might be unable to contain
themselves in front of a bowl of nuts.

Ben's much vaunted love of children had more to do with his
identifying himself as still being one of them than a desire to
interfere with them. My own experience as both his godson and as
a boy treble was that he was always sensitive to the insecurities and
uncertainties of being a child in an adult world. Indeed, I saw both
sides of his nature as I grew up; how he could be utterly charming to
the young, yet pretty unpleasant to adults. Though it did not happen
to me, young singers would be in favour while their voices were
innocent and unbroken but were then unceremoniously dropped
once they could no longer take part in a *Ceremony of Carols*.

Partly because of his affection for my father, despite the awkward
termination of their initial and intimate relationship, and partially
because Ben was strangely conventional in many areas of his life,
he was a wonderful godfather and I regularly received postcards
at Westminster Cathedral Choir School from exotic locations
around the world where he and Peter were giving recitals. Birthdays
and Christmas were never missed and five or ten pounds would
regularly wend their way to a delighted choirboy.

Visits to the Red House combined, in those early days, all the
excitement of being with someone who was a hero and a slight
nervousness at the court-like set-up at Aldeburgh. Ben was at once
oblivious to this and yet expected it. He rejoiced in school food
like Shepherd's Pie and Spotted Dick (though never seemed to add
weight to his slight frame), and regular, bracing swims in the North
Sea, regardless of the temperature of the water.

During one stay at the Red House, along with some other older
boys from Westminster Cathedral Choir School, the fair was in
town and Ben assembled us downstairs and announced that he
was going to drive us in to Aldeburgh and let us loose on the rides
and the dodgems. He then gave each of us a ten bob note (only
50p now but like £30-odd pounds in those days) and told us to go
up to our rooms, brush our hair and get our coats. We were wild
with excitement. As only small boys can – well come to think of it,
64-year-old boys too – I managed to lose my ten bob.

Embarrassed beyond belief I returned to the hall without my
coat, explaining that I did not feel too good (true!) and that I

thought I would stay behind. Remarkably, guessing what had happened and intuiting my fear of being shamed in front of my seniors, Ben told the other boys to go and get in the car. When they were out of sight he silently pressed another ten-shilling note into the breast pocket of my shirt and said, 'Now go and get your coat.' His feelings not only for the child but also for the potential outcast had prompted this most touching and unforgettable sweetness.

While I was at Westminster Cathedral Britten wrote his *Missa Brevis* for us boy choristers. Where, in *Billy Budd*, he supremely transcends the problem of eschewing female voices, in the Mass he does without adult male voices and not for one moment do you feel their absence. Lennox always thought the *Missa Brevis* the work of a wonderful composer but not of a believer. I think he felt that in the sheer facility of the composition some element of the sacred and profound was missing. However, it is unquestionably direct and dynamic and in the *Benedictus*, Britten creates one of his effortless and endlessly memorable melodies.

The first performance is engraved on my memory. George Malcolm was the Master of Music, a gifted but eccentric musician; he would lead us boys in procession into the Cathedral. In summer he eschewed underpants so that, on one occasion, as we passed over a grill concealing an air vent, his cassock rose up to reveal to an astonished group of nuns in the front pew a pair of very hairy legs leading up to exactly what you might expect. For the choristers bringing up the rear, the sight of his hirsute buttocks was hysterically funny. The premiere of the *Missa Brevis*, though, was no laughing matter. We were lined up along the balcony of the West end of the Cathedral in front of the organ. Being George, he both played and directed from the organ and since those at each end of the row could not really see him, we had to know the music virtually by heart.

I think there was an awareness that we were privileged to be taking part in something extraordinary and valuable. Decca recorded the Mass in situ and it, along with the Victoria *Tenebrae*, is a classic recording of that choir, and its forward continental tone, at its best. Since then that Mediterranean influence, combined with the movement of gifted choirmasters from Cathedral to Abbey and to St Paul's and King's College, Cambridge, has resulted in the English Cathedral sound changing from its cooing quality to a more nasally focused, cutting sound. It still retains its origins but has become a telling hybrid, a happy marriage of Latin and Anglican.

For a recording of his *Friday Afternoon Songs*, Ben was using the leading boy chorister from Westminster, John Hahessy (later to be the fine tenor, John Elwes). One of the songs requires a second treble to repeatedly imitate the sound of a cuckoo and I was recruited. I was much younger than John and not nearly such a fine or experienced musician and was so nervous that I kept mucking up my entry.

'Don't worry, Michael,' Ben said from the piano, 'Peter will be your own private conductor and bring you in.' This he did, mouthing with exaggerated gestures the word cuckoo at a somewhat trembling young boy.

Ben was insistent that since this was a professional engagement I must be paid and he asked me to choose anything I fancied from the Decca Catalogue. I asked for the Tchaikovsky *Sixth Symphony* and he wrote back to say that he heartily approved of this selection and that there was much I could learn from it.

I always had the impression that Ben, for all his performer's nerves, was completely aware of his prowess as a composer. A few years later Lennox took me to hear Ben and Peter perform *Winter Words* at the Wigmore Hall and I waxed lyrical about encountering the cycle for the first time. Ben was pleased but also clearly astounded that I did not already know the music: 'You mean you have not heard it until now?' I was mortified. I don't think that it was vanity on his part but genuine surprise that a young composer did not know all his recent compositions. The combination of Britten and Hardy was to create an even greater embarrassment for me only a few years later.

Throughout my early years Ben was always encouraging my composition. On one occasion I sent him a brass piece 'De Profundis'. I am somewhat horrified now to think of its amateurish inadequacies and its rather naive humanitarian aspirations. Yet Ben bothered to read it through, to make technical suggestions and to find promise, not only about the music, but also the philosophy behind the piece, which, he said, he shared. He was, I think, enjoying getting into my schoolboy skin, passions and mindset and, while I was this young, did not seem to mind my revelling in his influence.

I found Ben very easy to look up to and, indeed, to love because his qualities and failings were all too obvious. Lennox had been beguiled by Ben and in particular his gifts. I think he looked back on their closeness with gratitude, because it brought him into contact with all the things he aspired to as a musician. It was a meeting of minds as much as physical attraction and the potency of intellectual stimulation will usually outlast the merely physical.

Even after their slightly uncomfortable split, which coincided with Britten meeting Pears and then their move to America, Lennox and Ben stayed in touch. Britten remained a strong supporter of Lennox's music (as with many of his contemporaries) and commissioned and conducted several major works for Aldeburgh and for The English Opera Group. For his part, Lennox remained a devoted admirer of Britten's music and devoured the latest score as soon as it became available. He would often point out to me marvels of orchestration and how they were achieved.

As Tony Scotland points out in his perceptive *Lennox & Freda* (Michael Russell Publishing, 2010) there was in the Britten-Berkeley relationship a mutually joyous delight in music and texts. The older Berkeley learnt from the young Britten's precocious musical abilities and, for his part, Lennox, bilingual in French, shared with Ben his love of the French aesthetic: Rimbaud (BB's *Les Illuminations* was written in 1939), Baudelaire and Mallarme.

It was in Barcelona at the 1936 ISCM Festival that the two composers really got to know each other and heard together the first performance of the new Berg Violin Concerto. Many Britten works from that point on were to incorporate the saxophone, not least the powerful *Lament* in *Mont Juic*, the enchanting suite on which the two composers collaborated. Lennox described how Ben notated the Catalan folk tunes that they heard on the backs of envelopes *with unfailing accuracy*. Back in England they spilt the compositional work on a 50/50 basis – two movements each – but sharing ideas on orchestration throughout. For instance, in certain passages that I know Lennox wrote, I can clearly see ideas of scoring that are Ben's, and vice versa. With a wry smile Lennox said that the title, *Mont Juic*, came from an area of Barcelona which used to contain the infamous local prison and that it did occur to him that audiences might erroneously assume that the two composers were temporarily housed therein.

He always saw in Ben's clarity of thought a precise example of the difference between Britten and Michael Tippett. Where Michael ended up in Wormwood Scrubs as a conscientious objector, Britten convinced a tribunal that he should be determined exempt from military duty. He was, though, Lennox always told me, prepared to volunteer for the Merchant Navy, a truly brave thing to do given the fate of so many allied convoys in the Atlantic. As conscientious objectors, and what's more gay conscientious objectors, both Britten and Tippett fell foul of the establishment but Lennox, working in the BBC Music Department, fought tooth and nail to have their works broadcast.

Towards the end of Ben's life Lennox and I kept up a correspondence with him, but as illness began to take its toll we saw less of him. When Ben became unable to play the piano or act as accompanist, Peter Pears began to work with other musicians, like Murray Perahia, but, perhaps to save Ben's feelings and fearing that no one could understand or replace the symmetry that existed so effortlessly in his legendary performances with Ben, he tended to seek out instruments other than the piano and commissioned cycles for tenor and guitar (Julian Bream) or harp (Ossian Ellis).

As a semi-mature student I was enormously flattered to be asked to write some songs for tenor and harp. Since writing extensively for this instrument really requires expertise, I had some lessons with Ossian who explained how the pedalling changed the length of the string and hence its pitch, and the time needed to effect these changes. This had also been Ben's way; working closely with musicians like James Blades (percussion), Dennis Brain (horn) Julian Bream and Ossian, he learnt what their instruments could do and what, until then, had not been thought possible. A viola player and pianist, he already had an insight into how to write effectively for strings and keyboard.

Before posting off the resulting song-cycle, *Wessex Graves*, I asked Lennox to read it through with an ultra-critical eye. He felt that the songs worked and were good enough to send to Aldeburgh. So there I was, a young and vulnerable student, desperately keen to hear some sort of response. Nothing. Nothing for weeks on end. Then I ran into Ossian who said, 'What ever happened to your songs? Peter and I tried them out and we really loved them – they work so well on the instrument.' I decided to write to Peter and ask if I could have them back. They arrived without any letter or note. A couple of years later I was talking to the late and much lamented composer, Nicholas Maw, and told him this story and how it remained a complete mystery to me. 'No longer,' he said. 'I can tell you the answer because exactly the same thing happened to me with some songs I wrote for Peter and Julian Bream. Which poet did you set?' I said it was Hardy. 'Ah,' said Nick, wagging his finger at me. 'Not allowed!' Ben couldn't bear to hear Peter sing lines by poets he had set himself. My love and admiration for Ben and his music becomes, I hope, more credible if tempered by an acknowledgement of his considerable frailties.

As a devotee of Berg and Webern I can understand that for some musicians, Boulez in particular, some of Britten's music is, as Thomas Adès puts it, just too 'pat', that there is superficiality in the artifice and that the internal workings are slight, too easily attained. Controversially, Adès also ridicules the widely held view that Britten derives power from identifying personally with the drama of the outcast – the lone voice at odds with the community. This is crass, 'stupid' he says (*Thomas Adès: Full of Noise – Conversations with Tom Service*) and an insult to the way Britten 'factures' the music. Perhaps Adès was thinking of Janáček's dictum that great emotion does not necessarily lead to great music; quite the reverse, he said, 'the notes take fright and fly out the window.' Nobody could be more emotional than Janáček, a great favourite of Adès or, indeed, Tchaikowsky who Britten revered, yet both composers create music of power through structure and technique rather than simply and indulgently riding a turbulent wave of hysteria. Pathos rather than bathos. Indeed, as Milan Kundera put it, the essence of Janáček's music lies in 'capturing unknown, never expressed emotions, and capturing them in all their immediacy'.

Emotional immediacy is a quality that lies, without question, at the heart of Britten's best works and he wielded surgical precision in paring down his ideas to sharpen their effect. Nevertheless, all three composers have incontestably mined, at some profound level, their experiences of life, love and loss and these clearly shaped their personalities both as composers and as people. Britten's choice of texts is the best clue to what inspired him and it is pretty unequivocal, not least the repeated focus on the corruption of innocence.

Even though I do not entirely agree with them I am grateful to figures like Thomas Adès, Pierre Boulez and Alfred Brendel for challenging the accepted orthodoxy of Brittens's status, in this country in particular, because they have all at different times made me challenge my own feelings about the music, a challenge that has, by and large, only endorsed my appreciation of it.

Of course the unpleasant preciousness of the court at Aldeburgh (a hybrid form of it still exists) led to some amusing anecdotes as well as savage ones. William Walton loved to tease Julian Bream over his playing of John Dowland. William, in mischievous mood, had asked Ben and Peter why Julian, a festival regular, was suddenly absent. 'My dear,' came the reply, 'his Dowland – it's slipping!' After a couple of years Julian was considered to have hitched up his Dowland and was reinstated. But whenever Walton saw Bream, he would quip 'How's the Dowland, still slipping?' Wherever you get exceptional talent, surrounded by worthy keepers of the flame, this kind of pettiness becomes exaggerated, just as Auden prophesied it would in his famous letter attempting to prepare the young composer for the perils and pitfalls into which his extraordinary talent was likely to lead him.

No one seriously thinks that to be a great artist you need to be a wonderful human being. Indeed I would say that to write music you have to be ruthless with yourself, and probably with others as well. In Britten's case it was, additionally, the conundrum of being a brilliantly creative musician in an essentially philistine environment, of being gay at a time when it was illegal, of sensing that he was something of an odd man out in Suffolk, that all fed into making Ben the musical personality that he was. How lucky for us that this synthesis of time, place and nature led to a talent of originality and edge. One that makes us question the society that bred it and, indeed, ourselves. How lucky that he was, then, a *Lowestoft Lad* rather than *The Boy From Ipanema*.

Working with Britten

Janet Baker

Ben was a king. When he walked into a room the air began to crackle; everyone came alive, became more than themselves. When he left, he made us feel as though we had been better than our best, pleased with ourselves.

Approaching his kingdom, which begins for me where one leaves the A12 and makes that right turn 'to Aldeburgh', feels exactly like going home. It must have rained a lot over the years during Festival time but in my memory the town is everlastingly bathed in sunlight, the cornfield behind the old rehearsal hall is for ever gently moving in a soft breeze, and colleagues are sitting in shirt sleeves enjoying a coffee break in the open air.

They have been marvellous years. People would look at us, the young ones, as though we'd been given the *Good Housekeeping* 'seal of approval' if we were appearing at Aldeburgh; working with Ben did indeed 'seal' us – with quality. Once exposed to him a musician could never be quite the same again. It wasn't that Aldeburgh concerts were given endless rehearsal; on the contrary, I can remember a number of occasions when we felt decidedly pushed for time, but that's part of professional life in general. It was rather a widespread longing to do great things because Ben would be listening; after that it wasn't enough just to be at one's best for Aldeburgh, one tried to give the same dedication to every situation.

One of the most touching aspects of his personality was his deep understanding of performers and their problems. He was a performer of the very highest calibre himself and he knew from the inside exactly how we felt. This was the only level on which I could attempt to communicate with him. We talked once about the difficulty of the *Lucretia* rape scene; this is awkward for me since the tessitura lies just on the break in my voice around middle C.

The entire scene is full of drama, which is hard for me to achieve so low in the voice. Ben's comment when we spoke of this was: 'Oh dear! It's my fault, I've written it all wrong.' Of course he had not written is 'all wrong'; he had scored the piece for Ferrier whose voice was rich and full in that area but who had difficulty later in the opera where I felt more comfortable.

He once gave the cast of *Albert Herring* a piece of advice which I have never forgotten. He had watched a run-through which had not pleased him but which we all thought had gone well. He explained that in playing comedy one must not think the situation amusing oneself; that the characters were not in the least amusing or eccentric *to* themselves, which is precisely why an audience thinks them to be so. We must therefore take ourselves seriously and not try to make the characters funny; this fact is well known to actors but I had not come across the theory before and found it illuminating and true.

Ben was always ready to talk over problems. He discussed the character of Kate in *Owen Wingrave* at length as were sitting among the tombstones in Blythburgh churchyard. He warned me that she was not an easy person to play but that he wanted me to tackle her because of my ability as an actress.

In my experience of the 'good' women, like Penelope, Dido, Savitri or Charlotte, there is in all of them a perverseness which is their saving grace; none of them is too good to be true; they each have a flaw. Penelope, that paragon of fidelity, from some sort of strange cussedness, does not look at Ulysses for a long time in the Peter Hall production; perhaps she is paying him back in that moment for all the empty years. Dido knew perfectly well that Aeneas had a special destiny to fulfil; nevertheless, she defied the gods, took him, and paid the penalty. Charlotte is a model wife but an adulteress in her heart; Savitri won her husband from Death by a sort of trick. Such flaws do not mar a wonderful character; they make the person more real, more moving and more believable. In such contradictions lies the fascination of acting. It is exactly the same with bad girls. Dorabella, although only very mildly wicked, is young and thoughtless; Vitellia is indeed ruthless but she is also a very frightened lady and she bitterly regrets her behaviour; Kate is full of fear too, of insecurity and the vulnerability of youth, a product of an anxious mother, for whom she feel responsible; she behaves badly but there are reasons for her behaviour.

People would often say to me during the weeks of rehearsal for *Owen Wingrave,* 'Does Ben see you as this sort of character, because he has type-cast you all so carefully?' In that case, he must also have seen me as a teenager when I was already a woman of over thirty; that sort of logic is nonsense. What he did see was a singer who had to be capable of acting a difficult role and who looked right enough in shape and size to pass for a younger woman. The real key to Kate's character lies in the score at the moment when Owen's body is discovered and she realizes that she will spend her entire life suffering the most dreadful remorse for what she has done. Ben portrays Kate's anguish most vividly. A bad person feels no remorse. Kate is not a bitch and she is not bad; she is young, and she is without security of any kind, dependent upon the charity of the household, constantly and desperately mortified by her mother.

To work under Ben's baton was a joy of a special kind. The clarity of his beat and the sureness of his tempi gave a rare security. One was upheld by his marvellous shaping of the phrase but at the same time given room, a sort of freedom, to yield to the inspiration of the moment. Only the very greatest conductors have this ability. I imagine his accompanying at the piano was the same but I never had the opportunity to sing lieder with him on my own. There was an occasion during the English Opera Group's tour of Russia in 1967, when he played for Peter and me in a performance of *Abraham and Isaac*, which I shall always remember.

Whether he directed his own or the music of another composer, there was a feeling that the tempo he chose was the right one. The sheer kindness of his personality and the infinite patience with which he would iron out problems never made one feel restricted or dominated. People with his sort of charm allied to immense talent must find relationships easier than lesser mortals do. Of course there must have been a 'dark' side to him after all, he was a genius, not a saint. All I can say with perfect honesty is that I never saw it.

Ben's personal magnetism drew everybody towards him. My own decision not to allow myself to approach too close too often is one which I do not regret. I must have appeared at most of the Aldeburgh Festivals since the early sixties except for the odd year when Glyndebourne performances made it impossible to make the journey to Suffolk. Ben would get a bit huffy about Glyndebourne interfering with his projects but I would grin to myself and think, 'It's a jolly good thing not to be always available at the Master's call!' He knew perfectly well I considered Aldeburgh home and he knew also of the huge musical debt I owed both to him and to Peter. So did many musicians. One couldn't really do anything *for* him, though, except try to perform at one's very best, of course. But there was no way of returning a fraction of what he poured out to us and to his profession.

Now that he is gone, I feel very differently. The one thing he would ask is continued loyalty in every sense, to the place and to the School which is his superbly fitting memorial. That, at least, I can give; it is especially important that musicians who fell under his spell and were polished by his methods of working should pass on as much as possible to the young people involved in the Snape project. It is very greatly Ben's doing that English musicians have become a truly important international force in the years since 1945. If it is possible to sum up the reasons for this tremendous flowering of talent it might be in the word 'Excellence'. It is quality which divides the professional from the amateur, a dedicated, single-minded search for the best – in oneself – allied to the best in others. In work with Ben everyone was concerned with this search because it was his search too.

I have always believed that the creative person inhabits a world unknown to others. The gulf which exists between his world and that of the re-creative artist is wide indeed. Even at their most sublime, performers are still only able to go as far as the entrance and look from afar towards the land where the composer is perfectly at home. The suffering such a homeland exacts from an individual as the price he must pay for the original ideas he brings back to us is unimaginable. And yet, while there is no doubt that the composer wants no other country, it must be frightening and lonely there. Contact is far more easily made on the performing level and many people consider it to be as important as the creative one because performers bring a work to life. I cannot agree; even if a composition is never heard, the process of seizing an inspired idea, and shaping it into concrete form, makes the composer what he is. A woman is not less a mother because her child dies at birth; she has undergone the psychological and physical processes which make her so; the same with the creative genius, whether his music is heard or not, he has gone through the agony, and there it lies, the material for others to use.

I often used to wish I could communicate with Ben on his own level, the level of his creative work; an utterly futile wish. Yet when he was conducting and one gave him, heart and soul, of one's best in performance, the look in his eyes, the expression of gratitude on his face, made such a moment memorable and the best sort of communication one could possibly wish for.

The last rehearsal I did with Ben was on *Phaedra* during the summer of 1976; this is the last piece he wrote for me, a dramatic cantata. Dramatic indeed, full of passion and nobility. Phaedra – the words of the Robert Lowell translation which Ben used make her a woman who has loved, betrayed, suffered remorse – attempts to put right the terrible wrong she has done, and nobly dies; a character to glory in. Her music is towering, full of contrast, and the bars in which she announces the progress of the poison surging through her veins are among the most sublime of all Ben's music. I now have copies of the printed score but the much-thumbed, tatty, yellow-paper-bound, awkward-sized manuscript I had at first is more precious to me. I always revise from it. I began to memorize the score during my annual tour of the USA in January 1976, in a train going from New York to Washington. The first rehearsal was in the spring of that year and when Steuart Bedford and I met Ben in the library at the Red House the music was tucked safely away in my head; Ben was pleased I knew it so well at that early stage.

We worked for two hours that day. Steuart and I had run through the piece on our own the day before and he had started to play the first recitative section rather fast for me. It is marked 'agitative crotchets' and I could not manage the words 'My lost and dazzled eyes' clearly enough. I said to Steuart, 'I'm sure Ben will want me to sing the phrase at a speed which makes the words possible' and sure enough, the following day, Ben did comment on this very point. He would always see at once how to solve a difficulty according to the individual need. He also mentioned that the 'Aphrodite' a little further on should be sung marcato, a marking which is not in the printed vocal score. I asked him if I could start the final phrase 'My eyes at last give up their life', on C, instead of E as he had written it, because it gives the voice a moment to relax before that extremely taxing end; this he immediately agreed to.

On the day of the first performance, Ben, who had been at the previous day's rehearsal, appeared at the final run-through. He saw I was without score and said, 'You're a brave girl to do the first performance from memory.' I was suddenly terror-stricken and thought, 'My God! Perhaps I'm not as brave as I think I am!' and then that night I thought of the five months of study and decided to trust my memory. Responsibility for the work of any composer is a heavy burden, but the premiere of a piece with the creator sitting in his box twenty feet away is a terrifying one. I opened my mouth and out rolled the words 'In May, in brilliant Athens', beautified by the perfect acoustic at the Maltings. The performance went very well and everyone was stunned by the power and passion of Ben's writing at a time when he was so frail physically.

The following year, we repeated the performance and this time Ben was not in his box. Somehow the first summer without him was not a sad one. The air, the fields, the buildings, were all filled with his joyous spirit, free of the frail body at last.

A composer belongs to the whole world; but a composer has to live at a specific time in a certain place and is a human being like the rest of us; so Ben is also the special property of his country, and of the people who knew him. As a man, a musician and a friend he belongs particularly to those of us who were lucky enough to know him, to work with him, and to love him.

Britten and the Gang

Peter Parker

One evening in 1937 Benjamin Britten was dining with the novelist Christopher Isherwood and the film-maker Basil Wright. 'Well,' they said to each other when Britten momentarily left the table, 'have we convinced Ben he's queer, or haven't we?'[i] By this time, Britten was in fact well aware that he was homosexual, but – unlike Isherwood and Wright – was uneasy about it. 'Decisions are so hard to make,' he had written in his diary the previous year, '& it's difficult to look unprejudiced on apparently abnormal things.'[ii] This difficulty is one that has plagued those who have written about Britten's life and work. Donald Mitchell has argued that Humphrey Carpenter's 1992 biography was 'highjacked by the issue of Britten's sexuality', and that subsequent writers 'have perhaps been unduly influenced by his emphases and exaggerations and gone on to exaggerate them, copiously, and fantasize about them.'[iii]

While Mitchell is quite right to suggest that there are many other themes to explore in the composer's life and work, the relationship between Britten's sexuality and his music is both fundamental and inescapable. At the very least, it influenced his choice of subject matter and those with whom he decided to collaborate. Though audiences might not have recognized it at the time, the poetry of Rimbaud and the sonnets of Michaelangelo had a clear personal significance for the composer, as did those works of Herman Melville, Henry James and Thomas Mann he used as the basis for three major operas. Collaborators such as W. H. Auden, E. M. Forster and William Plomer were members of a distinct if discreet homosexual network in the arts, and it is unlikely that Britten and Peter Pears would have had such a long-lasting and definitive professional relationship had they not also had a personal one. In addition, the tension between sexual attraction and self-restraint,

48

particularly in Britten's relationships with a succession of boys and adolescents, fed into and shaped his work. It is both characteristic and wholly appropriate that his last opera, *Death in Venice*, should be based on an autobiographical account of a writer's obsession with a young boy, a Dionysian lapse from a life of Apollonian self-discipline.

Now that homosexuality has become part of the cultural mainstream and same-sex partnerships are sanctioned by law, it is necessary to remind ourselves that for most of Britten's life, until the passing of the Sexual Offences Act 1967 a mere nine years before his death, homosexuality was punishable by a two-year prison sentence and attracted widespread prejudice. The premieres of both *Billy Budd* and *The Turn of the Screw*, for example, took place against a backdrop of increasing public hostility towards homosexuality. In the wake of the defection to the Soviet Union in 1951 of two British diplomats, the homosexual Guy Burgess and bisexual Donald Maclean, there was a ferocious backlash against 'perversion'. Both Sir David Maxwell Fyfe as Home Secretary and Sir John Nott-Bowers as Commissioner of the Metropolitan Police saw it as their duty to stamp out this particular 'vice', and prosecutions for 'gross indecency' rose exponentially. Several trials – such as those of Rupert Croft-Crooke in 1953, and of Lord Montagu, Michael Pitt-Rivers and Peter Wildeblood in 1954 – received widespread publicity, and many people thought that John Gielgud's career would not survive his prosecution in 1953 for 'persistent importuning'. Britten himself was interviewed by Scotland Yard during this period, without further action being taken. Although he had been at school with Maclean, and one of Burgess's boyfriends had lived in his Hallam Street flat in the 1940s, it seems likely that Britten was questioned merely as a matter of routine: Cecil Beaton was interviewed at the same time.

Public opinion appeared to have moved on a little by the time Britten died in 1976 and much has been made of the fact that the Queen sent Pears a private letter of condolence. While Pears was no doubt right that this was 'a recognition of the way we lived', it was reported in the press that he had received the message merely 'as a representative of all who had worked with Lord Britten.'[iv] When Pears himself died, there was certainly no recognition in *The Times* obituary that this relationship with Britten had been a personal as well as a professional one. This relationship was both discreet and publicly decorous, but throughout their life together

they had been subject to innuendo. Back in 1948, for example,
Peter Grimes had provoked some unwelcome comments in the
Times Literary Supplement in the course of a review of Eric Walter
White's book on Britten. Grimes' 'only claim to our interest is that
he has been involved in the death [sic] of several small boys,' the
reviewer noted; yet the 'composer and librettist seem to be attaching
some mystical value to the mere fact of being in opposition to
society.'[v] This might be a coded attack on Britten's pacifism, but
the reviewer went on to note that the absence from the opera 'of
any feminine figure, except the purely maternal school-mistress
and the cardboard caricatures of femininity in its most unpleasing
or ludicrous forms [i.e. Mrs Sedley, Auntie and her two 'nieces'],
accentuates the extraordinarily emotional unbalance of the whole
plot.'[vi] Quite what this reviewer would have made of *Billy Budd*,
with its all-male cast and distinctly homoerotic atmosphere, or
even *The Turn of the Screw* (asked what construction should be
put upon his story, Henry James replied 'the worst possible'), is
anyone's guess.[vii]

Clearly, the subject of Britten's homosexuality could fill an entire
book, and it is only possible here to concentrate on one aspect: the
lasting influence upon Britten's life and work of the associations
he forged in the 1930s. Isherwood and Wright's rhetorical question
was partly a joke, but the fact that Britten was homosexual introduced him to a whole new world of people and ideas at a key
moment early in his career. Although his precocious talent would
always have brought him to the front rank of twentieth-century
composers, the circles in which he began to move in the 1930s both
shaped and helped to promote his work. Being 'queer' was not
merely a matter of who you went to bed with: it made you part of a
what Isherwood called 'the gang', a disparate but highly influential
group drawn together partly by sexual orientation but also by
shared interests and political attitudes, and by frequent collaborations. One of Isherwood's boyfriends from the 1930s, the former
chorus boy called Jack Hewit who (as if illustrating the point) was
also the lover of Guy Burgess and at one point became Britten and
Pears' lodger, described 'a sort of gay intellectual freemasonry'
that existed at this period: 'It was like the five concentric [sic] rings
in the Olympic emblem. One person in one circle knew one in
another and that's how people met.'[viii] An alternative family tree
could be drawn up showing how these people were related – by
love affairs or friendship or working together: between most of

them there were very few degrees of separation. Writing of the 1930s from the vantage point of 1951, Evelyn Waugh complained that 'certain young men ganged up and captured the decade.'[ix] This may have been something of an exaggeration, but a whole network of alliances – both personal and professional, sometimes buried, sometimes in plain view – played a significant role in the cultural life of Britain at that time.

It was during the second half of the 1930s that Britten, somewhat gingerly, entered this brave new world and underwent a profound change both personally and professionally. Christopher Headington argued that for Britten generally 'work and private life were virtually one', and nowhere was this more apparent than during these few formative years.[x] Britten turned twenty-one in November 1934 and had already written several works he considered substantial enough to grant opus numbers, including the *Sinfonietta* (1932), the *Phantasy* for oboe quartet (1932), *A Boy was Born* (1933) and the *Simple Symphony* (1934). Then, on 27 April 1935, he was invited to lunch with the film-maker Alberto Cavalcanti and the painter William Coldstream. Both men worked for the GPO Film Unit, which had been founded by John Grierson in 1933 and was at the forefront of what became known as the British Documentary Movement. Grierson's intention was to bring genuine creativity and aesthetic excellence to what were in essence public information films. To this end, he recruited writers and painters and musicians to work in collaboration with his core group of talented young film-makers. Coldstream was currently working on *The King's Stamp*, a short film about a special postage stamp issued to mark the Silver Jubilee of George V (himself a keen philatelist), and Britten was asked to provide the music. This useful (and not very taxing) commission not only led almost immediately to other work, but introduced the young Britten to sexually sophisticated and politically aware older colleagues, at least three of whom – Cavalcanti, Wright and Auden – were homosexual.

In July Britten had been taken by Wright, who worked as a director and producer with the Film Unit, to meet Auden, with whom he would be collaborating on a mining documentary titled *Coal Face*. Britten described Auden as 'the most amazing man, a very brilliant & attractive personality,' while Auden in his turn was startled by Britten's youth but at once recognized his musical talent.[xi] The two men would work together on several other films, notably *Night Mail* (1936) and *The Way to the Sea* (1936), which in turn led to further collaborations. One of the films Auden and Britten worked on, *Calendar of the Year*, provides an example of just how closely and complexly personal and professional lives could intersect and intertwine. In 1936 Britten was worrying in his diary about the influence upon his current favourite, the fifteen-year-old Piers Dunkerley, of the nineteen-year-old Giles Romilly when both boys were recruited to appear in this film. Romilly and his brother Esmond had achieved notoriety at Wellington College, where they had edited a highly subversive magazine, *Out of Bounds*. Among the school's staff were Coldstream (who had briefly taught art) and T. C. Worsley, with whom Auden would co-write a Hogarth Press pamphlet, *Education – Today and Tomorrow*. After running away from Wellington, Esmond worked for Grierson, where he met Auden (and resisted his advances). The more amenable Giles would be taken up by the Auden-Isherwood set and have an affair with Stephen Spender's former lover Tony Hyndman. When he and Hyndman set off together to fight in the Spanish Civil War, Isherwood and Gerald Hamilton (the model for his eponymous 'Mr Norris') accompanied them to the station to wave them off.

Meanwhile, convincing Britten that he was queer, or at any rate getting him to act on the knowledge, was Auden's self-appointed task, with Isherwood and Wright evidently lending a hand. It is clear from Britten's diaries that he needed encouragement. Shortly after joining the GPO Film Unit, he had dinner with his sister Barbara, who was herself homosexual. 'Long talks about troubles of life – rather overwhelming at the moment,' he wrote, presumably prompted by the new circles in which he was beginning to move; 'she is very good & nice on these matters.'[xii]

It has been suggested that one of Auden's motives in jolting Britten out of his sexual hesitancy was that he had fallen in love with the young composer. This notion rests largely upon two poems Auden dedicated to Britten, who subsequently set them to music. 'Underneath the abject willow' urges a reluctant lover into action, while 'Night covers up the rigid land' is written in the voice of a rejected suitor. It makes a neat little narrative, but there is no evidence that it describes the relationship between the poet and the composer. If the words of the first poem carried any weight for Britten, he effectively neutralized this by setting them to music he rightly described as 'very light & Victorian in mood!'.[xiii] Of the second poem, Britten merely noted in his diary that Auden had sent him 'another poem apropos of nothing.'[xiv] † Although there is no doubting the importance to both men of their collaborations, Britten's name does not appear in a list Auden compiled in 1947, commemorating what his biographer Edward Mendelson calls 'the sexual loves that had had the greatest effect on his work and life.'[xv] In his and Louis MacNeice's 'Last Will and Testament' (published in *Letters from Iceland* in 1936 and itself an extended catalogue of personal and professional connections, full of references that one had to be part of the gang to understand), Auden's wish that fate should soon send Britten 'a passionate affair' is not that of someone who considered himself in the running. Indeed, Auden had been in Iceland with Michael Yates, a young man he had known for several years, whose name *does* appear in the 1947 list, and about whom he was still writing love poems. Perhaps the real nature of Auden and Britten's relationship can be judged by what Auden wrote many years later about collaboration, with its clear distinction between sexual and erotic bonds: 'Between two collaborators, whatever their sex, age or appearance, there is always an erotic bond. Queers, to whom normal marriage and parenthood are forbidden, are fools if they do not deliberately look for tasks which require collaboration, and the right person with whom to collaborate. In my own case, collaboration has brought me greater erotic joy – as distinct from sexual pleasure – than any sexual relationship I have had.'[xvi] Whatever the case, Wright was surely correct to suggests that it was Auden 'who first awoke Ben's real imaginative and emotional life.'[xvii]

Quite how Auden shook Britten out of his 'unique and moping station' has never been fully explained. Isherwood, always more interested in practice than in theory, had taken matters in hand by getting Britten drunk and hauling him off to the notorious Turkish baths in Jermyn Street. Auden's approach is likely to have been more psychological. Isherwood recalled his own experience of Auden's methods: 'he intruded everywhere; upon my old-maidish tidiness, my intimate little fads, my private ailments, my most secret sexual

---

† It has been further suggested that Auden wrote the distinctly erotic 'To lie flat on the back' for Britten, who set it in 1937. In fact the poem was written in 1933, two years before the two men met. The reference to those who are 'brilliant at tennis' in the catalogue of the sort of passengers brought together by travel in *The Way to the Sea*, however, is almost certainly a fond bouquet to the film's composer.

fears. As mercilessly inquisitive as a child of six, he enquired into the
details of my dreams and phantasies, unravelled my complexes […] I
had found myself answering his questions, as one always must answer
when the questioner himself is impervious to delicacy or shame. And,
after all, when I had finished, the heavens hadn't fallen; and, ah, what
a relief to have spoken the words aloud!'[xviii] It seems probable that
Auden subjected Britten to a similar process. As Isherwood recalled:
'We were extraordinarily interfering in this respect – as bossy as a pair
of self-assured young psychiatrists – [Auden] wasn't a doctor's son
and I wasn't an ex-medical student for nothing!'[xix]

Not everyone thought this interference welcome. Marjorie Fass,
who had come to know Britten through her neighbour Frank
Bridge, told a friend: 'I'm having a bit of fun with Benjy by not
being bowled over with everything that Auden & Christopher
Isherwood do – I'm definitely *bored* with Christopher's adolescent
"smartness" & his unwise interest in prostitutes male & female –
and Benjy so hoped I'd like his last book called "Sally Bowles" that
he insisted on giving it me – & I find it even *more* boring & not so
good as "Mr Norris" […] Dear Benjy he is *so* young & *so* dazzled'.[xx]

Fortunately for Britten, Fass's influence in such matters was
waning. Auden and Isherwood may have been bossy, but at least
they weren't sentimental and patronizing. Before meeting them,
Britten was already in the too-cosy position Auden would later
warn him against, 'surrounded by people who adore you, nurse
you, and praise everything you do […] playing the lovable talented
little boy.'[xxi] There was a clear link in Auden's mind between sexual
and artistic maturity. By accepting and acting upon his homosexuality, Britten would not only be joining the gang but asserting his
creative and personal independence. To some extent he had already
broken free of his conventional upbringing and musical education
in his first major collaboration with Auden, *Our Hunting Fathers*.
A significant entry in his diary on 2 January 1936 records a day
working with Auden and Wright on *Night Mail*, after which
Auden comes to dinner: 'We talk amongst many things of a new
Song Cycle (probably on Animals) that I may write. Very nice and
interesting & pleasant evening. Preparing for early bed when Frank
B[ridge] phones and talks from 11.0 – 12.0 unceasingly. Very nice
tho' – he is one of the world's marvels & dears.'[xxii] It is likely that
Auden had also talked unceasingly, as he was inclined to do, but
one senses the he may already have seemed rather more of a marvel
to the young composer than the much older Bridge now did.

The following month, Britten lost his childhood home when his mother moved from Lowestoft to Frinton-on-Sea: 'I personally don't mind a scrap – except for the fact that one suddenly realizes that now, one's youth is so to speak gone. An era is passed.'[xxiii] His association with Auden and his circle undoubtedly directed his burgeoning political beliefs, and this increased his detachment from his more conservative family. Although he worked on *Our Hunting Fathers* while staying with his mother during the summer, the fact that she 'disapprove[d] very thoroughly' of a section he played her, far from worrying him, seemed 'almost an incentive'.[xxiv]

The cycle was written against a backdrop of increasingly alarming fascist advances in Europe – the occupation of the Rhineland, the invasion of Abyssinia, and the outbreak of the Spanish Civil War – all of which Britten commented on in his diary. Auden's 'Prologue', so densely written as to be ungraspable by audiences merely listening to it, nevertheless contains clear references to 'reformers and tyrants', while the last couplet of his 'Epilogue' adapts what he mistakenly thought were the words of Lenin (in fact said by Lenin's wife). Of the three central texts, which Auden selected and adapted, 'Rats away!' is clearly intended as a curse directed at the fascist vermin currently swarming over Europe. 'Messalina', although about the death of a pet, is a deeply-felt expression of grief, while the 'murdering kites/In all their flights' of Thomas Ravenscroft's 'Hawking for Partridges' suggest the military aircraft used by Hitler, Mussolini and Franco, a notion supported by the terrifying use of almost deafening brass and violently stabbing strings. The setting of the latter also takes two from the catalogue of hawks' names Ravenscroft supplies, 'German' and 'Jew', and isolates them, clearly articulated, at the end of this section, following this with the hunter's onomatopoeiac command 'Whurret!', sung by the soprano in a sobbing fall. At the premiere on 25 September 1936 many in the conventionally-minded audience were simply baffled by this electrifying piece, partly because it was utterly contemporary both in its musical language and in its political message. Bridge, though kind in his comments, clearly hadn't liked it. 'I feel he has a rather precious & escapist view of art,' Britten would comment a few months later '– but that is typical of his generation – & eminently excusable.'[xxv] Bridge would of course remain a key influence, but it was now clear which generation Britten sought to align himself with. Though disappointed by the cycle's reception, he nevertheless recognized its significance: 'It's my op. 1 alright,' he declared.[xxvi]

By now Britten had started working with the Group Theatre. Set up in 1932 by the dancer Rupert Doone and the painter Robert Medley, this theatrical co-operative was similar to the GPO Film Unit in that it sought to create something new by bringing together people from different disciplines. Its stated aim was 'by continually playing together and by using its own producers, playwrights, painters, musicians, technicians, etc., to produce a company which will work like a well trained orchestra.'[xxvii] Dance, mime and music were integral to the company's productions and the repertory was highly eclectic, including Shakespeare and Ibsen as well as plays by Jean Giono and Rudolf Besier and mixed programmes featuring extracts from the famous Victorian melodrama *East Lynne* staged alongside Rupert Doone embodying 'The Spirit of Cocaine'.

Gradually, however, the Group Theatre became known for what it called 'a theatre representative of the spirit of to-day', putting on experimental new plays, often with political themes, notably Auden and Isherwood's three collaborations, Louis MacNeice's *Out of the Picture* and Stephen Spender's *Trial of a Judge*.[xxviii] Again like the Film Unit, it took advantage of a network of personal relationships. Auden, for example, had been at school with Medley, who became the object of one of his first (secret) sexual passions. Auden's feelings had eventually dissipated, but the friendship persisted and he was asked to write a play for the Group Theatre soon after it was founded. Like the Film Unit, the Group Theatre had a distinct homosexual element without being a cabal. Doone (whom Britten, in a characteristically prim phrase, thought 'inclined to be too affectionate') and Medley were personal as well as professional partners and, as in most dance and theatre companies, a number of other members were homosexual.[xxix]

The Group Theatre already had a musical director, Herbert Murrill, who although only in his mid-twenties was Professor of Composition at the Royal Academy of Music. It was at Auden's suggestion that Britten was recruited in October 1935 to write 'what little music there is' for a production of *Timon of Athens*.[xxx] Murrill had provided the music for the first of the Auden-Isherwood collaborations, *The Dog Beneath the Skin* – 'very competently, but adding nothing to the show,' Britten noted. 'It was just clever & rather dull jazz – not as amusing perhaps as the original.'[xxxi] After his training with the Film Unit, for whom he had to provide many different kinds of music, Britten would prove more inventive when he took over from Murrill not only for *The*

Ascent of F6 and *On the Frontier* (which was dedicated to him), but also for MacNeice's *Out of the Picture* and *The Agamemnon of Aeschylus*. It was here that Britten became adept at setting the words of his contemporaries at a time when most composers chose older and more solidly established poems to set. Contemporary poetry demanded contemporary music and, as with *Our Hunting Fathers*, the very freshness and complexity of such texts kept Britten on his inventive toes.

The collaboration with Auden continued throughout the 1930s and beyond, during which Britten's versatility was honed and in some cases tested to the limit, as his diaries often record. The song cycle *On This Island* (1937) set five of Auden's recent poems for voice and piano, while several other settings that exist as individual songs may have been intended for a second cycle that never materialized. The first (private) performance of *On This Island* was given by Britten and Pears to an audience consisting of Isherwood and Britten's fellow-composer (and sometime suitor) Lennox Berkeley a month before its official premiere, and when the cycle was published in 1938 it was dedicated to Isherwood. At the same time Britten and Auden worked intermittently on a group of light-hearted, jazz-like 'Cabaret Songs' (1937–9), written for and dedicated to Hedli Anderson, a singer with the Group Theatre who would later marry MacNeice. In *Ballad of Heroes* (1939), honouring the International Brigade in the Spanish Civil War, Britten set Auden's 'Farewell to the drawing-room's civilized cry' (which the poet had written out for him before his own departure for the Spanish front in January 1937) alongside words by the communist poet Randall Swingler. Having introduced Britten to the works of Rimbaud and Christopher Smart, Auden was also indirectly responsible for *Les Illuminations* (1939) and *Jubilate Agno* (1943) and would later be credited by the composer as the person who developed his love of poetry, this leading to a substantial catalogue of songs and song cycles.

During the late 1930s Britten continued to receive what he called 'sound advice about many things' from Isherwood: 'I am terribly tempted always to make him into a father confessor,' he wrote.[xxxii] He was a frequent guest at the Isherwood family home in Pembroke Gardens, but the threads that bound all these people together were beginning to unravel. Intimations of the end were signalled by Auden and Isherwood's departure for China in January 1938 to report on the Sino-Japanese War. A rowdy farewell party was hosted by the Group Theatre, at which Hedli Anderson performed several of the Cabaret Songs. 'Beastly crowd & unpleasant people,' Britten noted. 'Christopher leaves in a temper' – and without giving Britten the spare key to his house, where Britten was supposedly spending the night.[xxxiii] Britten nevertheless came to Victoria Station to see the two friends off the following morning. Isherwood entrusted his latest boyfriend, the twenty-year-old Ian Scott-Kilvert, to Britten's care. 'I'd be only *too* delighted if you saw him occasionally, and, maybe, introduce him to some of the gang, as well?'[xxxiv]

It was while staying in New York on their way back from China that Auden and Isherwood decided to return to America the following year. *On the Frontier* opened in Cambridge in November, after which Auden and Isherwood (accompanied by Jack Hewit, who had replaced Scott-Kilvert in the latter's life) went to Brussels to complete their book about China, *Journey to a War*. Britten spent some time with them when he was in the city to take part in a performance of his Piano Concerto, and on the eve of their departure for America in January 1939, he and Pears held a small party. Hedli Anderson performed the Cabaret Songs, accompanied by Britten on the piano, and Pears sang Britten's setting (subsequently lost) of a poem by Stephen Spender. It seems appropriate that this party, which marked the end of an era, should have a guest list that once again showed the widespread interconnectedness of this circle. Stephen Spender, accompanied by his first wife, Inez, was of course an old and intimate friend of Auden and Isherwood. Olive Mangeot was the estranged wife of André Mangeot, for whom Isherwood had worked as a secretary in the 1920s and whose International Quartet had given the first performance of Britten's *Phantasy*, Op. 2 in 1933. Robert Moody had been at Oxford with Auden and at medical school with Isherwood, with whom he struck up an enduring friendship; he was also the brother of John Moody, a founder member of the Group Theatre who was married to the twin sister of Peter Burra, a close friend of Pears who had been killed in an air crash in April 1937. E. M. Forster had also known Burra well, had become an alternative father-figure to Isherwood, and was the dedicatee of *Journey to a War* and a supporter of the Group Theatre, where he had first met Britten, with whom he would later collaborate on *Billy Budd*. William Coldstream was accompanied by his wife Nancy Sharp, a painter with whom Auden was once 'on the verge of having an affair'; she subsequently became the lover, collaborator and muse of MacNeice, and then married Stephen Spender's brother Michael.[xxxv] The final three guests were Britten, Auden and

Isherwood's 'boys', as Coldstream put it: Wulff Scherchen (who was also a friend of Ian Scott-Kilvert), Michael Yates and Jack Hewit.

Auden and Isherwood had told everyone that they were merely visiting America, but they already saw their future in Europe as uncertain. The plans of Britten and Pears, who followed them at the end of April, were equally fluid – though in the case of both Isherwood and Britten, ending relationships that had become complicated (with Hewit and Scherchen respectively) was one reason for crossing the Atlantic. In the event, Auden and Isherwood decided to stay permanently in the States, while Britten and Pears remained there until March 1942. While they saw a good deal of Auden and even for a while lived with him in Brooklyn (where they worked together on *Paul Bunyan*), Isherwood had gone to California, where he proved elusive: 'Where is Christopher?' Britten asked plaintively. 'Dead?'[xxxvi]

Although enjoying considerable success in America, Britten was also feeling homesick, and this was increased when in May 1941 he came across a copy of the *Listener*. The BBC's magazine had Forster's close friend J. R. Ackerley as its literary editor and was more or less the house journal of the gang, many of whom had been regular contributors to it over the years. This issue published the text of a broadcast Forster had made on the Suffolk poet George Crabbe, and it was this that decided Britten to return to England and to write *Peter Grimes*. His first and perhaps least likely choice as librettist was Isherwood, with whom he had re-established contact. The opera might have raised even more eyebrows had Isherwood accepted this commission, but he could not spare the time and doubted that collaboration would be practical if composer and librettist were separated by the Atlantic.

While Auden and Isherwood appeared to be lost to America, other pre-war friends were still in England when Britten returned there. In a lecture he gave on Crabbe at the first Aldeburgh Festival in 1948, Forster announced that he would have liked to have written the libretto of *Peter Grimes* – a broad hint Britten would take up later that year. At the same Festival William Plomer (a close friend of both Forster and Ackerley) gave a talk on another local figure, Edward Fizgerald, best known as the translator of the *Rubáiyát of Omar Khayyám* but also of interest because of his long attachment to a Lowestoft sailor half his age called 'Posh' Fletcher. Plomer had written the introduction to John Lehmann's 1946 edition of Melville's *Billy Budd*, a book of immaculate provenance given that not only were the introducer and publisher members of the gang, but it also boasted an elegant dustjacket designed by the homosexual painter Keith Vaughan, for whom an admiring Isherwood would become a kind of agent in America in addition to buying one of his paintings as a birthday gift for Forster. It was this edition of *Billy Budd* that Britten said inspired him to adapt the novella for an opera – although he must already have known Auden's poem 'Herman Melville', written in March 1939 and published in *Another Time* the following year. It is also likely that he would have read *Aspects of the Novel* (1927), in which Forster holds up Claggart as an outstanding example of 'Evil […] labelled and personified'.xxxvii

The story admirably fitted Britten's recurring theme of innocence and its destruction. It concerns a beautiful young foretopman who, like Charles Dibdin's Tom Bowling in the song for which Britten wrote a ravishing arrangement some years before embarking on the opera, is 'the darling' of the crew, but whose very goodness goads the ship's master-at-arms, Claggart, into destroying him. For Eric Crozier, who as an experienced librettist had been called in as an additional collaborator, the subject matter of Melville's novella was a major drawback – not least because, set entirely on a warship, it had no female roles. For Forster, whose reason for abandoning fiction was 'Weariness of the only subject that I both can and may treat – the love of men for women & vice versa', this was a large part of its appeal.xxxviii In the notes he made for *Aspects of the Novel*, he had decided that Billy's 'goodness [was] rather alloyed by H[erman]. M[elville]'s suppressed homosex:', and he was determined that the opera should be about real people – 'human beings and the smell of tar' – rather than mere embodiments of good and evil.xxxix 'Evil is unspectacular and always human,' Auden had written in his poem, and Forster evidently had this in mind while writing a soliloquy for Claggart. He thought this his major contribution to the opera and was unafraid to tell Britten when he felt the music fell short. 'I want *passion* – love constricted, perverted, poisoned, but never the less *flowing* down its agonizing channel; a sexual discharge gone evil,' he complained. 'Not soggy depression or growling remorse.'xl Britten was deeply stung by this and it took all Crozier's diplomacy to get composer and novelist back on cordial terms once more.

J. R. Ackerley, whose job at the *Listener* covered the arts as well as books, had been consulted about which painters to approach to design the sets for *Billy Budd*, and in 1951 Britten asked him to recommend a librettist for a projected children's opera based on Beatrix Potter's *The Tale of Mr Tod*. After some discussion Plomer emerged as the most likely candidate. As his biographer puts it, although Plomer 'knew little about music and virtually nothing about modern opera', he was nevertheless 'in one sense [...] a natural choice, for he was associated in Britten's mind with the talented homosexual circle from which he had already selected Auden and Forster'.[xli] The Potter opera foundered on copyright problems, but Plomer went on to write the libretto of *Gloriana* and the three *Church Parables*, which came about largely because Plomer had urged Britten to see some Noh theatre while he was on a trip to Japan. (Plomer had lived in Japan during the 1920s and subsequently published a discreetly homosexual novel based on his relationship with a young man there.) Plomer's talks or readings would become a regular feature of the Aldeburgh Festival, while Ackerley, hearing that Britten had started writing the *War Requiem*, sent him his own copy of Wilfred Owen's *Collected Poems* because, unlike Britten's copy, this one contained a photograph of the poet. 'Here is Owen with his beautiful face,' Ackerley wrote in the accompanying letter. 'Do take, I would like to think of it being an inspiration to you.'[xlii]

Britten no doubt appreciated such gestures, but in spite of Isherwood and Auden's best efforts, he was never wholly at ease in any company that was too obviously gay. Peter Pears said that Britten 'was never drawn to what he described as the "queer society" in London, and had an abhorrence of camp.'[xliii] This is, however, more a matter of style than of substance: the substance is in the quality of his homosexual friendships and collaborations and the music that resulted.

Notes

[i]   Christopher Headington, *Britten* (Eyre Methuen, 1981), p35
[ii]   Diary, 5 June 1936: John Evans (ed.) *Journeying Boy; The Diaries of the Young Benjamin Britten 1928–1938* (Faber, 2009), p358.
[iii]   Donald Mitchell, Philip Reed & Mervyn Cooke (eds.) *Letters from a Life, Volume Three 1946–51* (Faber 2004), pp5–7
[iv]   Quoted Humphrey Carpenter, *Benjamin Britten* (Faber, 1992), p585
[v]   Quoted Carpenter, p303
[vi]   *ibid*
[vii]   William Plomer to Britten, 21 Nov 1964, quoted Carpenter, p337
[viii] Donald Mitchell & Philip Reed (eds.) *Letters from a Life, Volume One 1929–39* (Faber,1991), p606

ix   'Two Unquiet Lives', *Tablet*, 5 May 1951

x   Headington, p36

xi   Diary, 5 July 1935, *Journeying Boy*, p269

xii   Diary, 8 May 35, *Journeying Boy*, p261

xiii   Diary, 17 Nov 36, *Journeying Boy*, p389

xiv   Diary, 22 May 36, quoted Carpenter p81

xv   Edward Mendelson, *Later Auden* (Faber, 1999), p266

xvi   Auden's Berlin Journal (1964), 25 Oct 64, quoted Peter Parker, *Isherwood* (Picador, 2004), p176

xvii   *Letters from a Life, Volume One*, p379

xviii   *Lions and Shadows* (Hogarth Press, 1938), pp194–5

xix   Carpenter, pp188, quoting letter from Isherwood, 17 April 1980

xx   Marjorie Fass, letter to Daphne Oliver, Dec 1937, *Letters from a Life, Volume One*, p19

xxi   Auden to Britten, 'Saturday' [31 Jan 1942], quoted in Donald Mitchell, *Britten & Auden in the Thirties* (Faber, 1981), p161

xxii   Diary, 2 Jan 1936, *Journeying Boy*, p323

xxiii   Diary 19 Feb 1936, *Journeying Boy*, p334

xxiv   Diary, 11 June 1936, *Journeying Boy*, p358

xxv   Diary 1 March 1937, *Journeying Boy*, p413

xxvi   Diary, 30 April 1937, *Journeying Boy*, p248

xxvii   quoted Parker, p290

xxviii Group Theatre 1934 prospectus, quoted Mendelson, p266

xxix   Diary 11 May 1936, *Journeying Boy*, p353

xxx   Diary, 16 Oct 1935, *Journeying Boy*, p282

xxxi   Diary, 12 Jan 1936, *Journeying Boy*, p326

xxxii   Diary, 25 June & 29 July 1937, *Journeying Boy*, pp439, 446

xxxiii Diary, 18–19 Jan 1938, *Journeying Boy*, p462

xxxiv   quoted Parker, p370

xxxv   'Nancy Spender's Recollections of Wystan Auden', *W.H.Auden Society Newsletter* No.10–11 (Sept 1993)

xxxvi   Donald Mitchell & Philip Reed (eds.) *Letters from a Life, Volume Two 1939–45* (Faber, 1991), p658

xxxvii *Aspects of the Novel* (1927: Penguin edition, 1962), p146

xxxviii Diary, 16 June 10, Philip Gardner (ed.) *The Journals and Diaries of E.M. Forster, Volume 2* (Pickering & Chatto, 2011), p27

xxxix   E.M. Forster (ed. Philip Gardner) *Commonplace Book* (Scolar Press, 1985), p17; Forster to Britten, 20 Dec 1948, Mary Lago & P.N. Furbank (eds) *Selected Letters of E.M. Forster, Volume Two 1921–1970* (Collins, 1985), p235

xl   Forster to Britten, n.d. [early December 1950], *ibid*, p242

xli   Peter F. Alexander, *William Plomer* (OUP, 1989), p269

xlii   quoted Peter Parker, *Ackerley* (Constable, 1989), pp 340–1

xliii   *Journeying Boy*, p480

Auden, Britten and Night Mail

Blake Morrison

It is rare for the leading young talents in their respective fields to work together. It is even rarer for them to get on when they do. But in the years 1935–42, Britten and Auden collaborated on a series of documentary films, plays, song cycles and operas, and also became close friends. They even, for a time, shared a house in New York along with (among others) Peter Pears, Gypsy Rose Lee, Carson McCullers, Paul Bowles and Louis MacNeice, a convergence of talents memorialized in Paul Muldoon's poem '7 Middagh St'. As the younger man, Britten looked up to Auden and, like Stephen Spender, was more than a little in awe of him. For his part, Auden saw Britten as 'the white hope of music' and told him as much. Later, they drifted apart, for reasons touched on in Alan Bennett's play about their relationship, *The Habit of Art*. But they had accumulated a substantial body of joint work by then, including *Our Hunting Fathers, On This Island, Paul Bunyan, The Ascent of F6, Ballad of Heroes* and *Hymn to St Cecilia*.

Their closest collaboration was one of their first: *Night Mail*, the film they worked on for the GPO Film Unit. Directed by Basil Wright and Harry Watt, it was released in 1936, and became the Unit's biggest box-office success. Until then, despite the work of Robert Flaherty and others, documentary films were usually regarded as dull, pontificating tracts intended to fill the gap before the 'real' entertainment of a main Hollywood feature film. *Night Mail* changed all that, finding poetry, music, beauty and laughter in the story of the London to Glasgow 'Postal Special' and the men who worked for it.

The GPO Film Unit was established by John Grierson in 1933. Funds were limited but Grierson managed to recruit young men in sympathy with the Unit's left-wing sympathies and prepared to work for little money. Britten was hired in April 1935 and (so he later reported) was paid 'at the rate of £5 per week...with the possibility of it being increased to £10 per week.' W. H. Auden, who joined six months afterwards and was involved in fewer films, earned 'starvation wages' of three pounds a week – less than he'd been getting as a schoolteacher; he made ends meet by lodging first with his friend Basil Wright then with another of the Unit's recruits, the painter William Coldstream. Britten worked long hours and as well as writing soundtrack music carried out research for a film about the British mining industry, *Coal Face,* and for a projected film about the slave trade, *God's Chillun.* Auden's chief contribution was as a poet but he also worked as an assistant director. For *Night Mail* he was briefly in charge of the second camera unit as they shot mailbags being moved at Broad Street station. Basil Wright thought it 'one of the most beautifully organized shots in the film'.

Though they made contributions to *Coal Face,* the two men didn't meet until 5 July 1935, after it was finished. 'Auden is the most amazing man, a very brilliant & attractive personality,' Britten's diary entry for that day records. At 28, Auden was six years older than Britten and many years more mature; among the Unit's creatives, Britten was very much the baby. 'I always feel very young & stupid when with these brains,' he confided to his diary, 'I mostly sit silent when they hold forth about subjects in general.' Other entries speak of his 'pretty violent inferiority complex – these people know so much!' He and Auden had much in common, nevertheless. Both had been to the same Norfolk boarding school, Gresham's. Both were left of centre. And both were homosexual, though Britten was slower to admit as much, even to himself.

Employment by the Unit meant working long hours. Britten's diaries for the period describe him shuttling back and forth between the GPO's offices in Soho Square and its studio in Bennett Park, Blackheath (later the home of the Mass Observation project). It also meant being willing to compromise – to add, discard, shorten or lengthen material – as the director required. Harry Watt, who took over the directing of *Night Mail* from Basil Wright at an early stage, was unimpressed at having a poet and composer at his disposal. Of Auden, he said: 'I didn't give a damn if he'd written *The Ascent of F6* or whatever the hell he'd written. He was just an assistant director, as far as I was concerned, and that meant humping the gear and walking miles.' After seeing a rough assembly of the film, Grierson, Wright and the man in charge of sound, Alberto Cavalcanti, decided that something was missing and commissioned Auden to write a new ending. Watt couldn't see the point of a verse coda but, realising that he could shoot new material and incorporate footage he'd not found room for, he soon came round.

The revised ending of the film also made demands on Britten. By his own admission, Watt 'knew nothing about music but... had decided views on it', and when he met Britten – 'this shy, soft-spoken kid, with close-curled blond hair and a pale and sensitive face' – he played him an old-time jazz record to show what was needed. What Britten came up with wasn't jazz but he did catch the rhythms of a train, just as Auden had done with his verse:

> *This is the night mail crossing the border,*
> *Bringing the cheque and the postal order,*
> *Letters for the rich, letters for the poor,*
> *The shop at the corner and the girl next door...*
>
> *Past cotton grass and moorland boulder,*
> *Shovelling white steam over her shoulder,*
> *Snorting noisily as she passes*
> *Silent miles of wind-bent grasses...*

Auden wrote the poetry for the film on an old table in noisy, ramshackle surroundings in Soho Square, chopping and changing his lines as he watched the rough cut, or (as he put it) timing 'the spoken verse with a stopwatch in order to fit it exactly to the shot on which it commented.' Britten was similarly taxed by the need to make the music fit the words and time sequences – 'watch in one hand and a pencil in the other – trying to make what little ideas I have synchronize with the seconds.' He later reflected that the discipline of having 'to take exact instructions' was 'extremely good practice for me as a young composer.' Of all his joint ventures with Auden, *Night Mail* was the most genuinely collaborative: it wasn't a matter of setting an existing text to music; both the words and the music were written on the hoof.

The film had the working title 'Travelling Post Office' – TPO for short. Much of the footage was shot on location, from within, above or alongside a moving train. But the sequence with workers sorting envelopes in the mailvan was shot on a reconstructed set in the studio in Blackheath. To simulate movement, a piece of string was dangled and jiggled about, and the men sorting the mail – real post office workers, not actors – swayed in accompaniment. The music was also recorded in the Blackheath studio, as Britten's diary entry for January 15 1936 describes:

> *Up early & get to Soho Square at 9.45. Some bother over parts for orchestra but I eventually get down to Blackheath at 11.0 for big T.P.O. recording. A large orchestra for me – Fl. Ob. Bsn. Trpt. Harp…Vln, Vla, Vlc, CB, Percussion & wind machine – a splendid team. The music I wrote really comes off well – &, for what is wanted, creates quite a lot of sensation! The whole trouble, & what takes so much time is that over the music has to be spoken a verse – kind of patter – written by Auden – in strict rhythm with the music. To represent the train noises. There is too much to be spoken in a single breath by the one voice (it is essential to keep to the same voice & to have no breaks) so we have to record separately – me, having to conduct both from an improvised visual metronome – flashes on the screen – a very difficult job!*

In terms of duration, Britten and Auden's contribution was modest – a mere three minutes or so at the end of a 22-minute film. But the words and music were a necessary counterpoint to the dry facts and information overload that preceded them: the 500 million letters delivered annually, the 13 minutes the postal express is scheduled to stop at Crewe, the 34 points along the route at which mail is picked up or dropped off, the 48 pigeonholes each mail-sorter is in charge of, etc. The ending also reinforced the film's propagandist subtext – to celebrate the lives of the unsung proletariat, of whose night-time labours the sleeping bourgeoisie know little or nothing. The spirit of the film certainly infected both men. Never before or after was Auden's poetry so cheerily populist. And for Britten the film was a political education, pushing him further to the left. 'Write a long letter to Mrs Chamberlin (Kersty) in defence of Communism,' he reports in December 1935, 'not a difficult letter to write! It has shocked a lot of people that I am interested in the subject!'

Those brief six months left their mark in other ways. After leaving the GPO film unit, Auden wrote a poem for Britten:

> *Underneath the abject willow,*
> *   Lover, sulk no more;*
> *Act from thought should quickly follow:*
> *   What is thinking for?*

Your unique and moping station
  Proves you cold;
  Stand up and fold
Your map of desolation.

It's not one of Auden's best efforts, in part because the attempt to persuade Britten to loosen up is so transparent. Britten's diaries of the period, with their hectic round of musical commissions, dinners, concerts, games of tennis and visits to his family, do not suggest that he was moping or desolate. But he did come across as 'cold' or at any rate repressed, and Auden and his friends made it their business to help him come out or, as they put it, convince him he was queer. 'For my friend Benjamin Britten, composer, I beg/ That fortune send him soon a passionate affair,' Auden wrote in his jokey 'Last Will and Testament' in *Letters from Iceland.* 'We were extraordinarily interfering in this respect,' Isherwood later said, 'as bossy as a pair of self-assured young psychiatrists.' If Britten didn't respond as Auden hoped, nor does he seem to have resented the interference. When Auden announced that he was going to Spain, Britten was distressed: 'It is terribly sad & I feel ghastly about it.'

Britten didn't follow Auden to Spain but did follow him to America, where for a time their collaboration continued. But by now fortune had sent him Peter Pears and soon both the friendship and the collaboration came under strain. After the poor reviews of their operetta *Paul Bunyan* in 1941, Britten began to feel that the demands of collaborating with someone so bossy and uncompromising weren't worth the effort; 'Auden's stuff is desperately hard to set,' he complained, and for his later operas he looked to more amenable, workaday librettists, Montagu Slater, Eric Crozier and Myfanwy Piper among them. Before he returned to England in 1942, Auden wrote him a letter that accused him of being too bourgeois and conventional, and urged him to be more ruthless – rather than stifle in 'a warm nest of love', he should 'suffer, and make others suffer.' The appeal (or command) isn't so different from the one made in the poem 'Underneath the abject willow'. But by 1942 Britten was older, worldier, and in a stable relationship, and he resented Auden's chivvying. They never worked together again.

Nevertheless the six months they spent on *Night Mail* remained important to both of them. For Auden, the experience was the start of his withdrawal from Marxism: stubbornly individualistic, he couldn't adapt to the GPO film unit's communal ethos and became disillusioned with the idea that art can or should be *engagé*: 'poetry makes nothing happen,' he decided. Britten, by contrast, flourished in the team atmosphere and valued the apprenticeship of working to tight deadlines and with limited resources. He discovered organizational talents, too, ones that resurfaced when he founded the Aldeburgh Festival and surprised people with his financial acumen, practicality and ability to cope under pressure.

Night Mail will always be remembered for Auden and Britten's participation, and for Grierson's courage and vision in commissioning them. No film better expresses the concerns and ambitions of the British documentary movement of the 1930s. And no later collaboration between the poet and the composer ever quite lived up to it.

Auden, Britten and The Habit of Art

Alan Bennett

In his play The Habit of Art, *first produced in London in 2009, Alan Bennett imagines Benjamin Britten seeking advice from his former collaborator and friend W.H. Auden. During their (fictitious) meeting, Britten and Auden are observed and interrupted by, amongst others, their future biographer and a young man from the local bus station.*

By the time Auden came to live in the Brewhouse, a cottage in the grounds of Christ Church, in 1972, I had long since left Oxford, and in any case would never have had the nerve to speak to him. I'd first heard his voice in Exeter College hall some time in 1955. The lower end of the scholars' table where I was sitting was only a yard or two from the High Table where the dons dined and, hearing those harsh, quacking tones without knowing whose they were, I said to my neighbour that it sounded like the voice of the devil. Someone better informed put me right. It was Auden, at that time still with blondish hair and the face yet to go under the harrow.

I don't think I'd read much of his poetry or would have understood it if I had, but when Auden gave his inaugural lecture as Professor of Poetry the following year I dutifully went along, knowing, though not quite why, that he was some sort of celebrity. At that time I still harboured thoughts of becoming a Writer (and I thought of it in capital letters), so when Auden outlined what he took to be the prerequisites of a literary life, or at any rate a life devoted to poetry, I was properly dismayed. Besides favourite books, essential seemed to be an ideal landscape (Leeds?), a knowledge of metre and scansion, and (this was the clincher) a passion for the Icelandic sagas. If writing meant passing this kind of kit inspection, I'd better forget it. What Auden was saying (and he said it pretty regularly) was, 'All I do as I do,' which is what unhelpful writers often say when asked about their profession, though few with

69

such seeming conviction and authority as the newly inaugurated
Professor of Poetry. He used to hold court in the Cadena, but it
wasn't a café I cared for. There were undergraduates I knew at
whom Auden made passes, though I was still young and innocent
enough to find a pass as remarkable as the person making it.

When he died in 1973 his death seemed to me less a loss to poetry
– the poetry was largely over – than a loss to knowledge. Auden was a
library in himself and now all this store – the reading, the categories,
the associations – had gone down with that great listing clay-
coloured hulk. And though much of what he knew he had written
down and published, either as lectures or in reviews, there was
always more: the flurry of memoirs and reminiscences of the poetry
and his talk that began almost immediately on his death, not only a
testament to his life but an attempt to salvage some of the wisdom
he had discarded in conversation – and some of the unwisdom too.

In *The Hunting of the Snark,* Lewis Carroll, a Christ Church don,
wrote: 'What I tell you three times is true.' With Auden, also at Christ
Church, it was the opposite. What Auden said three times you would
begin to doubt, and when he'd said it a dozen times nobody cared
anyway. Auden somewhere makes the distinction between being
boring and being a bore. He was never boring – he was too extraordinary for that – but by the time he came back to live in Oxford
he had become a bore. His discourse was persistently pedagogic;
he was never not teaching and/or showing off how much he knew,
always able to make a long arm and reach for references unavailable
to his less well-read hearers. As he got towards the end of his life his
conversation and his pedagogy got more and more repetitive, which
must have been a particular disappointment to his colleagues at
Christ Church where, when he had been briefly resident in the past,
he had been an enlivening member of the common room. Now he
was just infuriating. What they had been hoping for was, under-
standably, some form of enlightenment and entertainment. This was
made plain early on in *The Habit of Art,* in a speech by the Dean
which had to be cut, as favourite bits of my scripts often are:

> *The Brewhouse is not a garret, quite – say sheltered accom-
> modation rather. A granny flat. But mark this. If the college is
> minded to provide this accommodation it's for nothing so vulgar
> as a poet in residence. This isn't Keele, still less is it East Anglia.
> No. We see it as providing a niche – young persons nowadays
> might even call it a pad – for one of our most renowned*

graduates. If it is a touch spartan, blame the Steward, but then the point of Parnassus was never the upholstery. Besides, the hope is that undergraduates will find their way up the stairs to sit not in the chairs but at these famous feet. But remember, we are not asking the great man to do. His doing after all is mostly done. No. We are asking him to be. Count the poet's presence here as one of those extra-curricular plums that only Oxford has to offer. Fame in the flesh can be a part of education and in the person of this most celebrated poet the word is made flesh and dwells among us, full of grace and truth.

But to everyone's disappointment – the college, the students, Auden himself – it didn't turn out like that. But say it had been Larkin at the same stage of his life – he wasn't much fun either at the finish.

In 1972, when Auden arrived in Oxford, Britten was well advanced in the writing of *Death in Venice*, his last opera. Neither poet nor composer was in good health, with Auden six years older than Britten. I never met or even saw Britten, but find I wrote about him in my diary in June 2006:

16 June. *Having seen the TV programme on which it was based, I've been reading* Britten's Children *by John Bridcut. Glamorous though he must have been and a superb teacher, I find Britten a difficult man to like. He had his favourites, children and adults, but both Britten and Pears were notorious for cutting people out of their lives (Eric Crozier is mentioned here, and Charles Mackerras), friends and acquaintances suddenly turned into living corpses if they overstepped the mark. A joke would do it, and though Britten seems to have had plenty of childish jokes with his boy singers, his sense of humour isn't much in evidence elsewhere. And it was not merely adults that were cut off. A boy whose voice suddenly broke could find himself no longer invited to the Red House or part of the group – a fate which the boys Bridcut quotes here seem to have taken philosophically but which would seem potentially far more damaging to a child's psychology than too much attention. One thinks, too, of the boys who were not part of the charmed circle. There were presumably fat boys and ugly boys or just plain dull boys who could, nevertheless, sing like angels. What of them?*

Britten and Peter Pears came disastrously to *Beyond the Fringe* some time in 1961. Included in the show was a parody of Britten written by Dudley Moore, in which he sang and accompanied himself in 'Little Miss Muffet' done in a Pears-and-Britten-like way. I'm not sure that this in itself would have caused offence: it shouldn't have as, like all successful parodies, there was a good deal of affection in it and it was funny in its own right. But Dudley (who may have known them slightly and certainly had met them) unthinkingly entitled the piece 'Little Miss Britten'. Now Dudley was not malicious nor had he any reason to mock their homosexuality, of which indeed he may have been unaware; I don't think I knew of it at the time. But with the offending title printed in the programme, they were reported to be deeply upset and Dudley went into outer darkness, as probably did the rest of us.

There's a story told in Tony Palmer's superb film about Britten, *A Time There Was*, of how when Kathleen Ferrier was working with the composer on *The Rape of Lucretia* there was quite a serious quarrel (though not with her). Britten tells the story against himself of how Ferrier took him on one side and said: 'Oh Ben. Do try and be nice.' And he says, slightly surprised: 'And it worked.' Both Britten and Auden's works were in better taste than their lives. 'Real artists are not nice people,' Auden wrote. 'All their best feelings go into their work and life has the residue.'

The Habit of Art was not easy to write, though its form is quite simple, because so much information had to be passed over to the audience about Auden and his life, and about Britten and his, and about their earlier association. Thinking of *Beyond the Fringe*, now nearly half a century ago, makes me realize how I have projected onto Britten particularly some of the feelings I had when I was a young man, not much older than he was and thrust into collaboration (which was also competition) with colleagues every bit as daunting as Auden. Recalling their early collaborations (in another passage from the play since cut), Britten remembers his slightly desperate attempts to keep up with Auden and make a contribution besides the musical one:

> *In those days I used to bring along a few carefully worked out notions I'd had for the film shots and sequences, but it was no good. Wystan, you see, could never admit that I'd thought of anything first.*
>
> *'Oh yes,' he'd say, as if I was just reminding him of something he'd thought of earlier. You could never tell Wystan anything, just remind him of it.*

> *Either that or he'd scamper off with your idea and make it*
> *his... and not merely an idea. A whole country.*
>   *Wystan was the first person to go to Iceland, did you know*
> *that? And Christopher Columbus didn't discover America.*
> *Wystan did.*

While this seems to me a true assessment of Britten's early relationship with Auden, it also chimes with my experiences in 1960. So, though in some ways I find Britten unsympathetic he, much more than Auden, is the character I identify with.

When I started writing the play I made much use of the biographies of both Auden and Britten written by Humphrey Carpenter and both are models of their kind. Indeed, I was consulting his books so much that eventually Carpenter found his way into the play. His widow, Mari Prichard, was more than helpful over this, though feeling – and I'm sure rightly – that I hadn't done justice to him as a biographer or as a personality. I had had the same problem in *The Madness of George III* when trying to fit in another character who was larger than life, namely Charles James Fox. To have given him his proper due would have meant him taking over the play. And so it is with Humphrey Carpenter, my only excuse being that he would have been the first to understand this and to be unsentimental about it. When he turned up on the stage he tended to hang about and act as commentator, often speaking directly to the audience. This was useful as he could explain points of fact and saved the main characters from telling each other stuff both of them knew already but the audience didn't. Even so, there was still a good deal of explaining left to be done. It's a perennial problem for dramatists and one which Ibsen, for instance, never satisfactorily solved, or, so far as I can see, ever tried to.

Towards the end of the play Carpenter mildly reproves Auden and Britten for being so concerned about their reputations, when their audience, Auden's readers, Britten's hearers, are anxious simply to draw a line under them both. They don't want more poetry; they don't want more music; they want – as they say nowadays – closure. Guilty at occasionally entertaining such thoughts myself apropos Updike's relentless output, for instance, I was reassured to find myself not alone in feeling like this. On the death of Crabbe, Lord Melbourne wrote: 'I am always glad when one of those fellows dies for then I know I have the whole of him on my shelf.' Which is, of course, the cue for biography.

A Haunting Relationship

Janette Miller talks to Hannah Nepil

Benjamin Britten knew how to make you love him. I first met him when I was aged 15, when he was looking for children for the Aldeburgh premiere of *Noye's Fludde*, in 1958. I was at ballet school at the time, but I'd had singing lessons so my teachers put me forward for an audition. I knew Britten's music – I'd seen his *Prince of Pagodas* four times at Covent Garden – and at the audition I recognised him from photographs. At my audition I said, 'Excuse me, are you Benjamin Britten?' and he said 'Yes, how did you know that?'. I think that must have helped me to get the part of Mrs Sem.

While in Aldeburgh I was made to feel like a nuisance and a silly little thing. It was clear that Ben had his inner circle – Michael Crawford, for instance, who played Mr Jaffet in the *Noye's Fludde* premiere, was a clear favourite. And it wasn't hard to see why. He was a brilliant actor, so inventive and a real Charlie Chaplin character. Small wonder he went on to become famous in his adulthood. Ben had a knack for discovering childhood talent.

David Hemmings, who created the role of Miles in *The Turn of the Screw*, was similarly charismatic. He and I both went to the Arts Educational School in London, so I knew him. Not that I spoke to him much. He was two years above me and already getting parts in TV plays and films. When I left for Aldeburgh, David was no longer playing Miles, but I do remember him telling me how envious he was that I was going to Aldeburgh and how much I was going to love it there.

But I didn't at first. It soon became apparent that young girls weren't really noticed. I was terribly naïve – I'd been brought up in a convent school when I was very young – but a friend took me aside and explained about homosexuality and about Ben's relationship with the tenor Peter Pears. She said: 'Some

74

men like other men the way your father likes your mother.' She told me that while I was in Aldeburgh, boys had the preference and I mustn't be upset about it. Nevertheless, Ben did notice me, choosing me to play Flora in Peter Morley's 1959 television production of *The Turn of the Screw* alongside Jennifer Vyvyan as the governess and Thomas Bevan as Miles. What I didn't know at the time is that Ben had already auditioned about 40 potential Floras. Eventually he had selected a tiny adult soprano, Olive Dyer, to play the part in the 1954 premiere opposite David Hemmings. Apparently she sang it beautifully, but she was fully mature and Ben wasn't content with the casting. Flora is a young girl – that's part of the fascination. She's an adult in a child's body. I was old before my time and, like Flora, had quite an isolated childhood, growing up in my grandfather's house in the countryside, so there were some similarities between us. Ben had a talent for type-casting. Thomas also looked very much the part. He may not have been quite a David Hemmings, but he had this highly angelic appearance, with the most incredible eyelashes you've ever seen.

I was invited to test-drive my part at Ben's flat in St John's Wood, North London. It was tiny and sparsely decorated: in the living room there was just a baby grand piano, two very uncomfortable armchairs and a lamp. Ben couldn't find the opera score. 'You may find this absurd,' he said. 'I know I write this music but I can't play it without the score.' And he and Peter proceeded to turn the flat upside down. Eventually somebody emerged with a triumphant 'I've found one!' and I sang through the part. At the end, Ben gave me no corrections. Instead he talked to me about the role. He seemed to be obsessed with Flora, which is strange because once we actually got into production nobody seemed to care tuppence about her. Some people think that Henry James made a mistake including her in his novel at all, as it interferes with the focus on Miles.

But for Ben, Flora was the strongest character in *The Screw*. She is highly manipulative, a natural rebel and used to having her own way. While her not-so-bright brother is something of a disappointment under pressure, she is a survivor. And without the major child-adult confrontation at the climax where Flora takes on the naïve governess, *The Screw* would be less effective dramatically. Compared with the 19-year-old governess from a sheltered country parsonage, Flora is socially and possibly even sexually more experienced – there is a suggestion that she has been abused by one or more of the ghosts. Many have wondered whether the ghosts in *The Screw* are real or a figment of the imagination. For Ben, they were real, and both children are haunted. Yet in most productions the boy takes precedence while Flora's side of the story is rarely promoted.

Ben told me that I had Flora 'just right', and in a letter to my agent he wrote that I would 'do'. Nevertheless, I found the filming difficult. After all, the part was written for an adult soprano and it's very demanding – quite similar to Schoenberg in some ways. Ben had told me that he would adapt it to make it easier for me. But he never did. I think the financial repercussions would have been too severe. The only person who helped me was our conductor, Charles Mackerras: he was aware that I was new to it all and he gave me extra time to go through my aria, although neither he nor Ben were given to tolerating musical mistakes.

I didn't see Ben at all during production; however we stayed in touch afterwards. I would go down to Aldeburgh during the summer with my mother. Ben set aside tickets for us and we would talk to him after performances. But I was never formally invited up until he decided to do *The Turn of the Screw* again at the 1961 Aldeburgh Festival.

We rehearsed at the Donmar Studios, in London, and I hardly saw Ben, except on one particular occasion. We had been working on the pussycat's cradle scene and I kept coming in a beat early. It didn't matter how many times we did it, I just couldn't get it right. Everybody was in fits. 'No Janette!' they kept crying. When Ben turned up to rehearsal that afternoon, our director Basil Coleman told him what we were rehearsing, 'and Janette can't get it right,' he added. We tried the part out. I got it wrong again, and there was a sort of 'ouch' as I came in. I could see curtains – I thought it was sack time. But instead Ben said: 'Well, let's figure this out,' and sat down at the piano. We tried it out. Of course it was wrong again. But instead of an 'ouch' this time there was a hush. Ben stood up and said: 'I don't know why none of you saw this. It quite clear what is going on. Janette's not wrong at all. It's Joy. She's coming in a beat early and throwing the whole thing out.' On his way out he gave me a pat on the shoulder. 'Don't worry,' he said. 'I'll make sure you're all right in Aldeburgh.'

My lodgings in Aldeburgh backed on to Ben's house, and when

I got there I was invited to use his pool. I hate swimming. There's nothing worse. But that's how I got used to going to Ben's house every day. He would ask me to come and sit beside him and we sang lieder together, or we would just talk. I remember Ben's colleague, Viola Tunnard, once asking me: 'What do you and Ben talk about when you are together?' I said: 'Ordinary things: opera, ballet, Gaudier-Brzeska, Schubert, croquet, china tea, sports cars, nothing much.'

One night after we had been rehearsing late Ben offered to take me home in his car. I had my bicycle with me, so Ben told me that he would put it in the back seat. Peter Pears, who was sitting in the back, began to protest. 'Get out, Peter,' said Ben, 'I'm taking Janette home. You can walk.' Peter emerged fuming from the car, Ben shoved the bicycle in the back, I climbed in the front and we drove off at an alarming pace. As we rounded the crest of the hill, Ben turned to me and gave me a good slap on the knee. 'That was fun, wasn't it?' he said.

I remember once remarking to Ben that he had so much. His reply was curious: 'But I don't really. Just a car; a few paintings maybe.' Even at the time, this struck me as rather sad. I think he would have wanted children of his own, and there are many stories of him taking on a fatherly role in his friendships with young boys. I recall reading about the case of one boy, Roger Duncan, the son of Ronald Duncan who wrote the libretto for Ben's *The Rape of Lucretia*. Apparently Ben asked Ronald's permission to 'share' Roger. He did something similar for me. Long after I had left Aldeburgh my sister told me that Ben had called my father and asked if he could spend more time with me. But the relationship fizzled out.

When I finished at Aldeburgh I studied production at the Guildhall School of Music. I met my husband at an ice rink – a GP, incidentally called Miles – and we moved to New Zealand, where I ran my own opera and ballet company for 14 years. Ben and I carried on exchanging Christmas cards for a while, but eventually those stopped too. Ben famously had this way of dropping people. While you were in his circle he would smile at you and acknowledge you in the street. Once you were out that was it. You were simply cut. Poor David Hemmings was cut after his voice broke in the middle of a performance of *The Turn of the Screw*. I took care to ensure that I never became one of Ben's 'ghosts'. The contact just faded naturally.

Nevertheless, I consider myself lucky to have got to know him as I did. Although the Ben I knew was possibly very different from the Ben of his other acquaintances, my memories of him are unanimously fond. He was such fun to be with. He gave me so much, even though at the time I took it for granted. And he made you feel as if you were the only person that mattered.

PART TWO

BRITTEN – THE MUSIC

Death in Venice: *A Personal Narrative*

Colin Matthews

Benjamin Britten, consistently perverse in his choice of opera subjects, has once again proved the impossible. Thomas Mann's 'Death in Venice', a compressed and intense story, an artist's inner monologue, lacking conversation, lacking plot, has against all the odds become a great opera.
Edward Greenfield, The Guardian, *June 18 1973*

Britten always tended to be sensitive about his projects becoming public knowledge, but in early 1971 it was well known in the Faber Music office, where I was working part-time as a copyist and editor, that plans for *Death in Venice* were well advanced. His touchiness about publicity had caused problems with operatic projects in the past – notably *King Lear* and *Anna Karenina* in the mid 1960s – the latter a collaboration with Colin Graham, which reached an advanced stage before it was abandoned when news of it became too widespread for Britten's comfort. So when a piece appeared in the *New Statesman* – I can't recall quite when, or who wrote it – on the lines of 'Rumour has it that Britten's next opera is to be *Death in Venice*. Please let it not be true', there was some concern that this might presage another aborted project.

Problems with the subject matter had already arisen: Britten had been advised to keep his plans under wraps because of the complicated negotiations with Warner Bros., who saw a conflict with Luchino Visconti's film which was in production at the same time. Britten first approached Thomas Mann's son Golo for his approval, which was freely given, in September 1970; the film was premiered at the 1971 Cannes Film Festival. Agreement with Warner Bros. was not finally reached until June 1972, by which time Britten had composed nearly half the work; but the negotiations had been

81

concluded in principle in time for Britten to start talking in detail to Myfanwy Piper about the libretto in January 1971.

I had met Britten for the first time in 1970 at the rehearsals for *Owen Wingrave*, for which I had collaborated on the fair copy of the full score with my brother David.[i] My first solo task for him was to edit the continuo part for his edition of the Bach *St John Passion* in April 1971, taking down as far as I could Britten's semi-improvised accompaniment. He did not begin work on the music of *Death in Venice* until the end of that year, and my own involvement with it began in April 1972. Graham Johnson, who was to be Pears' rehearsal pianist, had been recruited to prepare the vocal score, but it became evident that he would be unable to keep up with the pace of Britten's composing. I was asked by Donald Mitchell if I would take over the score, and I began work immediately; by this time Britten had nearly reached Scene 7, *The Games of Apollo* (at that stage called *The Idyll*).

There was a great deal to do; but as Britten's commitments, including the June Aldeburgh Festival, meant that he would have to take a two-month break from the opera, I had time to catch up. In some respects, making a vocal score for Britten amounted to little more than tidying up his sketch. He had always composed his operas as if writing for piano and would regularly play back what he had composed, both for himself,[ii] and for others to hear.[iii] But it was essential to make sure that the layout was properly pianistic, and above all that it would be very legible; part of the score had been engraved by the time of the first performance, but the great majority remained in my hand until the vocal score was published late in 1975. I worked from photocopies of the composition sketch (made laboriously by the thermofax process), sending back my pencil score by post as I worked in London, rarely in Aldeburgh, at this stage. I did not write in the words – this was left to Britten's principal music assistant Rosamund Strode.[iv] I had no copy of the libretto, and Britten's attitude to the words could be a little idiosyncratic. Rosamund also kept a careful watch over my handwriting : I learned more from her about the standards of music copying than from anyone else.

I would receive back from Britten pages that had been hand-corrected by him. I find it hard to believe now that I made the corrections and rubbed out his handwriting without any of us who worked with him thinking to preserve some of these pages and have them recopied. They represent a minor but now irretrievable stage of the composition process. I have a number of pages of later revisions in his hand, and some pages of the dye-lined vocal score with his writing on them, but the original marked up pages are gone forever.[v]

In June 1972 I was in Aldeburgh to help Britten with his performance of Schumann's *Scenes from Goethe's Faust*, whose orchestration he had retouched in a number of places. He returned to *Death in Venice* in July, although *The Idyll* scene caused him problems, and there were interruptions – he conducted two performances of *The Turn of the Screw* in August, and recorded Schumann's *Faust* in September. The latter tired him greatly, and probably as a result he decided to ask Steuart Bedford to conduct the first performance of the opera in June of the following year. (The Schumann was the last music he was ever to conduct himself.) On his doctors' advice he set aside most of his engagements over the coming months in order to concentrate on *Death in Venice*, and gradually he picked up speed, completing the sketch on 17 December. He spent a further week reworking the very end, whose first draft had dissatisfied him.

I had got as far as the end of Scene 6, Aschenbach's 'So be it', by the beginning of September, and at that stage this first section of the vocal score was finalized and sent off to be made up for the singers. Britten had not yet made up his mind about the act divisions at the time he had finished the composition draft, and in fact the work was through-composed without a break.[vi] But it had never been intended that the opera should be a single act of nearly two and a half hours (not quite as long as *Das Rheingold*); while separating out *The Idyll* as the second of three acts was dramatically inappropriate. In the event, the low fourth on B & E which followed Aschenbach's 'I love you', marked as a 'long pause', became both the final chord of Act One and the opening chord of Act Two.

But what, I wondered, would the first night audience make of this declaration of love? While preoccupied with the technicalities of making the vocal score I could not overlook what seemed to be a scarily autobiographical plot, and what I felt initially was music that was in many places under-composed. This latter was simply a misapprehension, deriving from the spareness of the sketch, largely alleviated as I worked on the full score, and completely dissolved when I heard the orchestral textures for the first time in rehearsal. But my concern about the subject matter itself and its treatment in the libretto remained, and to some extent still does forty years later, even though I never fail to be greatly moved by the work in performance.

One disquieting aspect of the story was that it seemed to have uncomfortably close parallels to Britten's infatuation with David Hemmings in Venice during the rehearsals for *The Turn of the Screw*, and that it revealed a side of Britten that, however innocent, was barely camouflaged behind the conflict between the Dionysiac and Apollonian impulses that underlies both book and opera. Britten would have deeply resented such an interpretation, and it was hardly something that I would have raised, having witnessed at first hand his anger when reading a critique of *Owen Wingrave* in *Opera* magazine – he hurled the magazine into a far corner.

But others were concerned : Pears is reported to have said to Sidney Nolan, 'Ben is writing an evil opera, and it's killing him.'[vii] What I found equally disconcerting was what seemed to me to be the over-simplification of a complex and multi-layered story : the very beginning, for instance, where, in Thomas Mann, Aschenbach is over-stimulated by too much creativity, finds the opera going in the opposite direction. Aschenbach cannot work, 'no words come'; and when they do, they tend towards the platitudinous : 'Light everlasting', chants the chorus, and Aschenbach responds 'Would that the light of inspiration had not left me'. 'They enter into the house of the Lord', 'Yes! From the black rectangular hole in the ground' – a line that I find particularly grating.

Such reduction of complexity to the more comprehensible narrative needed for staging made me anxious about its reception, although in the event this was almost entirely positive. Yet more than one commentator has been uneasy about these issues, notably finding *The Games of Apollo* as the weak spot of the opera – the games themselves more like school sports than Apollonian contests, with Aschenbach looking on like an elderly schoolmaster.[viii] But Myfanwy Piper was clearly simplifying the plot in a way that suited Britten – was indeed instigated by him – and ultimately there is no room in opera for the subtleties of Mann's writing, with its elaborate and intricate prose musings.[ix] Whatever my reservations, then or now, the opera works.

It was with *The Games of Apollo* that I resumed the vocal score. I was unaware at the time to what extent the libretto was being discussed and changed as the work was composed; and only after Britten's death did I learn of the notebook that he was using in order to sketch in outline the music that he was about to elaborate in the composition sketch. This unique document[x] represents the only time that Britten committed so much advance detail to paper instead of keeping it in his head.[xi] There are several other notebooks for work in progress, but nothing with this level of detail: it contains more than 30 pages of sketches, comprising over 100 entries.

I completed the vocal score by the middle of January 1973 – if I remember rightly it still had the unrevised ending, which had to be corrected at a later stage since the complete score had already been sent off to be reproduced for all the performers. More corrections had to be made as work on the full score threw up many minor changes[xii] – and one major change when it transpired that a tune in the Players' scene that Britten had assumed was traditional was in fact in copyright. Since the publishers of the tune in question were intransigent in demanding a large share of the Grand Rights for its use, Britten recomposed the whole number – fortunately before getting to it in the full score. But ten pages of vocal score had to be rewritten. A reworking of the Phaedrus aria in Scene 16 caused fewer problems, although again it meant replacing the vocal score pages; while many of Aschenbach's monologues changed as Pears began to learn them, and in the process suggested ways in which they could work more fluently.

Britten was racing against time to complete the full score, not so much because of the need to prepare the orchestral material in good time for the first rehearsals as because his strength was declining. He had been advised to have a thorough medical examination as soon as the score was finished. Nevertheless the speed at which he worked was remarkable, and although I came to Aldeburgh a number of times in February and March to help in writing out the score[xiii] – for which Rosamund Strode had prepared the layout, including all the vocal lines – the great majority of the full score, consisting of over 700 pages and completed by the end of March, was in his hand. I have a vivid memory from that time of having dinner with Britten and Imogen Holst in the Festival Club, when he seemed surprisingly relaxed, much more so than the other diners, who fell completely silent as he walked in.

The subsequent events were not happy. Britten had hoped that if an operation proved to be necessary it could be postponed until after the first performance of *Death in Venice*, but the examination revealed that the immediate replacement of a heart valve was essential. The procedure failed, in that all that was achieved was a stabilization of his heart which allowed him only three-and-a-half more years of life, with a greatly reduced capacity for work. His post-operative convalescence did not allow for any attendance at rehearsals.

I worked on the editorial details of both scores during April and May, and in early June was at Steuart Bedford's first orchestral rehearsal, for percussion alone, in London. There were several more rehearsals before the opera reached the stage, where my strongest memory is of entering the Maltings for the first time just as the rehearsal reached the powerful music at figure 230 in Scene 9, 'The Pursuit'. That passage never fails to send a shiver down my spine in performance, the memory of hearing it in its full glory remains so vivid.

Rehearsals were somewhat fraught, as without Britten's presence there was a tension between the protagonists. Pears, of course, had the confidence of having known the work from its inception, and seemed remarkably at ease in spite of the prodigious nature of his role; but Colin Graham and Frederick Ashton were often at odds, the latter, as Graham put it, 'somewhat stumped when confonted by long jumps and sprinting races.'[xiv] Ashton seemed excessively temperamental, and the two of them made life difficult for Steuart Bedford, especially when Colin Graham asked for cuts both in the Games and in Pears' recitatives.

Britten did not have the energy to deal with the proposed cuts; and he later restored most of them. I recall him, sequestered in The Red House during the rehearsals, being asked specifically about one cut in Scene 6, between figures 115 and 118. Steuart Bedford and I contrived a solution at Colin Graham's request, to which he made two small adjustments, written in ballpoint pen with a feeble hand.

Britten was advised to avoid any pressure during the Festival itself by getting away to his composing retreat at Horham, near the Suffolk border. There, as Rosamund Strode recalls,[xv] he was unable to resist the temptation to listen to the broadcast of the second performance, but was so disconcerted by a deep hum picked up from the stage machinery that he quickly switched the radio off. He did not hear a tape recording until August; a special performance was given for him at Snape in September.

I was, of course, present at the first performance on 16 June, but in retrospect it feels more like the culmination of the rehearsal process, in which I had been closely involved, than an event in itself. More memorable is the performance I saw in September of that year at La Fenice in Venice, where it was difficult to distinguish between the theatrical experience and the city itself.

Britten meanwhile continued to make revisions, and was well enough to come to London for rehearsals and performance at the Royal Opera in October. He phoned me with some of the changes that he wanted to make – the only time I can recall speaking to him over the phone, an instrument with which he was never comfortable. I was surprised how well the production, very much tailored to the Maltings, transferred to Covent Garden; and it was the first time I had seen Britten since April, looking much better than I had expected, although that may have been partly due to the elegant maroon velvet smoking jacket he wore. I was shocked therefore to see how much weaker and in poor shape he seemed at the recording, made in the spring of 1974 at The Maltings. He followed the sessions from a converted dressing room, isolated from everyone except Rosamund Strode and Rita Thomson, who had been his devoted nurse since the operation.

I continued to work on the vocal score: a major task was to put in the words of the German translation for the German premiere in Berlin in 1974.[xvi] But by the time of the recording most aspects of the score had reached a more or less definitive form, although the substantial optional cut that Britten had agreed to in the first scene was, to his subsequent regret, followed in the recording. The vocal score was published eighteen months later, in time for Britten's 62nd birthday in 1975. Work on the full score began before his death a year later, but he was not shown any of the proofs, and Rosamund Strode and I saw it through the press for its eventual publication in 1979.

* * *

It is difficult to disassociate my memories from the accumulated knowledge of the 40 years since the opera was composed. I know the work from the inside in a way in which I know few other works, in spite of which I think I can view it with a degree of objectivity. What remains a matter of concern for me is Britten's motive in choosing *Death in Venice* as the subject for what he may have suspected would be his final opera, and certainly the last major role he would create for Pears. I have already suggested that the subject was a kind of 'camouflage', allowing him to indulge private fantasies in a publicly acceptable way,[xvii] while I am aware that he would have vehemently denied that to be the case. Yet this was clearly part of Mann's own perception of the novella. He felt that it needed justification beyond the normal modes of literary criticism, writing, not long after its publication, of the central theme as 'passion that drives to destruction and destroys dignity'; while in a lecture given in 1940 he spoke of the work as 'a strange sort of moral self-castigation'. He even went so far as to describe the prose style of the work as Aschenbach's rather than his own, implying a kind of parody, or conceit.

Parody was certainly not Britten's intention, and he would never have thought to use a musical language that was not his own in a work of this kind. Self-castigation perhaps plays a part. But the one element that both works share is the autobiographical one. Thomas Mann freely admitted that all the events of the story were based on fact (although the outbreak of cholera did not coincide with the Mann family's visit to Venice in 1911: it occurred in Palermo). Remarkably the original of Tadzio, one Wladyslaw Moes, came forward in the 1960s, with his memories of an old man observing him at play on the beach.[xviii] (Mann's wife Katia was aware of what she called his 'fascination' with the boy, but maintained that, unlike Aschenbach, he did not pursue the boy all over Venice.)

An essential element that separates author and composer is that Mann was bisexual, more able to be dispassionate about the subject, and was at pains to dress up his infatuation behind a screen of Greek philosophy, something far simpler to do in words (note Myfanwy Piper's implied censure of 'extreme wordiness') than on the stage. An obsessive pursuit that Mann/Aschenbach can continually stand aside from to reflect upon, and disparage, becomes much more concrete in the opera's characterization of the protagonists. Britten would have said that he had no alternative, as he pointed out when *The Turn of the Screw* was criticized; Henry James' ghosts can remain in the imagination while they are on the page: in the opera they have to sing. But here we are somewhat uncomfortably aware that Britten's own obsessions are being made flesh.

The most significant decision taken by Britten and Piper, however, was that Tadzio, unlike the ghosts, should not sing (just as he is silent throughout the novella), and that his role should be that of a dancer. Recent productions of the opera have avoided straight-forward choreography in favour of what Britten – in the notes for the vocal score, approved by him – called 'stylized movement', to represent the world of the 'other' as seen through Aschenbach's eyes. The choreography was one of the failings of the original production, too elaborate and ultimately unconvincing. My own feeling is that relatively naturalistic movement works just as well: the gamelan-derived music associated with the Polish family, and the fact that they are effectively mimes, work to establish the sense of otherness to great effect.

Ashenbach is never able to speak to the family, so their silence on stage is appropriate. Yet without Mann's elaboratively descriptive prose Tadzio remains something of a cypher. There is no real 'dark side to perfection', the operatic Aschenbach's approval of Tadzio's antagonism to a Russian family, vividly described by Mann as 'glaring forth a black message of hatred'; nor any suggestion that Tadzio is less than beautiful. In the novella, Ashenbach, observing him closely, sees his bad teeth, and reflects 'he's sickly ... he'll probably not live to grow old', which gives him 'a certain feeling of satisfaction or relief'. This is not a theme that Mann develops, but it is completely absent from the opera.

The other major achievement of the libretto is the conflation of the various personae who make up the figure of The Traveller. This is implicit in Mann, notably by the strange motif of grimacing with bared teeth (surely intending a link to Tadzio in the description just cited) which is shared by the characters who in the opera become the Traveller, the Elderly Fop,[xix] the Old Gondolier and the Leader of the Players. The Hotel Manager and the Hotel Barber are far less sinister figures in the novella, notably the former, who is usually described as 'the soft-spoken little manager'; which makes their transformation in the opera is a striking invention, and the equation of all of them in the Voice of Dionysus a logical outcome.

And yet in spite of these felicities, for the most part the libretto is disappointingly prosaic. Mann writes 'The boy would be summoned to meet a guest ... he had an enchanting way of turning and twisting his body, gracefully expectant, charmingly shame-faced, seeking to please because good breeding required him to do so'. In the opera Aschenbach's reaction is the arch 'You notice when you're noticed', which becomes an irritating ritornello, almost the only music in the opera I would be happy to lose. Equally clumsy is the cod Italian of theVenetian characters, 'Il padre is sick, the bambini are hungry', a pointless attempt at local colour.

But musically there are so many golden moments: the holding back of the 'Overture to Venice' to the end of the second scene, and its brazen, glittering paean to the city; the 'view' music as Aschenbach sees the sea from his hotel room for the first time; the strangeness of the Voice of Apollo, for which Britten's uses the 2000-year-old Delphic Hymn; the darkness and intensity of the prelude to Act II; the beauty of the simple eloquence of the Phaedrus aria, and the noble brass peroration that follows it. Above all the sombre final bars, deep and foreboding as Tadzio's music disappears into thin air.

The music transcends criticism. A better, more sophisticated libretto would almost certainly have unsettled Britten, whose sense of theatricality outweighs any fault-finding. 'Consistently perverse in his choice of opera subjects' he may have been, but he had an unerring sense of what could and could not work, and Edward Greenfield's 'it has against all the odds become a great opera' is nothing less than the truth.

Notes

i   Britten had written out the full score at great speed and felt that it was too untidy for future use by other conductors; it was very unusual for a pre-publication full score not to be in his own hand.

ii   Britten never composed at the piano, but he would play through what he had composed each day 'to fix the music in time', as he once explained to me. He went on to say that he had once, during the composition of Billy Budd, written an extended passage without recourse to the piano, and that the timing had consequently gone wrong.

iii   Donald Mitchell describes being sole audience to a complete performance of the opera, with Britten taking all the parts, in December 1972, in his introduction to the Cambridge Opera Handbook *Death in Venice*. A subsequent 'performance' was given to a small audience of those who would be involved in the production, including Colin Graham and John and Myfanwy Piper.

iv   Rosamund Strode's account of the genesis of the opera in the Cambridge Handbook, A chronicle, is indispensable, containing greater detail about specific musical issues than I have given here.

v   The 350 pages of my handwritten vocal score are now in the Britten-Pears Foundation's archive.

vi   There is no division into acts in the composition sketch, and Rosamund Strode says that the final decision was not taken until December 1973. However, in a letter to Myfanwy Piper written in February 1972, Britten speaks clearly of 'Act I' and 'Act II'

vii   In Humphrey Carpenter, Benjamin Britten, p. 546

viii Other interpretations would doubtless have been made had Myfanwy Piper's suggestion that the boys dance naked been pursued. Donald Mitchell's description of this proposal as 'somewhat unworldly' (Cambridge Handbook p. 13) is a masterpiece of understatement. It is significant, though, that this is one of the few Britten operas where no children's voices are heard.

ix Myfanwy Piper writes of the difficulty of reconciling 'the comparative austerity of language required by the composer with the extreme wordiness of the text' in her account of the libretto in the Cambridge Handbook.

x See my article 'The Venice Sketchbook' in the Cambridge Handbook.

xi 'Usually I have the music complete in my head before putting pencil to paper. That doesn't mean that every note has been composed, perhaps not one has, but I have worked out questions of form, texture, character and so forth, in a very precise way so that I know exactly what effects I want and how I am going to achieve them.' In Murray Schafer, *British Composers in Interview* (1963: the interview was given in 1961).

xii Rosamund Strode says that in May 1973 she listed 346 corrections to the vocal score and 415 to Act I of the full score (Cambridge Handbook, p. 41).

xiii An invoice in the Britten-Pears Foundation archive shows that I worked 22½ hours in Aldeburgh during March (for which I was paid £2 an hour).

xiv Cambridge Handbook, p. 71

xv Cambridge Handbook, p. 41

xvi The German translation was made by Claus Henneberg and Hans Keller, but it was a collaboration in name only. I have a copy of the vocal score in which Henneberg's attempted alterations to Keller's translation are roundly dismissed. Keller's translation of 'I love you' as 'Ich liebe', altered to 'Ich liebe...' (implying 'Ich liebe dich') meets with a diatribe : 'There is, of course, no violent objection to the 3 dots, since one won't hear them, but I can't see why one should make a meaningless concession to an illiterate idiot : the sentence was the best translation in the opera.' Keller goes on to cite two uses of the intransitive in Schiller and one in Goethe.

xvii It is worth remarking that Warner Bros had little confidence in the viability of Visconti's film, since they suspected that the subject matter would lead to it being banned in the USA. Their fears were only allayed when the UK premiere was attended by members of the royal family.

xviii Mann was in fact only 36 years old at the time, 17 years younger than Aschenbach; Wladyslaw was not yet 11, as opposed to Tadzio's 14. See Gilbert Adair, *The Real Tadzio* (2001).

xix To the extent that his upper set of false teeth falls out as he leers at Ashenbach. The teeth of the hotel manager and barber go unremarked.

Peter Grimes: *Now Gossip is Put on Trial*

Nicholas Hammond

Gossip and rumour play differing but always significant parts in much of Britten's *oeuvre* post-*Peter Grimes*. The mysterious disappearance of Albert in the comic opera *Albert Herring*, for example, is made all the more enigmatic by the speculation surrounding him: as the character Florence puts it, the townsfolk find themselves 'starting fresh rumours to keep up the game'. In *Billy Budd*, Billy himself sees what 'the chaps tell me' in only a positive light, always believing what he hears, and culminating in his joyous greeting of Vere, just before Budd is accused by Claggart of posing the threat of mutiny, that 'the talk's got round' that he will be made Captain of the mizzen. The morally dark Claggart, on the other hand, manipulates everything he sees and hears (as Vere says of him, 'he has a hundred eyes'), creating gossip ('so foggy a tale' in Vere's words) to destroy Billy. The Earl of Essex's downfall in *Gloriana* is brought about to a large extent by the opaque rumours spread by the blind ballad singer in Act III, scene 2, and interpreted by the group of old men listening to him as pertaining to Essex. And Britten's final opera *Death in Venice* is dominated by the spread not only of disease but also of rumour and gossip. As Aschenbach declares in scene 9, 'Rumours, rumours. They should be silent. The city's secret, growing darker every day, like the secret in my own heart.'

Yet none of these operas is dominated by gossip to the extent that we find it to be in *Peter Grimes*. As Aschenbach's words above imply, there is a link to be made between love/sexuality and rumour/gossip; his concealed attraction for Tadzio seems to replicate the secrets of cholera spreading through Venice. Although sexuality is not the overt subject of this chapter, it certainly serves

92

as an undercurrent to gossip in *Peter Grimes* and many of Britten's operas. As Lloyd Whitesell writes of Britten, 'sexuality, though concealed, interacts significantly with the ethical, rhetorical, and aesthetic meanings in his operatic discourse.'[i] Indeed, when Peter Pears expressed his evolving view of *Peter Grimes* that 'the more I hear of it, the more I feel that the queerness is unimportant and doesn't really exist in the music (or at any rate obtrude)',[ii] there seems to be on the one hand a tacit acceptance of 'queerness' at the root of the work and, on the other hand, an explicit wish to downplay its significance. It is my contention that, as we will see, gossip plays a similarly double role.

Peter Grimes opens with an inquest. Grimes, the eponymous fisherman, is called to appear in court after the suspicious death of his apprentice William Spode. The verdict is eventually reached that the boy died in 'accidental circumstances', but Grimes is nonetheless advised not to take on any more apprentices.

Present at the inquest, in addition to the court officials and various witnesses, are what are described in the libretto as 'a crowd of townspeople'. This crowd make up 'The Borough', which is the title given to the long poem (comprising several Letters) by George Crabbe (1754–1832) and which was Britten's major inspiration for the story and name of the character Peter Grimes. Although Britten's title inevitably moves the focus away from the borough as a whole and onto one central character, the inhabitants of the town in the operatic version maintain the centrality which is explicit in Crabbe's title. Indeed, as a chorus, the townspeople act as the principal force which the outsider Grimes sees himself as having to face at every moment. For him, it is their gossip which is their most destructive weapon.

Interestingly, gossip as a directly expressed concept is an innovation by Britten and his librettist Montagu Slater, as the word does not appear at all in the Letter (XXII) which incorporates the story of Peter Grimes in *The Borough*.[iii] From the very first lines sung by the chorus in the opera, we find ourselves in the realm of gossip: 'When women gossip the result/ Is someone doesn't sleep at night.' The sentiments expressed here might appear to follow the long tradition of associating gossip with gender: women are the ones who gossip, men tend not to do so. But it would seem not to be as simple as that. The stage directions immediately before this utterance muddy the waters considerably: 'A slight hubbub among the spectators resolves itself into a chorus which is more like the

confused muttering of a crowd than something fully articulate.'
In other words, members of the audience will not receive this
statement about gossip in a straightforward manner. The misogynistic message will be buried within the confused muttering of the
chorus and will be received either subliminally or not at all. When
the same words are repeated later in the Prologue, again they are
smothered, this time by Grimes's defiant 'Then let me speak, let me
stand trial.'

Musically too we find the recurrence of what Alex Ross in his
book on twentieth-century music, *The Rest is Noise*, calls a 'gossip
motif'.[iv] Made up of the first four notes of the lawyer Swallow's
question, 'Why did you do this?', the phrase is repeated twice by
the oboes and bassoons (the latter of which are described by Britten
in *The Young Person's Guide to the Orchestra* as gossiping), first
staccato, then crescendo, and is subsequently taken up by the entire
wind section, becoming, as Ross describes it, 'a driving ostinato,
over which the chorus voices its growing suspicions of Grimes.'[v]

Gossip, therefore, is going to play an important role in the opera
on verbal, musical and dramatic levels, but the first utterances by
the chorus show that, although the question of gender forms an
indecipherable but present undercurrent, gossip will not constitute
a straightforward opposition between men and women or indeed
between Grimes and his critics, as we see later in the Prologue.
Once the townspeople have left the Moot Hall, where the inquest
took place, Peter (who is portrayed as much more of an idealist in
Britten's version than in Crabbe's poem, where he is primarily a
villain) is left alone with Ellen Orford, the woman he would like
eventually to marry.

The very first exchange which the two have in the opera is
revelatory. Whereas Ellen engages in the practicality of moving
Peter on from the immediate situation (as shown in the verb
'come away'), Peter remains rooted within a state of philosophical
questioning (marked by a verbless sentence consisting of nouns):

Peter
The truth – the pity – and the truth.

Ellen
Peter, come away!

Peter's immediate response shows the extent to which he has
absorbed the sense of himself as in perpetual conflict with the

borough. For him, not only those who populate the town become purveyors of malicious gossip about him, but even the inanimate objects which make up the town (the walls of houses) seem to be actively involved:

Peter
Where the walls themselves
Gossip of inquest.

Ellen, on the other hand, presents a crucially different view of gossip. As she replies to Peter,

Ellen
But we'll gossip, too,
And talk and rest.

By recognizing that gossip is something which she and Peter can themselves share, she is transforming the usually held negativity of gossip into something much more positive and affirmative of shared experience. Not only will their gossip neutralize the tittle-tattle which has surrounded them but it will also allow them to exist at peace within the community. What is more, their gossip will not be confined to women alone but will belong to men and women alike.

I have already mentioned that the traditionally misogynistic view of gossip, while present within the community, does not follow an expected course in *Peter Grimes*. However, this does not mean to say that gender does not play an important role in the expectations surrounding gossip. Indeed, Peter and Ellen's differing attitudes to gossip mark two major poles of the opera. For Peter, it emphasizes separation; for Ellen, it represents the possibility of inclusion.

Much of the opera hinges on whether Peter will accept Ellen's view or whether he will continue to see himself as an outcast. Certainly, his negative perception of gossip is perpetuated by the viewpoints of the two men who show themselves to be understanding of his plight. Although Captain Balstrode in particular and Ned Keene the apothecary to a lesser extent are generally interpreted as sympathetic characters, they seem to see gossip in apocalyptic terms which once more accentuate opposition rather than incorporation. In Act I, for example, as a storm brews and they are the only two to help Peter haul his boat onto the beach, Ned sings, 'We'll drown the gossips in a tidal storm.' Similarly,

although Balstrode attempts to liberate Grimes from his plight by
allowing him to express his viewpoint in the middle of the storm,
he does not offer to resolve the situation; instead he seems to accept
that Peter will remain cut off from the community:

> *This storm is useful. You can speak your mind*
> *And never mind the Borough commentary.*
> *There is more grandeur in a gale of wind*
> *To free confession, set a conscience free.*

Peter sees the solution to the gossips in purely economic terms.
If he works hard enough and becomes rich, then perhaps he will
silence them:

> **Peter**
> *They listen to money*
> *These Borough gossips*
> *I have my visions*
> *Fiery visions.*
> *They call me dreamer*
> *They scoff at my dreams*
> *And my ambition.*
> *But I know a way*
> *To answer the Borough*
> *I'll win them over.*
>
> **Balstrode**
> *With the new prentice?*
>
> **Peter**
> *We'll sail together.*
> *These Borough gossips*
> *Listen to money*
> *Only to money:*
> *I'll fish the sea dry,*
> *Sell the good catches—*
> *That wealthy merchant*
> *Grimes will set up*
> *Household and shop*
> *You will all see it!*
> *I'll marry Ellen!*

Peter's idea that economic prosperity will silence the gossips
continues in Act II, after he acquires a new apprentice, who is

brought by Ellen into the Boar pub in the midst of a storm during
Act I and after which the gossip theme is played obsessively by the
strings until the end of the act. Once again his vision is shown to
be in complete contrast to that of Ellen. While the townspeople
are in church on a Sunday morning, Ellen sits outside with John
the apprentice and discovers that he has been physically assaulted.
When Peter appears, ordering the boy to leave with him immediately in order to go fishing, Ellen confronts him about the bruise
on the child's neck. We find here the juxtaposition of differing
world views. At the same time that the gossiping townspeople are
uttering pieties in church, Ellen questions the obsession with work
and money, whereas Peter continues to see economic success as the
only answer to gossip:

Ellen
This unrelenting work
This grey, unresting industry,
What aim, what future, what peace
Will your hard profits buy?

Peter
Buy us a home, buy us respect
And buy us freedom from pain
Of grinning at gossip's tales.
Believe in me, we shall be free!

Choir
I believe in God the Father Almighty,
Maker of heaven and earth:
And in Jesus Christ his only Son our Lord,
Who was conceived...

It is at this point that Ellen realizes that her hope for the future,
where they will 'gossip, too,/And talk and rest', is doomed to
failure. Just as the town concludes its prayers, Peter resorts once
again to violence, and it would seem to be in response to Ellen's
overt rejection of his ideas about stopping the gossip and her recognition of failure:

Ellen
You'll never stop the gossips' talk
With all the fish from out the sea.
We were mistaken to have dreamed...

Peter! We've failed. We've failed.
(He cries out as if in agony. Then strikes her. The basket falls.)

Choir
Amen.

Peter
So be it! – And God have mercy upon me!

After this event, the borough's gossip-mongers come out in full
force. Britten brilliantly conveys both the claustrophobia and the
menace of the town in the chorus 'Grimes is at his exercise.' As
the townspeople gather to march upon Grimes' clifftop hut, gossip
would seem to be portrayed as unequivocally harmful, and this
is corroborated by the sympathetic Balstrode's comments in this
scene that 'When the Borough gossip starts/Somebody will suffer'
and (to some of the townspeople in particular) 'You interfering
gossips, this/ Is none of your business.' Indeed, even the chorus
seems to take up the challenge in placing Peter on the one hand
and gossip on the other as opponents on trial. Their atavistic
thrill (compounded by the beating of a drum) as they proceed to
confront Peter presents those who gossip in a predatory and bloodthirsty light:

Chorus
Now is gossip put on trial,
Now the rumours either fail
Or are shouted in the wind
Sweeping furious through the land.
Now the liars shiver, for
Now if they've cheated we shall know:
We shall strike and strike to kill
At the slander or the sin.
Now the whisperers stand out
Now confronted by the fact.
Bring the branding iron and knife:
What's done now is done for life.

Yet, from a dramatic point of view, instead of ending the scene
before the fourth sea interlude with these townspeople leaving in
pursuit of Peter, Britten, and Slater in particular, chose to close
with a quartet for female voices.[vi] Ellen sings with what have been
up to this point three of the most stereotypical female characters,

Auntie (the pub landlady) and her two flirtatious, not to say sluttish, nieces (described as the pub's 'main attractions'). If gossip were to be portrayed in an exclusively female and negative way, these three would surely have been at the head of the queue to find Grimes in his hut. But instead, we as spectators and listeners are left with a beautiful meditation by the four women on their lives within the community: 'In the gutter, why should we trouble at their ribaldries?' To see four women talking together might well in the traditional frame of things constitute gossip. Indeed, I would argue that it is a form of gossip, but it is not the aggressive gossip which characterizes Peter's perception but rather a kind of gossip which is more in keeping with the ideal which Ellen depicted in the Prologue. The fact that it is four women sharing this vision only serves to overturn traditional images of female gossip. The quartet also allows, in the case of Auntie and the nieces, previously one-dimensional characters to show their humanity and their capacity for (in a non-religious way) redemption or recuperation.

The final scene of Act II is set in Grimes' hut, where Peter and the apprentice prepare themselves to go out to sea. As the crowd with the banging drum approaches, Peter reiterates his belief that the 'Borough gossips/Listen to money,/Only to money.' He seems to veer between tenderness and violence towards the child, but when he becomes aware of the procession his obsession with gossip reaches its peak. For the first time, he separates himself further by placing Ellen and the boy in the ranks of those who gossip in a malicious way:

> **Peter**
> *Wait! You've been talking.*
> *You and that bitch were gossiping.*
> *What lies have you been telling?*
> *The Borough's climbing up the road.*
> *To get me. Me!*

In their hurry to escape from the crowd, with Peter distracted by the knocking on his door, the apprentice falls to his death from the cliff. Ambiguity remains as to what or who killed the child, but there is a strong indication that the crowd itself precipitated his fall. To a large extent, Peter's negative perception of gossip is therefore fulfilled. However, rather than seeing him as the passive victim of gossip, I would argue that it is both his rejection of

Ellen's model and his rigid insistence on his own model which are just as crucial in leading to his tragic end.

Act III only serves to support this theory. In scene 1, the towns-people in search of Peter seem to become the bloodthirsty pack of Grimes' darkest imaginings. In a grim mirroring of the 'confused muttering' of the chorus's first entry in the Prologue, their words disintegrate into a wordless assault at the end of the scene. In scene 2, Peter in his derangement remains as obsessed by gossip, as he picks up fragments of sentences which he has spoken or heard over the course of the opera, including 'Now is gossip put on trial.' By simply repeating his name in a ghoulish response to the crowd's incessant calling out of his name, it would seem that, as Alex Ross describes it, 'he sees himself only as the town sees him' (p.430). For a moment, he imagines that he is hand in hand with Ellen, but this dream is broken with his awareness of both his own failure to secure the friendship which Ellen offered and the triumph of gossip over him:

> *Take away your hand!*
> *The argument's finished,*
> *Friendship lost,*
> *Gossip is shouting,*
> *Everything's said.*

Could the intriguing finished 'argument' to which he refers signify his recognition that Ellen's sense of restorative gossip might have been more successful than his own?

It is significant that the other character who shares Peter's perception of gossip, Balstrode, is the one who persuades him to go out to sea and sink his boat, for Peter's failure is surely also Balstrode's failure to see, amongst other things, the possibilities of gossip. Ironically, the boat sinking is written off by one of those left on shore, Auntie, as 'One of these rumours.' Peter's death has been subsumed into the world of gossip and ignored. At the end of the opera, it is the borough as an entity which sings and not any individual, but instead of concentrating on ephemeral things, they evoke the eternity of the ocean's tide:

> *In ceaseless motion comes and goes the tide*
> *Flowing it fills the channel broad and wide*
> *Then back to sea with strong majestic sweep*
> *It rolls in ebb yet terrible and deep.*

Notes

i   Lloyd Whitesell, 'Britten's dubious trysts', *Journal of the American Musicological Society* vol. 56, no. 3 (Fall 2003), 637–94, p. 689.

ii *Letters from a Life: the selected letters and diaries of Benjamin Britten 1913–1976*, (eds) Donald Mitchell and Philip Reed (London: Faber & Faber, 1991), p. 1189.

iii For an account of the fraught history of the evolution of the libretto, see Philip Brett, '*Peter Grimes*: the growth of the libretto', in *The Making of 'Peter Grimes': essays and studies*, ed. Paul Banks (Woodbridge: The Boydell Press, 2000), pp. 53–78.

iv Alex Ross, *The Rest is Noise: listening to the twentieth century* (London: Fourth Estate, 2008), p. 424.

v   Ibid., p. 424.

vi The correspondence between Britten and Slater reveals that Slater in particular was keen to preserve the all-female quartet, in contrast to Eric Crozier, who suggested to Britten that the quartet be turned into a trio, with Balstrode replacing the Nieces. See Philip Brett, '*Peter Grimes*: the growth of the libretto', op. cit., p. 69.

Gloriana *as Music Drama:*
A Reaffirmation

Hans Keller

The younger one gets – the more, that is, one sheds those inevitable, almost instinctive prejudices with which one's civilisation, especially if it happens to be an old one, has burdened one almost from birth – the more easily things go right for one when they go wrong for the civilisation in general and for the critic in particular. Criticism tends to misfire in proportion as it is civilised, as it instinctively, pre-consciously judges the present in terms of the past: the law of precedent is the death of art – or, if art survives its application, the death of criticism. What is an opera? I don't know: it all depends on the next one, not the last one.

It is not only because I am going to write about *Gloriana* that I am singling out opera. Just because it is such an artificial art form, critics and indeed composers have always been guiltily anxious to establish its natural laws, which, of course, do not exist. The only general law I have been able to find is that librettos are bad unless or until the music is found good. Nobody loses a word nowadays about the idiocies that pervade almost the whole of *Il seraglio* and a substantial part of *The Magic Flute*. But you try, even if you are a towering genius, to write an opera on a comparable piece of non-drama or non-sense, and you are in for it. For a long time, I had my well-founded doubts about Goethe's musicality, but since he admired (and indeed continued) *The Magic Flute*, he must have understood the music.[i]

Things may be changing just now, but so far *Gloriana* has been the worst treated and the most neglected of Britten's operas; which is a pity, because there is none better except *The Turn of the Screw*. Actually, I have pinched this evaluation from my wife, who is an

artist and not a musician, which is why I have pinched it: as I grow
younger, I am getting less and less interested in expert judgement,
except of course my own. *Gloriana* is universal, because it is
complexity simplified by musical definition. So is *The Turn of the
Screw*, which goes yet deeper and therefore has to express itself
esoterically, chamber-musically: you have to be more musical (not
more expert!) for *The Turn of the Screw* than for *Gloriana*. Why,
then, was *Gloriana* a mitigated flop?

There are two answers. One is that it was not. Newspaper
criticism or lack of promotion may have put it temporarily on the
Index librorum prohibitorum, which, however, is not necessarily an
index of *vox populi*. The other answer is that I am over-simplifying.
There is no insignificant criticism, for no man is stupid alone. In
fact, shared stupidity is what is known as objectivity – whereas it
is, in fact, the purely individual discovery, unshared for a time by
anyone, that ultimately tends to prove the most objective. Original
sin is to share the stupidity – actively or, more often, passively
– of which one would consider oneself incapable if one were
placed outside one's social context. The persuasiveness of stupidity
cannot, in fact, be overestimated. No man is as stupid as are his
judgements. They are what they are because there are powerful,
infectious motives behind the lack of reasons.

It is hardly credible, but some of the criticisms of the premiere
13 years ago are not yet out of date. Martin Cooper today: 'It
was a commission for the Coronation celebrations and it must
be admitted that in the circumstances William Plomer's libretto
was, to say the least, tactless. It showed Elizabeth I on an unstable
throne, a pathetic and vindictive ageing woman attracted by a
much younger man.'[ii] In the first place, I could not care two
hoots what the libretto showed. I never read it – not without the
music. I know what the librettist wanted to do, because he said
it; and I know that the music did it, because I heard it. 'Reduced
to the barest outline,' William Plomer wrote, 'the theme of the
opera may be stated as follows. Queen Elizabeth, a solitary and
ageing Monarch, *undiminished in majesty, power, statesmanship,
and understanding*, sees in an outstanding young nobleman a
hope for both the future of her country and of herself.'[iii] Apart
from the wrong grammar of the last phrase, the summary
(whose italics are mine) is unobjectionable. It is a very different
characterisation from Cooper's, and it is the characterisation
that the music gets across.

In the second place, within this 'barest outline', a great deal more happens than meets the eye, yet no more than meets the hearing ear. (I have come to distrust the *listening* ear a little. The musical moralist or self-educator listens out for what is not there and so does not hear what is. A seer is a seer, not a looker.) Donald Mitchell is the only one who has said straight out that 'the Elizabeth-Essex relationship is a brilliant study in the ambiguities that can surround a great passion'.[iv] He sees the essence of the opera in its 'private face', of which 'the grand accumulation of pageant, pomp and ceremony' is a projection. So far, so excellent; but even Mitchell simplifies. Elizabeth's conflict is not merely one between duty and inclination (as Kant and Schiller would have put it), with 'inclinations' including her yearning for 'a vanished youth and freedom' (Mitchell). She does not only object to that in Essex that does not love her, nor only to that that pretends to love her and intends to misuse her. She also objects to the genuine part of his love, because she objects to her own. She objects to his re-arousing a conflict in her which she felt she had solved: "I hate the idea of marriage for reasons that I would not divulge to a twin soul" (to Lord Sussex).[v] Essex gets the worst of both her psychic worlds: she resents his loving her too little and she resents his loving her too much. When she signs his death warrant, she proves herself to herself once more – and it is not only her dutiful Queen's self that she proves, but also her personal, anti-sexual self, a guilty self of which her duties are, psychologically, a displacement.

But psychologically again, Essex himself deserves everything he gets. He does not so much play around with her as with his own feelings. 'How far,' asks Mitchell, 'does Essex love (and therefore flatter) the Queen because she is also the instrument of his ambition?' It all depends, as [C. E. M.] Joad would have said, on what you mean by love – or rather what Essex means by love. Without the music, the situation would be hopelessly ambiguous. With the music, it is well-definedly ambivalent: the truth – let's be honest: the touching truth – of Essex's feelings is no longer in doubt, but neither is his ability to marshal them in a way that will, he hopes, not only meet his purposes but also his conscience. His love makes him feel good, makes his ambition feel noble, but when we are shocked at her signing his death warrant, we should not perhaps forget that he would have signed hers far more readily, readjusting his feelings flexibly: he would not have felt any need to say, 'I will not sign it now: I will consider it'. Since he is actually able to make himself love, it would perhaps be an insult to call him a prostitute even though he tries to sell his love; on the other hand, maybe one insults one or the other prostitute by denying here that very ability.

In any case, two profound ambivalences – Elizabeth's and Essex's – encounter each other in this relationship between two complicated, but (musically) crystal-clear characters; so what more do you want? My rhetorical question responds to Cooper's review of first reactions 13 years ago: 'This strange relationship was felt by many to be *insufficiently substantial* [my italics] for an opera in which the only other love interest (between Mountjoy and Essex's sister) is pale and abstract.' And here is Cooper's own reaction to this one-time criticism: 'The Elizabeth-Essex relationship might be enough to carry the work, if only its exact nature was made clear and elaborated.' Does nobody ever listen to the music? The publication of a libretto outside the score ought to be prohibited before the music has been heard. Nor is it all that difficult to describe – better: report – what the music 'makes clear and elaborates': I have just done it, and the burden of proof, more firmly now than ever, is on the prosecution. My suspicion is that 'this strange relationship' is too substantial, not too insubstantial, for immediate success. What the old souls are crying out for is the type of simple love story in which the earlier stages of our old operatic culture abound. It's gone, my friends, it's gone, and you never noticed its departure. Where is the naive 'love interest' in the established operas of our day, Britten or no Britten? Do we find it in Berg's *Wozzeck*, Pfitzner's *Palestrina*, Schoenberg's *Moses und Aron*, Stravinsky's *The Rake's Progress*? It celebrated its mythical death in Wagner's *Tristan*, together with uncomplicated diatonicism.

It is gradually becoming clear why the musical world still reacts uncomfortably to *Gloriana*. The opera shows the inevitable obverse of nobility, majesty, courage, honour, rightful or righteous rebelliousness, poetic imagination – and, in fact, love. Now, we do not mind the obverse; we are not as naive as all that. What we do mind a little more is its inevitability, and it is such inevitability that good music tends to drive home without one's being able to do anything about it. Music has that wonderfully logical two-sidedness about it: since it always expresses itself through concrete, singular thoughts, never through more or less abstract terms (as does verbal art), it is capable of closely and comprehensively defining any given emotional situation; while on the other hand, the very depth and clarity of the definition shows it to be applicable to all similar situations, makes it immediately universal. So nobility, dignity, moral strength, etc., always look like that? Even such a thought might still be felt to be bearable if the automatic rider could be added gleefully: nobility is not what we fondly thought it was. That would be the conclusion of the third-rate psycho-analyser. But it is at this very point that masterly music delivers its master-stroke: investing nobility with nobility, majesty with majesty, love with love, it shows that when all is said and done, these qualities and feelings remain precisely what we fondly thought they were, despite the inevitable obverse underneath. To discover the muddy side of our virtues without being able cynically to throw mud at the clean side – that is something few of us can bear.

The motives, then, behind the absence of reasons in the opposition to *Gloriana* are motives of denial. The music critic of *The Times*,[vi] true to the traditions of his paper, has perhaps found the most civilised form, and certainly the most rational one, of denying the substance of the opera: he does not get himself involved in any evaluations at all. In a lengthy article on the recent revival, he concentrates, throughout, on details of performance. 'What about the work itself?' the bewildered reader asks, 'Is it any good?' He scans the article again, and becomes even more mystified. On the one hand, the piece can be read as a report on the performance of an established opera that does not stand in need of evaluation. But then, the reader reminds himself, it is not an established work at all. On the other hand, he now realises, it may be that Our Music Critic is just being non-committally tactful: let's not go into these complicated questions of evaluation of what, after all, is a jolly problematic work anyhow; the purpose, the function of my piece is a report on the production. Maybe, maybe not: Martin Cooper certainly did not think likewise. It is all very sad when one realises that, Mitchell apart, the last time anybody seems to have said anything sensible about the opera *in extenso* was 13 years ago, when John W. Klein wrote an essay that, although open at times to factual criticism, showed precisely the type of unprejudiced sensitivity, of spiritually youthful disregard for how an opera ought to behave itself, which one would expect from a critic of an important new work – if that critic is to have any artistic *raison d'être* at all.[vii] Am I begging the question by saying the work is important? Not even Cooper regards it as unimportant.

The operatic crisis started when opera acquired a conscience about its purpose – when it turned from entertainment (not *mere* entertainment, but entertainment nevertheless) to truth-telling. The time was the early nineteenth-century, and the place was *Fidelio* – or rather, to begin with, *Leonore*: Beethoven's own difficulties with the work were symptomatic of the revolution.[viii] I think Britten regards *Fidelio* as about the worst opera in the general repertoire. No matter: he has followed the only artistic tradition worth following – that of telling the truth.

Notes

Source: 'Two Interpretations of *Gloriana* as Music Drama: a Reaffirmation', *Tempo*, No. 79, 1966–7, pp. 2–5. Editorial notes in square brackets by Christopher Wintle.

[i]   [Keller's comment is obscure (even if he meant '(and continued to admire) *The Magic Flute*') Goethe, who had himself written *Singspiel*-type plays-with-music from about 1775–82, described his (manuscript) *Helena* as a piece that 'should begin as a tragedy and end as an opera', placing it alongside Mozart's *Singspiel*: 'Let the crowd of spectators take pleasure in the spectacle; the higher import will not escape the initiated – as with the *Magic Flute*.' His proposed composer for *Helena*, though, was Meyerbeer, who combined a 'German nature with the Italian style and manner'. (Johann Peter Eckermann, *Conversations with Goethe* (1836), trans. John Oxenford and ed. J. K. Moorhead, London: Everyman/Dent, 1970, p. 162 (Goethe made his remark on 29 January 1827).) For a more sceptical view of Goethe and music, see: Hans Keller, 'Goethe and the Lied' in: *Goethe Revisited: a Collection of Essays*, ed. Elizabeth M. Wilkinson, London: Calder, 1984, pp. 73–84.]

[ii]   Martin Cooper, 'Opera Revival', *Daily Telegraph*, 22 October 1966.

[iii]   William Plomer, 'Notes on the Libretto of *Gloriana*', *Tempo*, No. 28, June 1953, pp. 5–7. [One correction of Plomer's 'wrong grammar' might be: 'a hope for the future of both her country and herself.']

[iv]   Donald Mitchell, 'Public and Private Life in Britten's *Gloriana*', *Opera*, October 1966.

[v]   [These are the words of the real Elizabeth, not the operatic one.]

[vi]   William Mann, 'Characters of Britten Opera Captured', *The Times*, 22 October 1966. [By invoking the 'traditions of his paper', Keller typically castigates *The Times*'s music critic Frank Howes.]

[vii]   John W. Klein, 'Some Reflections on *Gloriana*', *Tempo*, No. 29, September 1953, pp. 16–21.

[viii] [See also: Hans Keller, '*Fidelio* at Covent Garden', *Opera*, Vol. 2, No. 8, July 1951, pp. 432–33.]

Britten's Last Masterpiece

Hans Keller

I see from a recent book on Britten that the reason why he dedicated his Third Quartet to me was that I kept 'prodding' him to write it. It wasn't, and I didn't really. Mind you, all I *know* about the dedication is that one day a note from him arrived out of the blue, asking my 'permission' for it: you can imagine my telegraphic reply. But many, many years ago, I had a long discussion with him about string-quartet texture in general, sonata structure in particular, and quite especially, about development: as I didn't tell him, the development section in his first movement of his great Second Quartet (written 30 years before the Third) had always struck me as being marginally below the level of the rest of the work's invention; in fact, I might now add that the beginning of the recapitulation is more of an intrinsic development than is the development section proper.

Anyhow, what I concentrated on in that protracted discussion was contrast – textural contrast so far as string-quartet writing was concerned, and the essence of sonata contrast from the formal point of view: I pointed out that successive analytic fashions, highlighting thematic contrast and tonal contrast, had not hit the very heart of the sonata's matter, which was *the contrast between statement and development, and its integration* – statement meaning stability, and development (continual modulation in tonal music) a labile structure which was not confined, of course, to the official development section.[i]

A long pause punctuated the end of our conversation, and then Britten said, "One day, I'll write a string quartet for you". Thereafter, there was no prodding for years and years. Came his heart operation and the partial paralysis of his right side: when he complained that he couldn't even move his right arm sufficiently to cover a full score, I wrote him a pseudo-jocular note suggesting

that this was the time for four staves, the more so since he was rid
of public commitments – the ideal time for a string quartet, for our
musical culture's private, personal work *par excellence*.

When I received an advance copy of the score, and after I had
overcome my initial, idiotic shock at the five movements, the
two scherzos very short (was this a bloody suite or something?),
my actual perusal of the opening movement soon disclosed
a stunningly novel answer to my lifelong preoccupations with
quartet and sonata – so specific a creative response that the
experience was that of a causal relation. My delusion? Maybe –
but it doesn't matter, for the musical relation is there, whether it's
causal or not, a question which is of little interest to anybody but
myself, anyway.

Myself apart, nobody has yet dared to call that movement a
sonata form in public, though there have been evasive whispers
about 'elements of sonata' and the like. The reason is that the
structure is so original, so precisely and pregnantly composed
against the background of sonata form that people who can only
think in terms of form (that which musics have in common) as
distinct from structure (that which they haven't) are confused: how
can these contradictions of sonata be called sonata? Easily – first,
because they can be shown to be closely related to that which
they contradict, and secondly, because the basic sonata contrasts
– thematic and tonal as well as developmental – are there anyway,
though things tend to happen in the wrong place.

But then, they've been doing that ever since Haydn started
contradicting sonata form; only, in due course, wrong places
become right places, which means that individual structure
turns into collective form so that you've got to find new wrong
places if you want to say something new – and this Britten does
to an extent which helps to make his opening movement one of
the most unprecedented sonatas of our time, our century even.
What's more, it's unprecedented as against the background
of any musical form, not only sonata: the coda, the stage of
eventual relaxation, is not eventual; it happens *before* the end,
before the recapitulation of the second subject, which thus takes
on the concluding job of the coda, with the truly eventual help
of the first.

How so, why? Because for the first time in the history of sonata,
the very material of instability's climax, of the development proper,
is used for *the* diametrically opposite purpose – extreme stability,

tonal relaxation, the coda before the coda. It must be stressed that technical as this may sound, the untutored, musical ear can take it all in at the first hearing, without any interruptions of the purely musical experience: Britten's clarity invariably increases with his complexity, demonstrably so.

There's nothing more essentially instrumental in the Western musical world than sonata – yet, paradoxically, Britten honoured this movement with an operatic title: 'Duets'. There is the most lucid method in Britten's apparent madness: the duets are the statements (exposition and recapitulation), whereas the development establishes extreme textural contrast by going so far as an octet and nonet – with the help of double and triple stoppings. And even though, to begin with, the development still evinces transitional duet structure, it can't be missed: powerful downbows and tremolando upbeat phrases throw you into the stage of instability which develops the syncopations of the first subject – and all you have to hear is sudden unrest.

But towards the end of the recapitulation, the resumed duet texture is interrupted – no, continued by those very double and triple stoppings which now re-emerge, against all expectations, 'very quietly', expressing rest with the help of pizzicatos: again, this extreme contrast on the basis of extreme unity can immediately be heard, because it is spontaneously experienced. At the end of it, for a bar or two, the developmental explosion recurs – to introduce the recapitulation of the second subject which, at the same time, unfolds or folds, the conclusion *after* the coda. The most contrasting quartet textures thus prove sheer functions of sonata structure, in which sonata form's own traditional contrasts are subordinated to the even more fundamental polarity between statement and development, and so create a new order of events which confuses the annotator and enlightens the analyst: if that's not inspired mastery, you can call me a music critic.

The remaining four movements, of which the final 'Recitative and Passacaglia' is the longest (over eight minutes) and the most moving, gradually reveal the entire work as having been composed against the background of what my first superficial glance feared to be its foreground – that of a suite or divertimento. The weighty, symphonic contradiction of this 'light' background has a long and distinguished history – from the Mozart String Trio, still called 'Divertimento', through Beethoven's early string trio in the same key and mould [as well as] his late B Flat Quartet, through Mahler and Shostakovich, right up to, into, Britten's transubstantiation of dance backgrounds into three of his five movements, where Beethoven's Op. 130 had four dances at the back of its six movements, and Mahler's Ninth two successive dances behind its four movements – like Beethoven's C minor Quartet and Eighth Symphony.

The lineage from Mahler's Ninth, moreover, is even straighter than that: the 'Rondo: Burleske', the second of Mahler's two successive dance inspirations, is not only responsible for the title – 'Burlesque' – of the second of the two scherzos that surround Britten's central slow movement, but has concretely stimulated its thematic characters – the movement's character, in fact. Whether the Viennese waltz that forms the background of the trio does homage to Mahler or pulls the dedicatee's legs, both of them, is not for him to say; a bit of both is the most likely answer – which, however, leaves the most important point unarticulated, to wit, the work's handshake with the Austro-German symphonic tradition, which is at least as firm as the Second Quartet's.[ii]

Nor is the Second Quartet itself only remembered by the [Third's] opening movement, which beats the Second's first movement at its developmental game. The extended C major that liquidates the slow third movement's tense middle section – an astonishingly free cadenza for the first violin whose dominant role gives the piece its title, 'Solo' – recalls the extended C major relaxation that is the coda of the Second Quartet's first movement – as if it had been yesterday. C major hovers in the background of much of the rest of the work, too, and indeed starts it: Britten's own key, this, the way *minor* keys are other great composers' personal keys, such as Bach's B minor or, in more major-mode times, Haydn's F minor, Mozart's G minor, Beethoven's C minor, Mendelssohn's E minor, Schoenberg's D minor ...

When I lectured on the work at Snape the other month,[iii] I analysed the heavily charged end, or non-end, against the harmonic background of the traditional interrupted cadence, and ventured that the only possible verbal translation of these last, unfinal notes was, 'This is not the end'. Whereupon Donald Mitchell, the composer's authorised biographer, recounted that in reply to the question what this end meant, Britten had said, "I'm not dead yet". Nor, 'advanced' phoneys, is his music.

Notes

Source: 'Britten's Last Masterpiece', *The Spectator*, Vol. 242, No. 7873, 2 June 1979, pp. 27–8. The notes are by Christopher Wintle.

i   [Keller was preoccupied in his last few years with the 'true' character of sonata form. See his 'The State of the Symphony: not only Maxwell Davies's', *Tempo*, No. 125, June 1978, pp. 6–11; reprinted in: *Essays on Music*, ed. Christopher Wintle, Cambridge: Cambridge University Press, 1994, pp. 106–10. Keller writes:

'… the elementary and elemental contrast in the sonata's modes of thought is independent of the contrasts between themes and keys: *it is the contrast between statements* (whether monothematic or polythematic) *and developments* (whether they concern themselves with the statements or not). In tonal music, therefore, it is the contrasts between harmonic stability and harmonic lability (modulation), while in atonal symphonism (such as, say, in Schoenberg's Third and Fourth Quartets), the differentiation is achieved by a variety of means, from which harmony is not excluded, and which encompasses both melodic and textural juxtapositions, as well as contrasts in rhythmic articulation.' (p. 132)]

ii   [See Keller's essay on 'Benjamin Britten's Second Quartet', *Tempo*, No. 3, March 1947, pp. 6–8, reprinted in: Hans Keller, *Britten. Essays, Letters and Documents*, ed. Christopher Wintle and Alison Garnham, London: Plumbago, 2013.]

iii   [Keller's involvement with Aldeburgh and later the Maltings, Snape, dated back at least as far as the early 1950s. He wrote on the first Aldeburgh Festival in 1948 for *Everybody's* (reprinted earlier in this book) and on the Festival of 1951 for *Music Survey*, Vol. 4, No. 1, October 1951, pp. 368–70; he 'composed' the FA No. 11, on Mozart's String Quartet in F major, K. 590, as an Aldeburgh Festival commission in 1961. Keller discusses this FA in 'From the Third Programme to Radio 3', *Music and Musicians*, December 1984, p. 15: 'When I asked [Benjamin Britten] why he had commissioned me, he told me that the analysis of his own work [the Second String Quartet] contained his pre-compositional thought, partly conscious and partly unconscious, and that so far as he could hear, it had contained nothing else. I watched his face when my Mozart analysis was performed at Aldeburgh, and saw from his multiple grins, often two or three a second, that he got every single point.']

Conducting Britten

Edward Gardner talks to Nicholas Kenyon

NK Can you remember the first music by Britten you performed?

EG As a treble in Gloucester Cathedral the *Missa Brevis* made a huge impression on me. It was instantly enjoyable to sing, and we fed off its clarity, its sense of fun, competition and playfulness. What an early introduction to bi-tonality, canons! That thrilling Sanctus with its bell-peal cycle of fourths; the neurotic Agnus Dei. Even then Britten's ability to engage a performer, whatever their age or level, was clear to me. Then, of course, there's that perfect little anthem *A Hymn to the Virgin* – absolutely extraordinary for a teenage composer. For me this showed Britten's connection to a text; the dialogue between Latin and Old English is remarkable. The ability to choose text and frame his music around it really defined him in many ways. Thinking of other very early compositions, I'm incredibly fond of the *Quatre Chansons Françaises*; they are an assimilation of French impressionist colour and harmony: they don't sound like Britten at all, but what assurance!

NK Being enjoyable to perform – is that a fundamental aspect of Britten's skill?

EG I would say absolutely: when I think of Britten's music, I'm struck by his ability to write uncannily well – both for any player or section of an orchestra, or for a singer. Vocal parts are sometimes based around the idiosyncrasies of original performers: all the roles written for Pears highlight a specific part of his voice – his glorious-sounding Es and Fs; for just about any other singer all those phrases are stuck in the *passaggio*, where the parts of the voice join up and mould together; 'the great Bear' in *Peter Grimes* is a particularly extreme example of this, where Grimes sits on a top E for ages!

Britten's music so often has such a clear identity that it's magnetic for a performer. I'm in the middle of rehearsing the *Sinfonia da Requiem* with a great orchestra which doesn't know the piece; yet even on a first play-through the essence of the music seems fundamentally clear, and what we're all aiming for: the keening quality of sound in the first movement, with those hugely expressive and precise hairpins, the pathos of the final movement, balancing to the warm colour of the alto-flute. Orchestras and singers always seem to sense what the aim of Britten's music is, and enjoy the experience of getting closer to it. The *Dies Irae* second movement, which I spent an hour or so on today, feels like an athletic pursuit, the game of the rhythm with its unpredictable ostinato all underpinned by a strikingly raw emotion. It's music that is a pleasure to rehearse almost as much as to perform.

I was struck by that from a really early age: Britten engaged so fully in the joy of childhood, that his music written for children, either for them to perform or to hear, is perfectly judged – centred around words, puzzles, competition – without a hint of being patronizing. *The Young Person's Guide* is such a good example of that, perhaps even heightened by the fact that while the text now feels so outdated, the music doesn't! It's fiendishly difficult to play for a good professional orchestra, but takes apart, plays with and gloriously reconstructs the music in such a joyful way. His music, generally, has this directness of contact with the performer and audience alike.

That brings me on to a word that's often used about Britten: how his music is 'effective'. This is a rather dangerous term to use about his music, and is by no means complimentary. But I really understand it and, through conducting a lot of the pieces, some of them a lot of times, I can't help but acknowledge it. I do find myself unable to identify with some pieces where the emotions, or drama, seem to be drawn on the surface by a master-hand, but where, certainly as a conductor, you feel somehow disengaged from the passion, the underlying emotion; or (to be even bolder) you feel the emotion is missing underneath it all.

On the other hand there are a few pieces that aren't instantly likeable that I have a very soft spot for, for example the Cello Symphony, quite impenetrable for an audience. Somehow I find, having lived with it, that it's become one of my favourite scores: its unremittingly craggy opening, working out to such warmth of humanity in the final movement, as the orchestra envelops the soloist. The Nocturne too, I adore; audiences immediately respond to the Serenade, but I find the Nocturne has hidden depths for a conductor and tenor, especially the way the work ends with that wonderful Mahlerian Shakespeare movement at the end – that is truly moving.

Music from the beginning and end of his life generally seems to speak to me most clearly; his official Opus 1, the Sinfonietta, is incredibly prescient of *Grimes* – the rolling waves – the second movement almost feels like a sketch for the 'Dawn' interlude. *Les Illuminations* has such vitality and brilliance: that was Britten's genius, even in his mid-20s, to set the impossibly colourful Rimbaud text. But then there's *Paul Bunyan*, a piece that seems to me written for a purpose, which I don't really enjoy.

At the other extreme of his life you have *Phaedra* which I find quite extraordinary, both for its emotion and the clarity and strength of what it expresses; one feels the poison coursing through her veins with those rising string chords. I see it as Britten's version of Berlioz's *La Mort de Cléopâtre*. I also love *Lachrymae*, written earlier, but orchestrated at the end of his life. It's a piece filled with darkness and austerity, but when the Dowland emerges through the mist like a viol consort – and I love to hear it played like that, without vibrato – the sense of relief and resolution is remarkably moving.

NK Britten clearly had a skill for writing music that would communicate?

EG   True, but in so many different ways, and achieving so many different things; and I don't identify with all of them. In the late '30s in the period leading up to *Grimes*, you have the Violin Concerto, a piece that certainly doesn't give everything up on one hearing but has perhaps one of the most haunting, heart-breaking endings in his music. Then you have the Piano Concerto, from the same period, but in a completely different style: more overtly virtuosic, Waltonesque in its exuberance. I would have loved to hear a recording of that premiere, Britten playing the solo part with Henry Wood conducting.

What Britten thought of conductors is a very interesting issue. You sense he wasn't happy with the level of performance he heard on the radio; he didn't like Adrian Boult at all. Later he loved working with the conductors who would take his music abroad, Giulini with the *War Requiem* for example, and we know he suggested to Solti he should conduct his music at Covent Garden. That would have been worth hearing! It's hard to analyze what he wanted from a conductor, but you can certainly say avoiding the routine, mundane was part of it: as his own conducting shows, the intensity of the performance is everything to him.

NK And then after that period there's this sudden eruption of *Peter Grimes*...

EG It's such an outpouring, *Grimes*, so visceral, and so meant. In one sense it's clunky: you can hear the structure of it, its bones. But it's as if he doesn't care about that because he means it *all*. It powers through its own framework, because it has this raw, elemental energy that generates such momentum. The more I do it, the more the piece sweeps you along. It hard to analyse why this is, but perhaps my experience of doing the Sea Interludes in concert helps me rationalize it. Whether for a performance of the Interludes on their own or as part of the whole opera, one prepares in the same way. In 'Dawn' you work on the intensity of the vibrato of the violins, the speed of the grace notes of the flutes and violins to give that nervous energy, the chords in the brass to make them seem as veiled as possible to start, leading to a wonderful climax; you work on the swell, the virtuosity of the 'Storm', then the warmth and humanity of 'Moonlight'; but in concert they never have quite enough of an effect. This is partially of course because they're miniatures. In the opera, however, at the point that they all come, they absolutely feed off the momentum of the drama that's come before, built up like a pressure cooker: the experience of those warm, yet nebulous chords in 'Moonlight' at the beginning of Act 3, after what's happened with the Apprentice, and what's happened with the wild mob demanding 'justice' – it's just so moving.

I often wonder why *Grimes* stands on its own in Britten's operatic output. Simply, there's a raw, almost feral quality to the music, to which he never returned. *Wozzeck* clearly lurks in the background – the devices like the stage band – but the influence is more than that though, isn't it? The character of Wozzeck himself is one example Britten found for the outsider in a society: Britten had so much admiration for Berg, and we know he had heard, and was blown away by, both *Wozzeck* and the Violin Concerto.

NK Was *Grimes* the first Britten opera you conducted?

EG   No. I had worked on *The Rape of Lucretia* at the Academy, and then assisted on *Albert Herring* at Glyndebourne. I admire both those pieces, but I have never quite got on with either. *Herring* must be one of the most effective pieces he ever wrote; people get it immediately – both players and singers – it has such a wonderful atmosphere around it, a conversational tone that works with such ease. I love the craft of it, the Threnody is superb and there are great moments like the end of Act 1 for Albert, but I don't get much beneath it. So yes, I enjoyed working on it because you can learn so much from it. But *Lucretia* I never really enjoyed working on. To be honest I have just never got the point of it, which is awful to say.

Peter Grimes, though, I certainly knew: I saw it quite a lot and I grew up with a video of the Tim Albery production in which Philip Langridge was Grimes, conducted by David Atherton. I had that from my teens, and it was a big influence; the strength of the music, but in that performance (and, my God, in so much else of Britten – the Nocturne, Vere in *Budd*) Philip's focus and intensity of expression through his inflection of text was such an example of the possibilities of performing Britten.

The first Britten opera I fully conducted was *The Turn of the Screw* at Glyndebourne. That's an amazing piece for an audience, but you feel a little outside it as a conductor because your job is to coach it, explain the drama to the players, and then somehow let them fly with it. It's the height of chamber music. You come away deeply affected by the piece because the story is so harrowing, however you play it. The ending would affect me every time: the fingernails on the timpani, the Governess completely destroyed. But you're watching: that piece is strangely voyeuristic for a conductor.

NK   Was *Peter Grimes* then top of your wish list when you took over at ENO?

EG   No, I was much more interested in doing nineteenth-century pieces to start with when I went to ENO, but I have grown into Britten more and more. The first Britten opera I did at ENO was *Death in Venice*, just after I had been appointed, as a cancellation for another conductor. That first time there were things in it I really didn't quite get. It's a piece which you have to do again and again, mainly because judging the emotional temperature of it is very hard: that's something Deborah [Warner, the director] was very good on: the music is so misty, it sits in the ether somehow, like the cholera pervading Venice. As a director or conductor of *Death in Venice* you have to be so careful what to shade, and what to leave open for a listener, an observer, rather than just pushing it out to the audience. The end of Act 1 is a good example of this for me, the exhilaration of Aschenbach as his mind corkscrews through the possibilities of why he feels the way he does about Tadzio, leading to the last words of the Act 'I love you'. I found the most effective way was to keep the music as bright and as pure as possible. An audience can react to these words with shock, horror, disbelief; but the music doesn't – that comes at the beginning Act 2 with the strange, tortured inert opening. That ambiguity in Britten is musical as well as dramatic: you have to allow the audience to have their feelings and their opinion. I find it also a ravishingly beautiful score, in an incredibly distilled way: that feeling of vertiginous excitement when the hotel manager shows Aschenbach the view, achieved in such a simple way (it's certainly no Alpine Symphony!).

The score also has a hazy colour built in; when one thinks of the brass music of St Mark's in the prelude, or the rocking of the Gondola, everything is seen through a gauze, musically: something the design of that production mirrored so well. And it is so subtle: if you compare the games in *Death in Venice* with something like the jousting scene in *Gloriana*, it's playful but so strange, the sonorities owing something to *Prince of the Pagodas* and the Balinese music he heard. *Grimes* became very important to do at ENO, but you have to wait for the right moment in terms of casting. We had Stuart Skelton over for some Janáček operas and it was clear that he was an important choice for Grimes, someone who could marry the heft and physicality of the role of Vickers with the pathos of Pears, so that took off. And it was wonderful to discover it with David Alden: an Aussie and American communing with the piece that's held to be the high point of English operatic composition! I relished that experience though: taking the piece a little away from its 'English context', whatever that means, because actually the piece isn't English – language aside it doesn't belong to that canon. That's a big dichotomy for Britten, isn't it: a man who will forever be seen as married to the Suffolk coastline, but who can't fundamentally be seen as being wholly in a British musical tradition.

NK   How difficult is interpreting Britten from his scores?

EG   This is a big issue for me; and one which I worked through when I first did *Grimes*. You look at the prologue to *The Turn of the Screw* where every note has a mark on it, a *tenuto* for the tenor or a staccato or a subtle shading of dynamic. Sometimes it feels that all you are there to do is to tease out what Britten means by every one of those marks, and find the way of achieving his wish. Of course you can say that of many composers, but Britten writes so precisely. The great artists then make it far more than that, but you're finding the inflection that he wanted and making it your own. But it's quite prescriptive, very prescriptive in fact. Tom Allen told me when he worked with Britten early in his career on one of his pieces he was rehearsing and thought he'd try a new inflection on a particular phrase; Britten came up to him and grabbed his arm and said, 'just do what's in the score, and it'll be fine'!! Even in *Grimes*, the score tells you so much of what you need to know. It's in that Mahler tradition of trying to tell you everything you could possibly need. Like Mahler, it anticipates your musical instincts and sends you down a particular route. I was just really scared about this straitjacketing. I found it hard to get under the surface of it, to be honest.

It was Britten's own recordings that gave me the confidence to put myself into performances of his music. When you listen to him at work, for example in that great *Grimes* recording, he really performs it. It's not about obeying the score, it's about using everything he wrote, every marking, accent and phrase-mark, and then allowing the performance to explode. I then understood what all the markings were about: yes, they were strict indications, but they were about Britten's fear of his music being performed generically, without a real commitment to character. (This seems to chime with his thoughts on the quality of British conducting.) In his recording of *Grimes* he stretches the piece: he takes what's there and pushes it in different, extreme directions. If you grew up with later recordings, and there are several very good later *Grimes* recordings, there are wonderful, beautiful things. But I don't think any of them replicate that raw performance energy. I suppose he had a lot more experience of conducting by then [1958], but, my God, it really hits home.

And yet his character was so superficially reserved! There's a bit of archive that's always struck me, of Britten rehearsing and speaking very politely to the orchestra but then whipping over the pages of the score with feral energy − a lot of suppressed emotion there! So this was the lesson to be learned: to start from the notes and the marks, but to get far beyond them. I find the sound he gets from orchestras extraordinary, and not just in his music: his *Gerontius* is strangely wilful and dessicated (you can tell a composer is conducting). But then I think of the beauty of phrasing in the St John Passion recording: it's no wonder his music speaks so clearly to the performer, because he was one of them!

But it's in his own music that he comes alive as a conductor. His recording of the *Sinfonia da Requiem* with the New Philharmonia has an intensity, especially in the string playing that is so arresting, and incredibly hard to get near. And the orchestral sound in the Cello Symphony with the ECO, the muscularity of the string playing, and the brutal timpani sound: he was outwardly so different to Rostropovich, for whom that piece was written, but there was something similar burning inside.

NK   What's been your experience of conducting Britten abroad?

EG   Interesting. Rehearsing *Death in Venice* in Milan was a fascinating experience because they're a great opera company who have had a pretty limited repertory, especially in the contemporary area. They had never played anything quite like it before, even though it's about Italy! We started with the swaying of the gondola on the way to the lido and they just didn't understand what was going on. That is in part because of the haziness, the untidiness of the music, which is deliberately smudged; even at ENO the first read-throughs were a bit of a mystery, and that's an orchestra which really understands Britten. In Milan we did three or four readings and they were increasingly intrigued by it. But then, and this was the big moment, we did a *Sitzprobe* and the chorus came in with all the chorus roles, and suddenly seeing their eyes light up and their ears open was extraordinary: they saw how direct the inflection of the language could be, how effective the musical commentary and emotional temperature could be, not from the detached beauty of a *mezza di voce*, but perhaps the *tenuto* the orchestra shared with Aschenbach on a particular note, or the way they painted an image of haziness around one of his phrases. I'll always remember the first read-through of the Games of Apollo with them. In Britain we're used to that choral tradition, but seeing it through their eyes it is intensely virtuosic and descriptive, in a unique way. Suddenly it wasn't nineteenth-century *bel canto*: it was a completely original concept for them, that an opera could have that direct a discourse and be that direct linguistically, dependent on the words: that opened my eyes to it as well.

NK However, it's clear you have some problems with quite major Britten works...

EG To be honest, yes. We recently did *Billy Budd* at ENO, the orchestra loves playing it, the male chorus enjoys it, composers talk to me about it being one of his best constructed pieces, some people say it's his most moving opera. It is the smoothest dramatically, and you're not aware of the construct in the way that you are with *Grimes*, and yet it leaves me a little bit cold. The battle scene is fantastically effective – that word again! – but it doesn't really go deeper for me. There are exceptions, the non-interview scene with those orchestral chords portraying something that didn't happen on the stage, where pure music takes over for a few minutes: that's a really great moment. Vere's final monologue, the trial – great scenes, but it just doesn't add up to a great piece for me. There are some issues with the story, both the original and the libretto, and you ask why Britten set it. Of course there is this central theme of the outsider, and something hauntingly claustrophobic about the piece, especially with a totally male cast, which gives it a strange atmosphere. (It was very odd rehearsing it at ENO when the only woman in the room was the fight director!). While doing it, I tried to analyze why I wasn't connecting with it. I feel the music is painted beautifully on the surface, but somehow doesn't live underneath. *Grimes* and *Death in Venice* have that elemental momentum; I don't feel *Budd* does.

NK What's your reaction to Britten being called a conservative among twentieth-century composers?

EG I think this goes back to his relationship with his musicians and his audience. It's a generalization, but his aim at any point in his life, with whatever compositional devices and within whichever framework, was to make the music, or music-drama, speak as clearly as possible. I see some interesting links between Britten and Lutoslawski, whose Centenary is also celebrated this year. There's something similar about the two men: with Lutoslawski you can't quite make the connection between this very polite, serene, noble man (like Britten he would always wear a tie for a rehearsal!) contradicted by the intensity of the music which burns with passion underneath. Now in one sense Lutoslawski was far more adventurous than Britten with the aleatoric freedom he gave his performers. Britten was so controlling of his compositions. He perhaps couldn't face the risk of it not working out! Lutoslawski was a magician, with his wonderful matrices of 'controlled chance'. Lutoslawski knew how the probability would tend to work out, and the sonority that turning an orchestra into a collection of soloists would produce. Britten experimented a little with this, and the effect at the beginning of *Death in Venice* is a remarkable portrayal of writer's block and an overactive mind. Freedom is such an interesting concept to discuss in Britten, in both composition and performance, because there's so little of it: *Grimes* and *Death in Venice* don't have much to connect them, but in them both Britten seems to allow himself unusual freedom, in a way I don't feel in a lot of other pieces.

NK Is the impact of a Britten opera different from that of other great opera composers?

EG Well, the natural rhythm of a Verdi or a Donizetti opera allows the audience to come in and out, build to a climax in an aria or an ensemble and then relax for a while. Britten doesn't allow you that – especially not in *Death in Venice*. The audience in Milan was completely gripped from start to finish, you could feel that, but it made big demands on them because there was no respite. Partly this was because of Deborah's amazing production and the wonderful performances, but the work has a lot to do with it – you do not know how to feel where you are in the piece and you are swimming around looking for bearings.

Working on the scores, I've come to the conclusion that the detail of the music is so essential to how the work comes out; you need to find a way of absorbing all that detail. A generalized approach, just letting it happen, works even less than it might for some earlier opera composers. Now at ENO we are very lucky because we know how to approach Britten – the company has historically done a huge amount of his work and so we have a shorthand for approaching it. How to shape a phrase through the discipline of the writing? These things really matter for the voices and instruments alike.

NK And will his music last?

EG It will be interesting to have a discussion of Britten in another 100 years! Composers will come in and out of fashion, but I'm convinced that Britten's reputation, and more importantly, the desire of people to see and hear his work, will grow. The way he wrote means that his music will never date. Certainly with the operas, Britten gives us something no other composer addresses so frequently or with such clarity: the lone man against all facets of humanity, the tension between the individual and community. That topic is timeless; it will never stop being relevant.

A Britten Childhood

Ian Bostridge

Many of Benjamin Britten's works – one might even say his compositional identity itself – are grounded upon and immersed in childhood. This is often seen less as an artistic choice than as a personal predilection, part of his sexual makeup; or as the result of a species of arrested development, which left him longing for a return to the simple verities of prep school life, Jennings or Adrian Mole reborn as *Wunderkind*. Britten's preoccupation with childhood – in works as diverse as *Turn of the Screw, Death in Venice* or *A Midsummer Night's Dream* – and his composition of a stream of works for children, both as singers and as instrumentalists, is indeed celebrated. But it is just as often condescended to and apologized for, explained, as if it were an eccentric piece of his personal constitution which connived in stopping him from producing the mainstream, grown-up masterpieces which might have been expected.

He didn't, as it turns out, write the Anna Karenina opera he had contemplated; he didn't, as some others had hoped, write an opera for Maria Callas, remaining instead bound to the voice of his lover and muse, Peter Pears, whose timbre, one witness relates, was eerily reminiscent of that of Britten's own mother. He remains for many (and for opera audiences in particular) outside the loop, no competition in box office terms to Puccini or Strauss; and this despite his resolute loyalty to diatonic harmony and, in the US and the UK, despite (or perhaps because) of his English language libretti. His most popular opera, embedded in the repertoire as a twentieth-century classic, *Peter Grimes*, is in many ways atypical of the mature composer, who endlessly subverted the generic straitjacket of 'grand opera' – reinventing chamber opera, writing a full-scale opera without any women in it, writing major roles, and major works, for children.

124

The intellectual preoccupations of the mid twentieth-century, with Freudianism at their core, are difficult to recapture or appreciate (Hitchcock's plundering of the Freudian treasure chest is one notable marker). However, these preoccupations ought to have rendered a composer who was obsessed with childhood not as unlikely or peripheral, but as groundbreaking and, somehow, necessary. It's a measure of how uncomfortable Freud's 'discovery' of childhood sexuality makes us, that Britten's works are still sometimes uncomfortable to listen to and watch. As Freud's work has slipped into the intellectual background – some of its terms now mere commonplaces, Freudian rigour diluted in the world of therapy, therapy itself sidelined by a more literally materialist psychiatry with drug treatment at its core – the culture at large has turned Freud's psychoanalytic epiphany on its head. For Freud, the crucial discovery was that his patients had not been abused but rather had experienced the sexual feelings typical of childhood. Without discounting Freud's insights, we're now more likely, with good reason, to problematize the disturbing prevalence of sexual abuse in society and in its families; but in the broader culture, the fear of paedophilia at large continues to take on of some of the qualities of a witch hunt.

Britten's life has made him an object of suspicion. Much of Humphrey Carpenter's sympathetic biography is given over to the question of whether the relationships he formed with adolescent boys could be construed as abusive (no, we are told). John Bridcut's illuminating study *Britten's Children*, cannily reconfigures the personal problem, seeing Britten as a man for whom being with thirteen-year-old boys, and in a sense being a thirteen-year-old boy, was Britten's necessary escape. What emerges from Bridcut's work on Britten's relationships is the sheer complexity of his emotional attachments, something typical of a human being but all too often ignored in the consideration of artists we should like to explain. One strand of those relationships – Britten's parental urge – is often underplayed when attention focuses on his sexual identity.

There's perhaps a larger historical point to be made here, about shifting relations between adults and children. Ours is an age of anxious parenting, in which fathers worry much more about the extent of their presence or absence in their children's day-to-day lives. For mothers too, this is an anxiety, with an unprecedentedly large number of women working outside the domestic economy. There is perhaps some underlying connection here with the nervousness felt about others being too close to our children and usurping that role. Britten's adoption of children of his friends – especially his 'sharing' of Roger Duncan with his father Ronald – may have been par for the course in the 1950s, but it now seems a little creepy, on both sides. It is certainly true that surrogate parenting plays a crucial role in many of Britten's operas, from the boy in *Grimes* to *Death in Venice*, via *Turn of the Screw* and *Midsummer Night's Dream* (in which Oberon and Titania's squabble hangs on the fairy king's desire to have Titania's adopted changeling boy to be his own 'henchman'). One of Britten's greatest, and least known works, the first Church parable *Curlew River* is about the supreme pain of a parent losing a child. Having foregone the joy and pain of having his own children, Britten's constant return to the theme of the care of children may have been at least partly a working through of that lost opportunity for renewal.

Regardless of these biographical shifts and turns, the work has remained troubling, as if it were at best a surrogate and at worst propaganda for paedophilia. Misreadings abound and Britten's late masterpiece, *Death in Venice*, has suffered from them more than almost any other part of his output. An opera which is predominantly concerned with issues of universal concern – with ageing, the desire to be young again, with humiliation, with professional stagnation – has been pigeonholed as a pervy manifesto, fascinating for the light it throws on the obsessions of a great artist but, as art, a falling away, precisely because it draws back the veil and reveals too overtly the creative driving force behind the composer. Britten did indeed see *Death in Venice* as 'everything that Peter and I have stood for'. Whatever else he meant, he cannot have intended to recommend the work as some sort of pederastic testament. It would be closer to the truth – though the declaration remains rather gnomic – to say that Britten's and Pears's utter embrace of a life of art rather the family life he (sometimes) envied, an art to which, in the writing of his last opera he was, quite literally, sacrificing his life's blood, is at the centre of Aschenbach's predicament.

The irony is that the psychoanalytic culture in which Britten's works were, albeit obliquely, embedded (they don't deal directly with psychoanalytic issues, but they do breathe the psychoanalytic atmosphere of their times) has encouraged a biographical approach to the work which has been too obsessed with personal pathology. Britten's own psychological formation and biases no doubt set the ball rolling, drew him to certain subjects and to the composition of important music for and about children. That is worthy of note and of examination, of course. But his works – and their salience – sprang more crucially from the intellectual and aesthetic climate in which they were conceived, and from Britten's own mastery of his musical and theatrical crafts. More investigation of this area would be welcome, as would an appreciation of the sheer brilliance of those works which, written for children, can too often be skated over as mere *jeux d'esprit*. Britten is partly to blame for this. He often wrote off major works as minor (the *Serenade for Tenor Horn and Strings* is a case in point – 'not important stuff, but quite pleasant, I think'); and insisted that his variations on a theme of Purcell (which end with one of the great fugues in our musical tradition) keep its original, unpretentious title, *A Young Person's Guide to the Orchestra*. But if any body of musical composition is to be considered as great, as worthy of a certain reverence, Britten's works for children – a *Ceremony of Carols*, *Noye's Fludde*, the *Children's Crusade* – deserve that imprimatur as much as the more obviously serious works of his contemporaries.

* * *

2012 saw the release of Wes Andersen's film *Moonrise Kingdom*, and a relieved, or maybe surprised, feeling among Britten aficionados that the master's music was back in contention as part of mainstream culture. Andersen's films are, of course, self-consciously quirky, but it is undeniable that a movie audience was being exposed to Britten's music in a new way. *Friday Afternoons*, *Midsummer Night's Dream*, the *Simple Symphony*, the *Young Person's Guide* and *Noye's Fludde* were all included in a soundtrack which they dominated, besides forming an integral part of the film's narrative structure. The two runaway children at the heart of the story meet during a production of *Noye's Fludde* in the early 1960s, they take an LP of the *Young Person's Guide* with them on their adventuresome journey, and the selection of Britten's music amounts an authorial commentary at various points of the film. As Andersen himself put it:

The Britten music had a huge effect on the whole movie, I think. The movie's sort of set to it. The play of 'Noye's Fludde' that

is performed in it – my older brother and I were actually in a
production of that when I was ten or eleven, and that music
is something I've always remembered, and made a very strong
impression on me. It is the colour of the movie in a way.

The only possible downside is that notion of 'colour'. The very
quirkiness of the film gives us a sense, as we watch that creaky
production of *Noye's Fludde* taking place in a small American
township, that this is the past, something foreign to us, and that
the piece is being used to reinforce a certain quaintness. It's only
when the opera returns, as a storm of almost Biblical proportions
threatens to engulf the community, that its seriousness of purpose,
as well as its thematic centrality in the movie, is definitively
confirmed.

My own experience of singing Britten started in childhood
with some of those very pieces which Andersen features. We
sang the unison songs *Friday Afternoons* in class at my prep
school, re-enacting the purpose for which they'd been written
(Britten composed them for his teacher brother Robert to use in
his own prep school), though whether we sang them on Fridays
I don't recall. In 1972 my school staged *Noye's Fludde* and,
aged seven, I took the part of one of the smaller animals (a rat
I think). More obviously significant to my musical development
were performances of a *Ceremony of Carols*; and of Britten's own
semi-parody of *Billy Budd*, the vaudeville for boys, drum and piano
written for the Vienna Boys Choir, *The Golden Vanity* ("write us
something without girls' parts" they had begged; a sentiment I
would have agreed with, having suffered as the Queen's Lady in
Richard Rodney Bennett's *All the King's Men* the year before our
Golden Vanity production).

After that, and until I became interested in becoming a singer,
I didn't take much interest in Britten – latency they call it. But
the seeds had surely been sown. Britten was, of course, always a
practical composer. His 1964 Aspen Lecture had put practical use
at the centre of his musical philosophy, a point that was well worth
making vis-à-vis the juggernaut of a sometimes infantile avant-
gardisme. Part of that practicality was reflected in his work as an
opera composer, both in the writing of chamber operas accommo-
dated to the financial needs of the immediate postwar period, and
in the provision of workable and workmanlike – qualities which
have never precluded genius – operas for established opera houses.

Britten's music for children was likewise a brilliant practical coup, not only because it provided a handy resource for communities like the fictional New Penzance in Wes Anderson's movie, or my own school in South London, but also because it introduced the Britten style and the Britten aesthetic to successive generations of children, effectively propagating a taste for his music.

Listening – on a CD – to *Noye's Fludde* for the first time in forty years (my memories of that 1972 school production are slim, but I do recall standing in a queue of animals, the music coursing into my musical cortex), I was struck by a particular feature of Britten's music that must somehow have insinuated itself into my tastebuds as a performer. I'm not an educated musician – I didn't learn music theory or an instrument as a child, and until I became a professional singer I learnt almost all of my music by ear – and so Britten's compositional fingerprints can only have passed into me unconsciously, as it were. But they are perhaps all the more powerful for having taken that insinuating path. The bitonality that is such a strong feature of Britten's music – intensely at work in *Les Illuminations* or the *War Requiem*, two works I perform constantly – draws me to itself with particular force. *Noye's Fludde* must surely be the source of the fascination. What's more, the equivocation about key that bitonality represents, the struggle between values for which it can sometimes be a proxy, indeed ambiguity more generally – these are all features of Britten's work that make it theatrically compelling and sophisticated in a literary way which few operas achieve.

Another feature of *Noye's Fludde*, one that links it to the wider Britten oeuvre, and that has perhaps been underplayed, is its Cold War context. *Billy Budd* – written like *Noye* in the anxious 1950s – is as much a Forsterian conflict between duty and personal feeling ('If I had to choose between betraying my country and betraying my friend, I hope I should have the guts to betray my country'), between public and private honour, as it is a psycho-sexual drama – the aspect, clearly drawn from Melville's novella as it is, that tends to receive the most emphasis nowadays. *Budd* is, then, very much a Cold War opera. The famous bugle calls of *Noye's Fludde* are indeed, as John Bridcut has argued, reminiscent of the cadet force on parade in the school playground, a typical Britten touch; but they also surely underscore the sense of threat at work in the opera, a foretaste of the trumpets-as-bugles in the later *War Requiem*, and a reminder that the deluge that awaits the protagonists of the opera is a metaphor for the brooding threat of nuclear annihilation.

*   *   *

As an adult singer, my definitive return to Britten came in two stages. First of all, I was utterly seized by his setting of the *Holy Sonnets of John Donne*, which I first got to know through a recording I discovered in the local record library, Peter Pears singing, Britten himself at the piano. A muscular engagement with the text is combined with the creation of a compelling musical image for each poem to create an unlikely masterpiece; for who would think in the abstract that verse with such a strong and idiosyncratic verbal music of its own could find a composer to master it ? The other quality that Britten seemed to have as a writer of vocal music in English was an ability to make the language sound like itself when sung. Not for Britten the 'singerese' beloved of so many English composers. The close relationship with Pears doubtless honed this ability to mould together pitch and the complex blend of vowel and consonant, but Britten's gift was evident from much earlier on, something allied to and consanguineous with his fabulous ear for both harmonic effect and the use of timbre. Since I was devoted at the time to German song, it was inspiring for me to find an English composer who responded to words with the fantasy and intensity of a Schubert, a Schumann or a Wolf. I went on to devour his other poetic cycles, those with piano and those with orchestra.

It was Britten, too, who converted me to opera. If the Captain of the *Golden Vanity* was my first and only leading operatic role as a child, Lysander in *A Midsummer Night's Dream* was my first (semi) professional foray into opera, first in a British Youth Opera production in London and then in Baz Luhrmann's famous Raj production for Australian Opera, produced at the Edinburgh Festival in 1994. I have moved on to other Britten roles since, roles more fascinating to engage with, offering ambiguity and subtlety in a way which few other operatic roles do: this is Britten's gift to us, and one for which tenors must be thoroughly grateful. What remains for me most of all of *Midsummer Night's Dream*, deeply embedded and treasured, is the music of dreams and the unconscious, the children's music, twentieth-century music, emerging from those mysterious glissandi that open the opera, and ending with a pavane of rare beauty, 'Now until the break of day', shared between boys' voices and the countertenor Oberon. 'Dreadful!

'Pure Kensington' was Auden's snap judgement on it, presumably
with a nod to Peter Pan in the park. How wrong he was. Coming
from the composer one of whose earliest musical enthusiasms was
Alban Berg, Vienna circa 1900 would have been a better call.

A Dancer Before God:
Britten's Five Canticles

Roger Vignoles

Every summer in the Spanish city of Santiago de Compostela there
is a music festival called 'Via Stellae'. In 2010 I staged a performance there of Britten's *Five Canticles*, in a tiny theatre on one of
the city's stone-paved streets. We presented them as a continuous
sequence, using the space between the piano at one side of the
stage and the harp at the other to create a metaphor for the journey
travelled by the tenor in the course of the five works.

As I explained in a pre-concert talk, the sense of a journey was
intrinsic to our performance, and nowhere was this more appropriate than in that beautiful pilgrimage city. After all, the fourth
Canticle, a setting of T. S. Eliot's *Journey of the Magi*, tells the
story of the most famous *via stellae* of all: the journey of the three
kings travelling to Bethlehem to witness the birth of Christ. But
I also wished to stress that these five works, though composed
at different stages of Britten's career, seem to me to embody a
biographical journey. Put quite simply, they can be read as a mirror
of the composer's own life. Not quite Seven Ages of Man, but at
the very least Five Stages of Britten.

They begin with a youthful declaration of love – *My beloved
is Mine* – which, though ostensibly religious in context, surely
celebrates his relationship to his lifelong partner and inspiration,
Peter Pears. They continue with his setting of the Chester Mystery
Play *Abraham and Isaac*, a story that touches on the perennial
Britten theme of youthful innocence and its abuse, corruption or
betrayal by the older generation, as memorably emphasized when
he returned to both the theme and the music of the canticle in one
of the most bitter passages of the *War Requiem*.

War itself is the setting of the third Canticle, *Still falls the Rain*,

132

whose poem (by Edith Sitwell) was written during the bombing raids on London in 1940. Seventeen years separate it from its successor, *The Journey of the Magi*, years during which Britten was at the height of his powers. But with increasing fame and success came the growing shadow of heart disease, and Britten may have felt a resonance, both personal and professional, in Eliot's Three Kings, who note the passing details of an event that will change their world forever, and see their power superseded by a new dispensation.

By the time he came to compose the fifth Canticle, 'The Death of Saint Narcissus' (also to a text by T. S. Eliot), Britten had undergone heart surgery and suffered the stroke that would put an end to his piano-playing career. At this point, therefore, the piano falls silent and is replaced by the more liquid, fragile tones of the harp. I invited the Spanish audience to imagine the piano melting and softening like one of Salvador Dali's watches, and the landscape described in that canticle has indeed a Daliesque quality to it. But the transition is also a moving metaphor for the composer's failing physical strength.

Britten of course never conceived the canticles as a unit, and on the rare occasions when all five are performed in concert, one might expect to end with the longest, most dramatic and most approachable, *Abraham and Isaac*. Yet for me the chronological sequence creates a far more interesting narrative. It also works exceptionally well musically. To begin with, there is an uncanny way in which the end of each canticle seems perfectly to prepare the ground for the beginning of the next, as if they had been composed as one. (I am thinking especially of the step down of a major third from G to E flat – typical of Britten's beloved Schubert, among others – between Canticles I and II.) But beyond that, the scoring of the five works means that essentially they form a palindrome: Canticles I and V are for solo voice, Canticles II and IV are for multiple voices, while Canticle III is for voice plus a solo instrument (horn).

Fortuitous it may be, but this is a detail I believe Britten would have appreciated. One of the outstanding features of his song cycles is their meticulous sense of structure, in which palindromes and pairings of songs are frequently evident. The eight songs of his *Winter Words*, for instance, are essentially palindromic in arrangement: working inwards towards the middle, the first and last address the issue of time and human existence, the second and seventh are about boys on the railway, the third and sixth have a strong ornithological element (Wagtail and Baby and Proud Songsters), while the fourth and fifth balance a domestic cameo (The Little Old Table) with the dramatic heart of the cycle (The Choirmaster's Burial). A similar pairing of songs can be observed in the *Songs and Proverbs of William Blake*, where the churning quintuplets of *London* are echoed by the restless quavers of *Tyger, tyger* (one of Britten's most brilliant evocations of animal movement), and the barefoot skipping of *the Chimney Sweep* by the buzzing semiquavers of *The Fly*.

But there is an even more striking example of structural organisation, in *The Holy Sonnets of John Donne*, composed in 1945, two years before the first Canticle. The emotional core of the cycle is the sixth sonnet, a setting of *Since she whom I loved*, written on the death of Donne's wife. One of Britten's most poignantly expressive melodies, the entire song is developed from a single three-note motif: G – A flat – F and its equivalent intervals, i.e. a rising or falling semitone followed by a rising or falling major or minor third. Remarkably, if you take the nine sonnets in three groups of three, the key centres of each *triptych* match this pattern precisely, i.e. B-C-E; F sharp-G-E flat; D-E flat-B. Knowing Britten, this cannot have been an accident. He famously wrote the Donne Sonnets in a fever, contracted after returning from a tour of the concentration camps with Yehudi Menuhin, but it is fascinating to observe that even in as highly-strung a state as this, his intellectual control remained paramount.

Composed in 1945, the Holy Sonnets can be seen as the high point of Britten's absorption of Purcellian rhetoric, brilliantly articulating both the complexity and the emotional profundity of Donne's verse. Writing about his song-writing in general, he had declared:

> *One of my chief aims is to try and restore to the musical setting of the English language a brilliance, freedom and vitality that have been curiously rare since the days of Purcell.*

It was an aim he had already triumphantly announced in the fanfare-like opening of *Let the Florid Music Praise*, the first of his Auden cycle *On This Island (1937)*, and the same qualities are evident in the first Canticle. It was composed in 1947 and first performed at the memorial concert for Dick Sheppard, founder of the Peace Pledge Union. Here the Purcellian influence is as much structural as stylistic: its four sections mimic the cantata-like shape of Purcell's longer Divine Hymns, for many of which Britten was even then writing the brilliantly idiosyncratic realizations of Purcell that he and Pears included regularly in their recitals together. The text is by the seventeenth-century poet and divine Francis Quarles, who took its title 'My Beloved is Mine and I am His' from the Song of Songs. On the surface, it is an extended and beautiful expression of the relationship between a human being and his Redeemer, but such is the reciprocity it describes – 'He's my supporting elm and I his vine' – that its application to a more earthly love is not far below the surface. Such formulations were not uncommon in seventeenth-century religious poetry, but for Britten it would have been hard to resist the line 'I give him songs, he gives me length of days' when composing for Pears. In fact, *My Beloved is Mine* joins the *Seven Sonnets of Michelangelo* (composed seven years earlier in 1940) as a work in which Britten was able to give expression to a homosexual love while keeping it under the public radar, so to speak.

The *Michelangelo Sonnets* themselves were a *tour de force* of heroic gesture, imbued with Renaissance spirit, and they ended with a paean of praise to the beloved, of which Britten himself identified Pears as the object. (The final playout is marked 'sempre *pp*', which as Britten once confided to Graham Johnson, was indeed meant to signify 'always PP'.) *My Beloved is Mine* brings that same spirit home to the domesticity of the English countryside:

> *E'en like two little bank-divided brooks / That wash the pebbles with their wonted tide / And having ranged and searched a thousand nooks / Meet both at length at silver-breasted Thames...*

and to start with Britten's opening music is equally unassuming, the piano's right hand meandering gently above a barcarole-like bass, pausing only to utter the refrain 'So I my best beloved's am, so he is mine'. But then the momentum resumes with quickening excitement, and with the words: 'And after long pursuit/Ev'n so we joined' becomes the very music of hunt and capture. First the right hand chases the left from the top to the bottom of the keyboard, then the tenor gives voice to an extraordinary melismatic outburst, supported by an ardent undertow of glowing triads: 'for I was flax, and he was flames of fire', that only burns itself out after extending the last word 'fire' for a full four bars of urgently syncopated semiquavers.

There is an intriguing similarity between this dramatic opening
and that of *Boyhood's End*, the four-section Cantata that Michael
Tippett (another Purcell enthusiast) had composed for Britten and
Pears in 1943. A setting of prose extracts from W. H. Hudson's *A
Boyhood in Argentina*, it begins equally quietly, but then explodes
into a whole series of ecstatic, hocketing melismas on the words
'want' and 'dance', and goes on to test both singer and pianist
to the limit. In a congratulatory letter to Tippett on his fiftieth
birthday, Britten asked rather plaintively 'Why do your piano parts
have to be so difficult?', and it is hard to believe that he did not
have this model in his mind when composing *My Beloved is Mine*.
After all, his love of winning on the tennis court has been well
documented, and his competitive instincts were no doubt equally
acute when challenged by the only contemporary who could rival
him in the field of composition.

The Canticle continues with a brief recitative-like section full
of tinkling fanfares suggestive of the 'glittering monarchs' with
their empty wealth ('counter to my coin'), followed by a scherzo-
like *presto*, where again the two hands of the piano, and the piano
and voice, play catch-as-catch-can with each other, continuing the
imagery of pursuit and capture. With its clearly audible canonic
imitations and inversions, it's a brilliant example of Britten's
ability to write quick music that really sounds quick (a skill that
many of his more avant-garde contemporaries have notably failed
to acquire). It also provides the perfect foil for the rapturous *Lento*
that brings the Canticle to a close, underpinned by warm triadic
harmonies in the piano part. These resonate, bell-like, in a reverse-
dot rhythm that is reminiscent of Purcell, but that also seems to
have had a special significance for Britten, since he used it again in
the fairy's chorus that ends *A Midsummer Night's Dream*, where
it imparts the same sense of satisfactory closure. Here, supporting
the arpeggio-like phrases with which the voice reiterates its refrain
'That I my best beloved's am', it brings to completion a work that
truly embodies the idea of love as a partnership of equals.

The second Canticle, *Abraham and Isaac*, was composed in
1951, and ultimately owes its origin to Britten's founding of the
English Opera Group. In 1952 Britten and Pears went on a fund-
raising tour for the EOG, together with Kathleen Ferrier (for
whom Britten had composed the leading role in his first opera
for the group, *The Rape of Lucretia*) and it was with this tour in
mind that Britten composed the work. With its combination of

naïve characterization and dramatic dialogue, its medieval text is already charmingly immediate, but Britten forges it into a brilliant mini-drama through a series of spectacularly simple, but original devices. The most obvious of these is his use of the combined alto and tenor voices to impersonate the voice of God, speaking from the heavenly clouds suggested by the piano's harp-like chords.

Significantly God speaks in E flat, while Abraham's earthly existence is represented by a pastoral A major – a key as far removed as you can get from E flat, perhaps suggesting what Britten sees as the vast divide between the cruel Divine command to sacrifice Isaac, and the humanity it is going to test so severely. As the drama develops, the opera composer in Britten knows to keep the piano out of the singers' way, often using simple spread chords and *tremolandi* for the dialogue between father and son. These extend even to a chain of root-position added sixths, a chord at the time frowned upon by purists for its 'vulgar' connotations but whose harmony lends a searing poignancy to the scene when Isaac kneels to beg his father's blessing. (Sixty years on, it is extraordinary how Britten's commitment to tonality, deeply unfashionable at the time, has been vindicated by every bar he composed).

There follows the terrifying passage where Isaac is bound and blindfolded, with father and son answering each other on an increasingly desperate monotone. If the piano's dark background of threatening octaves in the piano part seems to foreshadow certain passages in the *War Requiem* this is not surprising. For it was of course to the music of this Canticle that Britten would return in his setting of Wilfred Owen's *Parable of the Old Man and the Young,* which bitterly turns the story on its head, with Abraham slaying 'half the seed of Europe, one by one'.

In the Canticle, however, all ends well (the re-emergence of the voice of God from a clap of thunder at the work's climax is a veritable coup de theatre); God relents, Abraham has passed the test, and the piece ends with an *Envoi* for the two voices, now united in God's key of E flat, their opening music transformed into a medieval carol accompanied by pealing bells.

With the third Canticle however, darkness descends. It was composed in memory of the gifted young Australian pianist Noel Mewton-Wood, who committed suicide in 1953 at the age of thirty-one. (A close friend of Britten and Pears, his recording with Pears of Tippett's *The Heart's Assurance* – another highly challenging work – is a lasting testament to his virtuosity and musicianship.)

Britten's decision to set sections of a long poem by Edith Sitwell may have been influenced initially by its title, *The Canticle of the Rose*, but the text gave him the scope to express both his humanity and his pacifism. Subtitled 'The Raids. 1940. Night and Dawn', it is a essentially a painful and eloquent questioning of Christ's sacrifice in the face of man's inhumanity to man.

Though punctuated by repetitions of the refrain 'Still falls the rain', the poem reads on the page as a free, unstructured train of thought, which Britten sets as a continuous, extended recitative. But he ingeniously gives it structure by repeating a device he had recently used to great effect in the opera *The Turn of the Screw*. In the opera he linked its succession of scenes with a series of orchestral interludes, each of which was a variation based on a twelve-note theme (no atonality intended or implied). In the canticle the horn and piano punctuate the text with a series of variations on an opening theme whose dark tones and brooding character recall the Blake *Elegy* of the sick rose from the *Serenade*.

Each of the variations is vividly characterized to reflect the text: for example, in Variation I repeated chords suggest the hammering of nails – 'the nineteen hundred and forty nails', and in variation V the brash, braying hunting-horn motif picks up from 'The tears of the hunted hare'. It is only at the end of the canticle, when Christ himself speaks, that voice and horn are joined, in a fusion that recalls the voice of God in *Abraham and Isaac*: 'Still do I love, still shed my innocent light, my Blood, for thee.'

Towards the end, there is a surprise interpolation in text and music. It's a short passage of *Sprechstimme*, when the singer declaims the words 'O Ile leape up to my God: who pulls me doune? See, where Christ's blood streams in the firmament'. The words are a quote from Christopher Marlowe's *Doctor Faustus*, and it's a dramatic interjection in what is otherwise a gradual 'dying of the light' – a slow diminuendo over three pages of music.

Like the *Serenade, Still falls the Rain* is a night piece, and its horn part was composed for the same artist, Dennis Brain, whose life was tragically cut short only three years later. In retrospect this seems to add an extra layer to its elegiac quality, and to the very special glow the instrument imparts to the music. 'One is left aghast,' Britten wrote, 'when one thinks of the loss sustained by English music in these two deaths [Mewton-Wood and Brain] and that of Kathleen Ferrier, all young artists at the beginning of dazzling careers, in the space of only two years.' For Britten, composing for friends was always of vital importance, and the Canticles celebrate several of his musical friendships – with Pears of course, with Kathleen Ferrier and Dennis Brain, but also in the fourth canticle with James Bowman and John Shirley-Quirk, and finally in the fifth, with the harpist Osian Ellis.

If *Still falls the Rain* forms a kind of pendant to *The Turn of the Screw,* the fourth Canticle, *The Journey of the Magi,* was written (in 1971) as a pendant to the opera *Death in Venice* and composed for the same trio of soloists, Pears, Bowman and Shirley-Quirk. Technically it derives some of its procedures from the three Church Parables, whose spare textures and vocal lines are frequently derived from specific medieval plainsong chants, often combined in overlapping layers to create so-called 'heterophony'. Interestingly this is an effect that Britten had already anticipated in the Hardy setting *The Choirmaster's Burial,* when at the mirac-ulous appearance of the angelic musicians by the graveside, the pianist's two hands play the identical music at several octaves, but rhythmically out of sync, creating a sense of overlapping echoes. In Canticle IV, at the point at which the three Kings arrive at the stable, the piano plays the melody of *Magi videntes stellam,* the Antiphon before the Magnificat at first Vespers for the feast of the Epiphany, and it is another moment when Britten's scoring recalls the *War Requiem,* in the passages for boys' choir and bells.

There is no doubt that the music of Canticle IV is drier and less approachable than its predecessors. Like the *Songs and Proverbs of William Blake,* it is slower to yield up its secrets, and the language is less melodically and harmonically comfortable. But in the context of a performance of all five canticles, it has its own wintry eloquence, and Britten's own recorded performance brilliantly emphasizes the cold, hard ground and the background glitter of snow and ice. I am sometimes reminded of the wonderful Brueghel painting *Hunters in the Snow,* while the jolting camel ride is just another example of Britten's extraordinary gift for conveying rhythmic movement: think of the points-crossing rattle of the train in *The Journeying Boy,* or the Governess's arrival in *The Turn of the Screw,* not to mention the restless padding footsteps of the tiger in *Tyger! Tyger!*

But the dry musical idiom is also surely intended to match the dryness of T. S. Eliot's famous text. With its deliberately matter-of-fact language (as though in the words of a civil servant delivering a departmental report) it is not an obvious candidate for musical setting, and perhaps only Britten could have brought it off. But what is interesting is that where another composer might have adopted a conversational, narrative approach, Britten instead comes up with an extremely stylized form of vocal delivery. This no doubt evolved from his decision to employ three voices, where Eliot's texts suggest a single narrator.

At the outset the three voices sing together, the word 'cold' (as in 'a cold coming we had of it') forming the basic triad from which the whole piece is developed, the word 'coming' repeated hypnotically as if in a dream. As their story progresses we hear them sometimes singing in chords, sometimes in canon with each other. Sometimes they share sentences, even single words between them, which can lead to a problem – rare in Britten – with audibility of the text. But at its best the effect is hypnotic, as in the trance-like passage in 5/4 time, to the words 'At the end we preferred to travel all night, sleeping in snatches, with the voices ringing in our ears.' The implication is that their memories are sometimes unanimous, sometimes more fragmented, and when it comes to the most famous line of all, the Magi's description of the Stable: 'It was (you may say) satisfactory', Britten draws out the moment with several solo repetitions of the word 'satisfactory', as though the Magi are each reflecting on the meaning of the experience.

There follows the crux of the poem, an extended unison passage in which the Magi recognize Christ's coming as heralding the end of their own era: 'There was a Birth, certainly...' Throughout the canticle Britten's acute aural perception has been at work, inventing novel ways of combining the voices with the piano, and with each other. Now, at the words 'Like Death, our Death', he conceals within a sequence of falling semitones, a *rising* seventh (to top G sharp) for the tenor, creating an emotional tension that the listener registers without quite knowing where it comes from.

When he composed this music, Britten was already suffering from serious heart disease, no doubt conscious of his own mortality, and that a new generation of composers was ready to take over. By 1974, when he composed the fifth and last Canticle, he could no longer play the piano. His position as accompanist to Pears was ceded to Murray Perahia, but he also composed a number of works for Pears to sing with the harpist Osian Ellis, of which the most significant is *The Death of Saint Narcissus*. (Ellis had worked with Britten for years – the Suite for harp was written for him – and combined his virtuosity with an unassuming but supportive manner that would have endeared him to the often-sensitive composer.) Once again, the text is by T. S. Eliot, reputedly by then the only poet Britten would read. As its title suggests it combines the world of Ovid's *Metamorphoses* with the *Christian Lives of the Saints*, so that the hero becomes a strange combination of Narcissus and Saint Sebastian.

In contrast to *The Journey of the Magi* the text is remarkably sensual, touching on beauty, youth, age, desire, pain, above all flesh. It is also remarkably tactile:

> *Then he knew that he had been a fish / With slippery white belly held tight in his own fingers, / Writhing in his own clutch, his ancient beauty / caught fast in the pink tips of his new beauty.*

This tactile quality is strongly reflected in Britten's writing for the harp, which employs every kind of articulation, from watery arpeggios to the most acute *sforzandi*, in which the fingers positively bite into the strings. Britten of course had long ago done his homework into the technical characteristics of the instrument, as shown in both the Ceremony of Carols and the Suite for Harp: this is neither harp-like piano music nor piano-like harp music, but totally idiomatic harp-writing.

So what drew Britten to this particular text at the end of his life? What for instance did he make of the following passage:

> *Then he had been a young girl / Caught in the woods by a drunken old man / Knowing at the end the taste of his own whiteness / The horror of his own smoothness, / And he felt drunken and old.*

Let alone this?

> *Because his flesh was in love with the burning arrows / he danced on the hot sand / Until the arrows came... and satisfied him.*

With its overt physicality, its masochistic sexuality, this is a far cry from the sublime tone of *My Beloved is Mine*, and it is significant (and contributory to the palindromic mirror-effect of the five works) that whereas the first canticle began with a joyous coupling, the last ends with a climax of an altogether different kind. Here – as in the opera *Death in Venice* – one has a sense of Britten finally confronting darker, less controllable elements in his own personality.

For all his fascination with evil and its corrupting influence, some writers – including his admirers – have detected a certain sanitization in his music, a pulling of punches at the last resort. In this his very facility and technical brilliance may have had a part to play. Certainly, if one compares the smooth, bright articulacy of *My Beloved is Mine* with the clogged, inchoate richness of its forerunner, Tippett's *Boyhood's End*, it is hard not to feel that where Tippett was happy to get his trainers muddy, Britten preferred a well-polished pair of brogues. But here at last, in Canticle V, there is a sense of the protective layer having been stripped away, the flesh allowed to shine through, and the impulse to tidy abandoned, right down to the casual and apparently inconclusive ending:

> *Now he is green, dry and stained*
> *With the shadow in his mouth.*

Britten was a master of endings, not least in his song cycles. Think of the magnificent Renaissance splendour of *Spirto ben nato* from the Michelangelo Sonnets, or the great Purcellian ground-bass *Death be not Proud* in the Donne cycle, let alone the final song of *Winter Words*, with its longing to return to a state not just of innocence, but of non-feeling. And what could be a finer musician's epitaph than the last song of the *Hölderlin-Fragmente*, and the triumphantly affirmative chords of E flat major with which it ends?

> *Was hier wir sind, kann dort ein Gott ergänzen, / Mit Harmonien und ew'gem Lohn und Frieden* ('What here we are, can there by a God be completed / With harmonies, eternal recompense and peace').

But these were all composed with his strength intact. Now, faced by his own mortality, he contemplates not an apotheosis, but the very snuffing out of his physical existence. In Canticle I he may have written 'I give him songs, he gives me length of days', but by now he knew he would not even reach his biblical three-score years and ten. And so the music of Canticle V ends as a quiet slipping-away: there one moment, the next gone for ever.

If, as I believe, *The Death of Saint Narcissus* represents some kind of personal summing-up, there is one line above all that seems me to have a special resonance. It occurs twice in the Canticle, accompanied by a saraband-like rhythm on the harp: '... [he] became a dancer before God.' There is a rather nice story from the Middle Ages about a juggler, who was asked by his local priest why he never came to church. He replied 'I worship God in my own way' and it so happened that one night the priest went into the empty church and there, in front of the altar, he saw the juggler all alone, performing his routine for God.

Benjamin Britten was probably more of a sceptic and humanist than a conventional Christian. At the end of his life he received many honours; he was accepted by the great of the land and was well-off beyond the dreams of most composers. But as an artist he had a divine spark. His greatest music includes that in which he speaks for the outsider, for the individual against society, in the end for all humanity. And through his music he was indeed a 'Dancer before God'.

'Almost Miraculous': Britten's Music for Orchestra

Guy Dammann

It is often remarked of Benjamin Britten that of all the qualities he wished his music to exemplify, that of 'being of some use' was, for him, among the foremost. It is a concern which set him in surprisingly good stead in the context of a musical culture whose concerns, in the main, were of a more highfalutin nature, and it allowed him to evade becoming trapped between the two extremes of twentieth-century musical culture – of resolute progressivism on the one hand and a desire to keep traditional artistic fires burning on the other – and instead to plough his own rather singular furrow. At the same time, his deep-rooted sense that his music should have some practical value, whether this was construed in terms of his music serving a dramatic and colouristic function in opera, or in the rather grander terms of broadening and enlivening the tastes and expectations of the local community, nonetheless caused him occasional problems, when he was called upon to compose (or when he called upon himself to compose) music of a more straightforwardly abstract nature. Even a casual glance at the catalogue of Britten's works – a catalogue which in itself is by any comparison prodigious – will quickly reveal something of a lacuna in the traditional 'absolute' musical categories. Where are the ranks of numbered sonatas and symphonies through which composers, since the dawn of the nineteenth-century, have marked out their serious intention?

He started well enough, completing at the age of thirteen a grand Symphony in D minor. The manuscript runs to 117 pages, scored for a giant orchestra featuring no fewer than eight French horns. It was never performed. There are of course a few instances of the word 'symphony' scattered across the list of evocative titles that form Britten's catalogue proper, but on closer inspection these reveal little continuity with the idea of any symphonic tradition, be it that of the Austro-German 'mainstream' – which, in his student years, dominated his musical imagination but which afterwards became something from which he was keen to dissociate himself – or from the domestic tradition of English symphonists such as William Walton and Ralph Vaughan Williams, towards which he was less than charitable, perhaps somewhat disingenuously so. Rather, Britten's orchestral music reveals a consistent effort to evade the generic associations of its principal forms. One looks in vain for any traces of sonata form or developing variation in the four beautifully crafted light dances that make up the *Simple Symphony* while the more ambitious and at times distinctly *Mahlerian Spring Symphony* turns out to be more of an oratorio than a symphony, each of its twelve movements setting a different poem, in each case by a different poet. While the neo-baroque flavour of the former foreshadows Britten's lifelong fascination with the pre-history of the age of absolute music, the brooding, knowing sentimentality of the latter reflects his willing embrace of aspects of the twentieth-century's darker aesthetic range.

Britten was born at a time when the creative effort to forge a credible musical style and language demanded more and more of a composer's effort. In comparison with many of his contemporaries, then, Britten was an extraordinarily fluent musician. He typically worked at great speed, drawing on a seemingly inexhaustible, if always immediately identifiable, palette of techniques and colouristic devices to produce music that crackled with the energy of its creation. It is instructive to consider, then, that the principal times at which Britten's cornucopia-like fount of creativity deserted him all occurred when he was engaged in large-scale, absolute music projects. With the exception of the ballet score, *The Prince of the Pagodas*, the comparatively slow composition of which left Britten drained and exhausted ('I feel as if I've been just let out of prison after 18 months hard labour', Britten's only creative blocks came during the composition of major orchestral works. The only other time occurred when he was fresh out of the Royal College.

This early episode is less unusual for when it occurred than for the manner in which it was overcome. After graduating from the Royal College of Music in 1933, following a fruitful and busy career at the conservatoire, during which Britten took advantage of the built-in opportunities for arranging performances of his own music, he found life outside the structured environment more challenging. He had never before been stuck for ideas about how to proceed musically, but the combination of his return to the isolated cultural milieu of his parents' house in Lowestoft and the pressure of transferring school and college successes to the real world of BBC commissions and publishing contracts somehow cowed the young composer into a period of comparative inactivity. His big hope on leaving the Royal College had been to travel to Vienna to study with Alban Berg, but permission was refused by his parents, following the advice of one of his former professors (he did make it to the city the following year, but without meeting Berg). His one major achievement of these two years – the *Simple Symphony* – came from patching together, albeit with immense skill and lightness of touch, various of the ideas and sketches that had come to him so easily in his youth. The relief, when it eventually came, did so from an unexpected quarter: the new Film Unit of the General Post Office approached Britten to supply the music for a short documentary entitled *The King's Stamp*.

Although Britten was initially rather sniffy about the subject matter, the commission provided manna from heaven in more ways than one. Given Britten's absolute determination to earn his living through composition, an offer of work so firmly rooted in the real world must have seemed auspicious indeed. More auspicious still, however, was the specific nature of the task: not only was Britten forced to work to a very tight set of deadlines, providing music to precisely specified lengths (the film had already been cut and edited), but he was also forced to bring all his ingenuity to the task in a ways that clearly appealed to the young composer's ability to solve dramatic problems through musical means. As he later recalled, he had 'to write scores for not more than six or seven players, and to make those instruments make all the effects that each film demanded. I also had to be ingenious and try to imitate, not necessarily by musical instruments but in the studio, the natural sounds of everyday life.'

Britten's twenty-minute score for the film contains music of great charm and energy and his success in writing music to order led, initially, to three similar one-off commissions before he was invited to join the film unit's permanent staff at a comparatively generous rate of £5 a week. As a key part of the team, Britten's involvement in each project could begin at a much earlier stage, an element which made further demands on the energetic young composer's ingenuity. The most ambitious of these films was a short documentary called *The Coal Face*, on which Britten was asked to collaborate from its inception. The task of documenting the hazardous world of coalmining could only have fallen under the brief of the film unit of the General Post Office in the loosest possible terms, and the film in fact had its origins in an extended set of footage from miners and mines, mostly in County Durham, which had somehow found its way into the unit's hands. This suggests that the project was in many ways an article of faith for the team, an opportunity to pay tribute to an industry which at the time saw the death of five of its workers every day. The film is extraordinary in its focus on the extent to which the lives of miners and their communities was dominated by the underground, and is in part a poetic tribute to the men and their work ('Coalmining is the basic industry of Britain', runs the refrain), in part a forthright critique of their working conditions and society's culpability in failing to see them improved. Britten collaborated on the script as well as writing and recording the music. The score, probably the most adventurous of the early film scores, was produced and recorded within a period of two weeks and is remarkable for its oratorio-like grandeur and extraordinary blending of text-setting styles, from homophonic choral passages to chant and accompanied speech. The range of effects is also dazzling, Britten extending the traditional range of percussion instruments to include sandpaper and wind machine, used in combination to imitate the noise of a train in motion. At one moment, when the coal train enters a tunnel, Britten managed to recreate the muffled sound of a train approaching by recording a cymbal clash and then playing it backwards, so that the vibrations grow louder rather than softer.

Another memorable moment in the score is Britten's setting of the poem contributed by the poet W. H. Auden. In contradistinction to the other films on which the two men collaborated – such as *Night Mail* and *The Way To the Sea* – Auden's contribution to *The Coal Face* is somewhat over-represented. He only joined the project after most of the script was finished. He did however supply the memorable seven-line lyric, 'O lurcher-loving collier', which is set at the end of the film's third section and at its dramatic climax insofar as the depiction of miners as ordinary men is concerned, showing as it does a miner with his wife and child after the end of the shift. The passage, set for piano and four-part boys voices, is extraordinary for its fleeting lyricism and for the way the narrator's lines seem simply to fade away at this moment, conveying the impression that the narrator, whose primary responsibility is to document the miners' lives in facts and figures, no longer has the words to describe the simple family scene he is witnessing.

In addition to providing the perfect foil for Britten's musical ingenuity, the strongly left-leaning environment of the GPO Film Unit, led by the Scottish producer John Grierson and peopled by directors of ambition and achievement such as Basil Wright and Alberto Calvalcanti, also proved influential in enabling Britten to conceive of his musical gifts in terms of a wider political and intellectual effort. The collaborations with W. H. Auden were especially important in this respect as a deep friendship and mutual respect between the two young men grew. Though the composer remained somewhat shy and reserved around the brilliant Oxford set which Auden gathered around himself, their intimacy and friendship deepened Britten's confidence both in himself and in the value of his art.

It is also significant that Britten's first great creative release as a professional musician came from the rather seat-of-the-pants environment of working in film. The GPO film unit was no Hollywood studio, and at times the young and impatient Britten expressed frustration that others involved in the films couldn't work as fast as he did himself. But the aspect of working to deadlines, using music to achieve very particular atmospheres and effects, and – perhaps most importantly of all – having a particular narrative or dramatic framework into which to place his musical ideas suited him to a tee, and the doldrums of his months after graduating from the Royal College of Music soon became a distant memory. It should not be surprising in this respect that what is probably Britten's best known orchestral work also began life as a film project.

The virtuoso concerto for orchestra now performed all over the world under the title of *The Young Person's Guide to the Orchestra* was initially conceived for a film sponsored by the Ministry of Education called 'The Instruments of the Orchestra' and scripted by Britten's friend and collaborator, the director and librettist Eric Crozier. Britten reportedly described the process of writing the work as 'a chore', but this claim is rather belied by the exuberance and grandeur of the score and Britten's evident determination that its didactic intentions should not occlude the musical experience.

As is well known, the theme on which the *Young Person's Guide*

is based is taken from a hornpipe Rondeau by Purcell, originally composed as part of his incidental music to Aphra Benn's 1676 play *Abdelazer* (or *The Moor's Revenge*). As well as providing apt, stately material, easily memorized by the listener on first hearing and thereby suitable for ornamental development through the variations for the individual instrument groups, the choice of Purcell is significant as a statement of stylistic loyalty to a tradition of British music-making older and, as Britten felt, far superior to that of Elgar, Vaughan Williams, Walton et al. with whom Britten kept an uneasy peace during his lifetime.

Perhaps because of its popularity, the Guide has come in for fairly regular criticism for pandering to orchestral clichés and for exemplifying what Britten's critics have sometimes felt to be his suspicious fluency. But the music is in fact far from clichéd. The piece is, of course, duty bound to display something of the character of each of the orchestral instruments, so the sections are bound to 'run to type' in some basic respects. In others, though, the characterizations run against the grain. The double basses soar with glorious lyricism while the violins' variation, with its chains of thirds and compound arpeggios, traces more of a Britten signature than a traditional violin one. The bassoon part, too, is undoubtedly among the more sinister variations, resisting any hint of avuncularity – contrast this with, say, the bassoon part in Prokofiev's *Peter and the Wolf*, with which the *Guide* is frequently paired. More importantly, perhaps, the grand fugue in which the instruments combine in the same order in which they were originally introduced remains one of the most exhilarating demonstrations of the complex make-up of orchestral timbre in the repertoire. If it educates, it does so thrillingly.

Britten's desire to imbue his music with political significance was evident in the piece which he initially meant to dub his First Symphony, and which he intended as a chilling statement of the pacifism which, following Auden and Isherwood, led him to leave his home shores for America after the onset of the Second World War. The somewhat bizarre circumstances of the work's commission, however, almost caused the gesture to backfire. It is hard to guess what must have been in the composer's mind – or not in the composer's mind – when he accepted a commission from the Japanese government as part of their planned celebrations of the 2,600th anniversary of the Mikado dynasty. Although the commission came over a year before the Japanese attack on

Pearl Harbor, the country's military ambitions and political affiliations were hardly a well-kept secret. Had the grand premiere of the
work, completed in 1940, taken place as planned, with Britten in
attendance in Tokyo, it is difficult to imagine how the composer's
domestic reputation, already damaged by his anti-war stance and
retreat to the US, could ever have been repaired. In the event, the
dark and foreboding atmosphere of the *Sinfonia da Requiem* – as
the work came to be known – with its unmistakably Christian
message and remembrance of the dead in the name of peace, didn't
please the Japanese at all and they refused to accept it – citing,
with laudable politeness, that the scores had arrived too late for
adequate rehearsal; nor did they ask for their money back. The
premiere was instead given to the New York Philharmonic at a
concert conducted by John Barbirolli.

Although the premiere was a success, it was a performance of the
work the following year, in Boston under Serge Koussevitzky, that
proved pivotal to Britten's entire career. For it was Koussevitzky's
profound admiration of the Sinfonia that prompted him to offer
the composer a fee to write an opera, and the resounding success
which this opera – *Peter Grimes* – eventually went on to meet
altered the course of Britten's composing career for good. He
didn't exactly turn his back on pure orchestral composition, but
his quickly gained sense that his musical and dramatic instincts
would find their surest creative outlet through the opera closed off
in Britten's mind any thoughts of a career as a symphonist.

While there is some irony in its having been the success of
Britten's 'First Symphony' which indirectly led to this chain of
events, that should not distract us from the fact that the *Sinfonia*,
above and beyond its openly declared political charge, is far from
being a symphony traditionally conceived. Written in three as
opposed to the usual four movements, it also lacks the kind of
thematic argument and development associated with the genre. In
its place is a potent combination of immediately thrilling gestures
– such as the terrifying timpani strikes which mark its opening, or
the furious disintegration of the Dies Irae scherzo – with an astonishing tautness and economy of composition, a feature which lends
the piece a far greater sense of weight and gravity than its twenty-
odd minute duration might lead one to believe.

Unlike the *Young Person's Guide*, the *Sinfonia's* critical reputation
has been consistently high. This is in part due to the astonishing
efficacy with which Britten achieves his dramatic and textural aims,

but also because, in contradistinction to much of Britten's orchestral oeuvre, it is a piece which is immediately heard to be rooted in the historical and musical context of its epoch. In addition to its origin as a wartime work specifically, it is also a work which seems to bear a more general testimony to the darker currents of its era. The last movement in particular seems to offer stylistic kinship not merely with Mahler but also with Berg – in the rising and falling motif given to the saxophone, considered by some to be a direct reference to Berg's violin concerto – and even Stravinsky. The enormous success of Britten's music in his homeland, to the extent in his later years of becoming a kind of de facto national composer, has often led people to conclude mistakenly that his music is in some sense parochial and unadventurous. From such a perspective, the *Sinfonia da Requiem* has always appeared to be an exceptional work. But while this confusion was understandable in the context of the exceptional polarization of debates surrounding music of the post-war era – to the extent that any music 'giving in' to tonal urges was seen by an influential minority as automatically compromised and reactionary – the *Sinfonia* is better understood as being central rather than exceptional among Britten's mature oeuvre. Besides, of all his orchestral scores, it is the one to which the troublesome etiquette of 'masterpiece' is least troubling applied.

Britten's early musical allegiances were, if anything, resolutely un-British by the standards of many of his contemporaries. Largely due to the early influence of Frank Bridge, much of the music Britten wrote while a student at the Royal College would have veered towards the progressive end of the current aesthetic spectrum. He became furious when the college library refused his suggestion to stock a copy of Schoenberg's *Pierrot Lunaire* (which he first discovered in 1933), and it was the college's influence that prevented him, on leaving college, from cultivating the links with Alban Berg that he had so counted on. The one major work which survives from his student years, the *Sinfonietta*, later published as Op. 1, is in an important sense a response to Schoenberg's seminal first Chamber Symphony. This is not to say that the music is superficially akin to Schoenberg's in some way, but that it takes its inspiration from the absolute tightness evident in the three-movement work's thematic construction. The melodic material of the entire piece is presented in a continuous line which spins in an almost hocket-like manner across various instruments. The orchestration is on the sparse side, Britten achieving astonishing textural variety which offers a counterbalance to the thematic uniformity. It is also remarkable for the play of bare dissonances and the use of pentatonic and modal scales.

The seven years separating the *Sinfonietta* (1932) and the *Sinfonia da Requiem* (1940) saw, largely thanks to the creative explosion that followed Britten's appointment to the GPO film unit, the composer's most productive period in terms of purely orchestral music. His output during this period includes the first versions of the violin (1939) and piano (1938) concertos, the wonderful sparkling, Rossini inspired *Soirées Musicales* (which also began life as a film project), and the *Diversions* for left-hand piano, commissioned, like so many such works, by Paul Wittgenstein. Given the composer's superb facility as a pianist, many might have hoped for something weightier in the way of a piano concerto from Britten, but the work is definitely on the sprightlier, bubblier side of his output. Britten described it as a 'bravura concerto with orchestral accompaniment' and it eschews any symphonic ambitions in favour of a baroque-style structure, rather anticipated by the labelling of the movements in the style of a dance suite: Toccata, Waltz, Recitative and Aria, and March. The work has never been as completely established in the repertoire as its composer might have hoped, but in recent years, as Britten's catalogue of orchestral music has begun to re-emerge from behind the impressive shadow cast by his stage works, the concerto has found itself becoming programmed rather more often. A similar waxing of popularity is being enjoyed by the violin concerto, long overshadowed by its more straightforwardly melodious contemporary by William Walton.

Only the second movement of Britten's violin concerto shares the atmosphere of fun-poking exuberance exemplified by the piano concerto. It is a movement of tremendous energy and exuberance, couched within a three-movement scheme which elsewhere adopts a much more serious tone than its piano predecessor. The opening gesture on the timpani recalls Beethoven's concerto, and the formal confidence displayed by the still relatively young Britten barely suffers by the comparison. The confidence and skill with which the latent energy of the opening gesture is sublimated in the material that follows it – in the violin's soaring melody and and in the way the bassoon and horn maintain, apparently indifferent to the violin, the basic rhythm – is certainly extraordinary. Britten also saves the cadenza for the transition between the second movement and the finale, as a way of reintroducing material from earlier in the work, before gliding straight into the brooding atmosphere of the Passacaglia.

Perhaps the most significant statement of Britten's quality as an orchestral composer to date from the period leading up to the *Sinfonia* comes from his 1937 *Variations on a Theme of Frank Bridge*. Indeed, it was more or less conceived as such by its composer. The loyal testimony to his composition teacher, and portrait of various aspects of his character and musical tastes and influences, is supplemented by the confidence and individuality of its style. Few of Britten's works from the 1930s are as unmistakably Britten-ish as the *Variations*. The main theme is taken from Bridge's second Idyll for string quartet, but it is handled with such skill through the brilliantly contrasted characters of each of the short, fiercely compact movements that the whole work shines with an originality which shows the former pupil has now become the master. Though scored only for string orchestra, the textural palette seems as rich and varied as any of the works for full orchestra, and the lack of self-indulgence in the slow, romantic and brooding second variation and the gloriously wistful fourth – entitled 'Romance', whose long and winding melody seems to glide through the air suspended like strands of gossamer – and the lightness of touch applied to the more ironic sketches, such as the exuberant 'Aria Italiana (fifth variation) and whirling 'Wiener Waltz' (seventh movment), whose spiralling energy distils magnificently in the central slow passage.

Nothing in this beautifully crafted work – except perhaps the sense of its conception in a single breath of inspiration – reveals the hurried circumstances of its composition. But the whole twenty-minute work was sketched within the period of a week in response to an urgent call for help from the conductor Boyd Neel. Neel needed a virtuosic piece by a contemporary English composer in order to show off his crack ensemble, the English String Orchestra, which had been invited to perform at the 1937 Salzburg Festival, on condition that it perform a new British work. Following Britten's successful playthrough of the sketch to the presumably delighted conductor, the work was completed and scored within a further four weeks, leaving an ample six weeks for the ensemble to rehearse the work. Its success with the Austrian audience outshone even the favour it found when brought back home, a testament to the fact that Britten's aesthetic was at the time in much surer alliance with continental tastes than British ones. Among the work's early champions was no less influential a figure than Herbert von Karajan, who recorded the piece with the Philharmonia Orchestra in 1952.

Had Britten's celebrated first foray into the world of opera not met with the extraordinary success that greeted it, and its composer, soon after returning to England to settle permanently on the Suffolk coast, Britten's post-war catalogue of orchestral works might not appear quite so thin. But anyone studying the earlier works from the *Sinfonietta* onwards, and with some knowledge of the kinds of subject and situation which would most reliably stimulate in the composer sustained and inspired activity, would not be surprised that his greatest artistic gifts came to lie in the field of music drama and vocal music more generally. As it is, aside from the *Young Person's Guide*, the principal pieces for orchestra from the last four decades of the composer's life are the lugubrious 1963 Cello Symphony, the ballet score for *The Prince of the Pagodas* which, as we saw, despite its verve and sparkle cost Britten so dear in terms of creative effort, and his last work for orchestra, the 1974 'Suite on English Folk Tunes'.

The Cello Symphony, one of seemingly innumerable works commissioned from his (equally innumerable) friends by the indefatigable Russian cellist and conductor, Mstislav Rostropovich, followed the sparse but electrifying Cello Sonata, also written for the Russian. Britten's choice of the term 'symphony' for the work was intended to differentiate it from the kind of virtuosic display and dramatic opposition between soloist and orchestra traditionally associated with the term 'concerto'. But while the work is decidedly 'democratic' in the musical partnership, and the first movement amounts to what is probably Britten's most rule-abiding exercise in composing in sonata form, it is really no more of a 'symphony' than any of the other works that invoke or play with the genre description. The opening minutes contain little in the way of the grand statements that one would expect to find anchoring such a substantial, multi-movement form, and the soloist's *style-brisé* entrance has a purposefully indistinct quality, exaggerated by the irrational rhythms. Equally, much of the rhetoric of the piece – and particularly the vocally-inspired gestures of the cello part – seem more concerned with their immediate context than with developing long-term correspondences.

The Cello Symphony is a deeply rewarding work when sensitively

performed and, just as importantly, when one has become famil-
iarized to its dark orchestral palette and unusual makeup. In mood
it has perhaps more in common with the *War Requiem*, composed
the year before, than anything else. It also has a raw, emotional
quality which suits beautifully the cello's distinctive timbre and
which makes a virtue out of the generic compositional difficulty
associated with works for cello and orchestra, which is that the solo
instrument is all too easily overpowered. Superficially, the Suite on
English Folk Tunes could not be more different. Its flow has none of
the cello symphony's awkwardness, and few of its dark orchestral
colours. The material is of course also completely different, drawn
as it is from the folk songs collected by Percy Grainger inter-
spersed with dance tunes from 'The English Dancing Master' and
concluding with an original setting of Hardy's poem 'Before Life
and After' (from where the quotation in the work's subtitle, 'A
time there was', is taken). The carefully plotted composition and
beautiful, jewel-encrusted handling of the folk material confirm
that Britten's labours on the work were ones of love. Indeed, its
luminous scoring and precisely voiced emotional registers spawn
a totally unsentimental breed of nostalgia which must have been
extraordinarily difficult to pull off. In this sense the work does
have something of the emotional rawness of the Cello Symphony,
but here the glance looks backward rather than starkly ahead, as if
seeking to glimpse something of a lost plenitude – to 'a time there
was' – which can no longer be exactly captured.

   Britten's brilliance as an orchestrator tends to hide behind his
remarkable genius as a musical dramatist. This is perhaps as it
should be when one considers that it was in the field of opera that
Britten's musical skills were at the most 'useful', as it were. All
the same, however, very few of the dramatic and musical images
operagoers have come to cherish over the past sixty years would be
nearly so successful without that characteristic sparkle associated
with Britten's orchestral writing. Our sense of the ambiguous
allure of the sea and its abilty to turn from a mysterious, glittering
balm for mankind's moral bewilderment to a pure, raging killer
– such an important structural metaphor for *Peter Grimes* (not
to mention *Billy Budd*) – gains so much from the way in which
the portrait of its swirling currents is now splashed with glinting
sunlight, now smothered in fog. Similarly, the taut brilliance of
the story-telling in *The Turn of the Screw* relies on the precision
of its musical elements and their alignment in the hands of

the thirteen-part chamber orchestration. As another of Britten's composition teachers, John Ireland put it – while admitting that he didn't quite like the work – *The Turn of the Screw* 'contains the most remarkable and original music I have ever heard from the pen of a British composer. What he has accomplished in sound by the use of only thirteen instruments was, to me, inexplicable; almost miraculous.'

Britten and the Piano

Stephen Hough

Most composers play the piano and many of them use the instrument as a tool of creation, whether improvising at the start of the process or editing and checking in the final stages. Some are such good pianists that the piano becomes an inseparable part of their compositional identity – Chopin, Liszt and Rachmaninov spring to mind. Others carry the timbre of the piano in their heads and transfer it to the orchestra – Debussy and Ravel's transparent waves of sound are clearly influenced by the piano's strings shimmering with overtones held by long sustaining pedals. Still others seem to have avoided altogether the influence of pianistic colour in their music – Berlioz, Wagner and Verdi were clumsy pianists but superb orchestrators.

Benjamin Britten is a case apart and a puzzling one. From the evidence of the many recordings he left as a collaborative chamber musician, he was a great pianist. His control of colour and nuance was at the highest level of virtuosity; he had total command of the keyboard. But he wrote nothing substantial for piano solo and only one mature work, the short 'Night Piece' (*Notturno*) which was commissioned as a test piece for the first Leeds International Piano Competition in 1963. His early piano concerto (1938), written for himself to play, clearly indicates that he had fingers to burn in addition to his more lyrical gifts, and yet its glittering passages were his rite of passage from youth to maturity. Never again would he attempt to write for the concert pianist except his 'Diversions for Piano and Orchestra' (1940), significantly for left-hand alone.

The pianist-composer finds his instrument a constant companion to creation. The familiarity of keys under hands is part of his identity and style – the figuration is covered with his fingerprints, the sonorities fit like old gloves. But Britten was not a pianist-composer in this sense. He didn't write at the piano, and while he obviously loved his instrument, perhaps he felt he needed to get away from its patterns to find inspiration. He needed to remove the gloves to dig deep into a different musical reservoir. Hammers striking strings, arpeggios flying up and down the keyboard, ten fingers seizing chords ... all of this was probably a distraction for him. The piano's shapes were too set, its stock gestures too familiar, the risk of cliché too present. It was only with the human voice (and the singer who became his life-partner) that he discovered his own voice as a composer.

I don't think this was so much a decision made as a destiny reached: Britten preferred to make music or to be on stage with other people, and particularly with friends. His life-partnership with Peter Pears was a well-known, unique example of artistic fecundity with decades of masterpieces flowing freely from their intimate relationship – truly a Musical Offspring; and his friend-ships with Mstislav Rostropovich, Julian Bream and Osian Ellis led to a series of important works for cello, guitar and harp respec-tively. Perhaps it is similar to writers: some spend their creative lives utterly absorbed in introspective autobiography, whereas others are more interested in observing other people's lives.

Despite the fact that a number of the most important characters in Britten's operas are loners or outsiders (Grimes, Budd and Aschenbach for example), their aloneness is not a self-sufficiency; it requires others to spark off, to react to, or to walk away from. The solo pianist is a confident, self-contained entity, and the piano recital is not just a one-man show but a fearless public display of individualism. I think the man writing quietly, privately, close to his roots in Suffolk, would have felt awkward assuming such a role. Britten's music is powerfully communicative to those sitting in the auditorium, but it appears that for him there needed to be a communication between more than one performer on stage too.

Britten and the Race to the Finish

John Bridcut

His last work is, surprisingly, one of his least known. Britten mapped out his *Welcome Ode* in the torrid summer of 1976, for Suffolk schoolchildren to perform for the Queen's Silver Jubilee the following year. He had gone to Norway in a vain search for relief from the heat, freshly ennobled by Her Majesty but physically weaker by the day. He returned with a composition sketch for his musical inkslinger Colin Matthews to orchestrate.

This cheerful, five-movement frolic gives no hint of his parlous state of health at that time. He had often turned his hand to a Tarantella or a Moto Perpetuo – even an Irish Reel. But the second movement of the *Welcome Ode* is his one and only published Jig, and it just belts along for one minute twenty seconds, with not a single musical grey hair to betray the three years of debility since his major heart surgery, or the thirty years since the coruscating finale of *The Young Person's Guide to the Orchestra,* or indeed the 48 since he had been crowned *victor ludorum* as the outstanding athlete at his prep school. The race to the finish was in his blood, as Colin Graham knew all too well from the nearly twenty years he had worked with Britten on the staging of his operas. 'He was what the French would call *sportif*. He was besotted by youth, and he tried to maintain it in himself in his own life, until the day he died.'

'Do you *always* have to win?' asked Imogen Holst in March 1953, as they squabbled over who was to finish off a bottle of 'an excellent claret'. 'Well, I get very cross if I don't,' Britten replied – and indeed, it was she – as Britten had insisted – who downed the last glass. This competitiveness was an essential ingredient in Britten's musical personality, and infuses even some of his most reflective pieces. Take, for example, the *Serenade* for tenor, horn and strings. Amid the muted colours and lengthening shadows of 'the fainting sun' comes Ben Jonson's Hymn to Diana the huntress, the 'goddess excellently bright'. The horn-player is whisked into a gallop, competing with tenor and pizzicato strings in a dash to the winning-post. It is the perfect way to set up the breathless beauty of the final song, Keats's 'O soft embalmer of the still midnight'. But it is also Britten having fun on his own account, testing the agility of every performer.

Mrs Britten had started it all. In that irritating way that some parents have of being over-ambitious for their offspring, she kept talking of her beloved Benjamin as the fourth musical B, after Bach, Beethoven and Brahms. Luckily it didn't put the boy off music for life, although it did ensure he was fairly rude as a young man about most of his competitors. As he matured, he turned against Beethoven and Brahms too, although Bach managed to survive relatively unscathed.

The competitive streak first expressed itself in sport, and that stayed with him nearly all his life. Thanks to his mother's tireless ministrations, his headmaster was induced to shout from the boundary of the cricket field, when the ball was in the air: 'Britten, don't catch it!' – in case it damaged his precocious pianist's fingers. What his team-mates made of this is not recorded. But the boy did throw the thing quite skilfully, and rejoiced that his distance record stood for several years after he had left the school ('until broken', as Britten only half-teasingly put it, 'by a beastly little boy in a gale'). He was no footballer or hockey player, but his tennis was lithe and cunning, as his schoolfriend David Layton recalled: 'Most people hit the ball hard straight back over the net until they win. But he didn't. He'd slice it and put it in the corner.' And he always won.

Tennis was a lifelong obsession. He first got to know The Red House in Aldeburgh through playing lawn tennis with Mary Potter in her garden. Eventually they swapped houses, so for him tennis was virtually on tap. All his visitors knew there could be only one winner. The teenager, Humphrey Maud, was given no quarter, 'absolutely none. We played quite fiercely,' Maud added, 'and there was no question of him being beaten.' Squash was another compulsion: he played against Eric Crozier for an hour a day while writing the *Spring Symphony* in 1948: 'I was no real match for him,' Crozier noted. 'He was faster than I was and had more stamina, and he always played to win, delighting to outwit his opponent by a series of unexpected shots that were impossible to return.' Perhaps the squash court is the proper context for 'Fair and fair', the symphony's unrelenting duet (maybe duel is a better word) for tenor and soprano.

Croquet was a less energetic but equally aggressive contest. David Hemmings, the first Miles in *The Turn of the Screw,* would pair up with Stephen Potter against Britten and Pears. 'I was actually rather a good croquet player, and Ben was slightly pissed off about this. He didn't like being beaten. Stephen and I used to say, "Ah, we've got you this time!" – well, we got them every time, actually.' The opera's producer, Basil Coleman, was new to the game, and was surprised at how touchy Britten was when Coleman managed to beat him at his first attempt.

As both librettist and opera producer, Crozier may have fallen out with him later, but their closeness over many years informed his shrewd remark that Britten's 'enjoyment of the sheer physical pleasure of playing games and of winning by a combination of swift thought and economy of effort, was reflected in his piano-playing and his conducting. From the first bar he was on top of his form, like a trained athlete beginning a race, nervously intense, poised, determined to succeed, and revelling in his mastery – and at such times he radiated a kind of magnetism that inspired everyone who played or sang with him.'

The pianist Ronan Magill confirmed the flow of nervous energy with his visceral description of the 'shudder of electricity' that coursed through the composer's body in performance, and Britten's agent Sue Phipps, who often was his page-turner in recitals, found it terrifying to watch his hands going down on to the keyboard, because they were 'absolutely a-quiver'. Yet, she marvelled, they produced 'this glorious sound'. Humphrey Stone, who often stayed with Britten in Aldeburgh as a boy, described him as 'a coiled spring' – and this is clearly audible in the out-takes of Britten's recording of the *War Requiem,* where he turns the pages of his own score with alarming ferocity.

Britten's physicality was not confined to the tennis court or the piano keys. It is one of the most distinctive features of his music. The opening of 'Rats Away!' in *Our Hunting Fathers* bristles with physical tension, as quick-fire fragments are tossed between the players in shudders of fear, as though rats are scurrying all over the furniture. Vaughan Williams may have had to remonstrate with the orchestra for fooling around like schoolboys in rehearsals for the premiere in 1936, but at least they had got the point. Britten too is playing the fool, but with fierce self-discipline. When he wrote the breathlessly fast three-part canon in 'This Little Babe' in *A Ceremony of Carols*, he was throwing down a gauntlet to his choristers. Not only does he require each boy to hold his own against the other parts singing the same music fractionally ahead or behind, but he tests their breath control and oral dexterity in spitting out the words. As the three parts finally coalesce into unison, to the words: 'If thou wilt foil thy foes with joy...', you can almost hear Britten chuckling at how close they came to being foiled.

Britten's working pattern was mostly puritanical, but he did allow himself the one luxury of fast cars. This 'boy racer' knew the thrill of the chase, preferably in a convertible. He tried to convince himself that he could safely keep the hood down in the rain, on the grounds that if he drove fast enough, the rain would be forced above the car in a curve, leaving its occupants completely dry. Before the war, he was lent an AC sports car by Lennox Berkeley, which he took great pride in driving from London to Brighton at 90 mph. Although his musical inspiration seldom failed him, there was one occasion in America in the early 1940s when he had 'writer's block' and consequent depression. His cure was to drive up and down a beach on Long Island at high speed for several hours. The next day he was happily back at work.

Later, as he moved away from using conventional Italian tempo markings, Britten frequently chose the word 'Quick', rather than 'Fast'. His performers had to be sharp-witted as well as speedy, because agility in his lexicon was mental as well as physical. This was the composer who doodled noughts-and-crosses, played Happy Families and Dover Patrol, or spoke a gobbledygook which involved putting the letters *arp* before every vowel. Harpe darpid tharpis rarpegarpularparlarpy warpith tarpeenarpage barpoys harpe barpefrarpiendarped. Most people begin to wilt by about the fourth word, but not Britten. He even told Peter Pears: 'Arpi larpove yarpou!'

In a similar way, Britten never tired of writing in canon. In the late 1940s he realised he was in danger of overdoing it. 'I must stop myself too much "canonizing"', he told Pears. 'Probably more entertaining to write than to listen to!', he added (though the blur of the canon in 'This Little Babe' is undeniably thrilling for both performer and listener – when it works). There may sometimes be a sense that he begins a canon without being quite sure where it's going to take him. But, with his remarkable gift for setting himself musical conundrums which work out in the end, he reaps rich rewards in *Spring Symphony, Noye's Fludde* – or indeed, his children's song 'Old Abram Brown is dead and gone', a funeral march with a difference.

Variations and the passacaglia form appealed to him because they offered similar challenges – intellectual and mathematical. As a schoolboy he found he was solving algebraic puzzles in his sleep, and there is a boyish boastfulness in the way he often chose to present his variations first, with the full theme only at the end, as if daring his audience to guess what it was. This was how he shaped his wonderful viola piece *Lachrymae*, as well as his *Nocturnal* for guitar – variations with their own enigma, which Elgar, as a fellow devotee of puzzles and word-games, might have appreciated.

Britten was often criticized when young for being 'clever', and it is hard to imagine that a composer who maintained that boyish competitiveness all through his life found such an accusation entirely disparaging. From childhood in Lowestoft he had been the blue-eyed boy, and one of the root causes of the collapse of his friendship with W. H. Auden was that he felt himself intel-lectually inferior. This was tolerable while Auden was lavishing praise on 'Bengy dear', the 'lovable talented little boy', but when he turned to barbed criticism, it was too much. Britten had to be top of the class. Imogen Holst noted that, when he took a group to rub brasses in Orford church, 'Ben *straight away* did his very much better than anyone else!' – and he was then 39.

Problems with 'cleverness' arise only if there is no musical profit. To this day there are those who find Britten's music artful but bloodless, though how anyone can say that about the *Four Sea Interludes* from *Peter Grimes* – let alone the full opera – defeats me. It would certainly be in character for Britten to have been tickled pink by his own ingenuity in devising a canon for the *Grimes* chorus that sounds like a traditional song, and yet is written in very untra-ditional 7:4 time. 'Old Joe has gone fishing' plays an important part in the drama – not only in the ebb and flow of the first Act, when it apparently relieves the tensions created by Grimes inside the pub and the storm outside, but in the opera as a whole. The relationship between the crowd on stage and the crowd sitting in the theatre is crucial. So beguiling is the 7:4 tune and the clever way the round works that the audience finds itself identifying with the mob it will come to disown. Then, as Grimes himself interrupts and wrecks the round, he demonstrates his isolation from the rest of the community and ratchets up the tension even higher, whereupon his new apprentice arrives at the pub door, cold and bedraggled. As he is dragged off into the storm once more by Grimes, Britten propels the final bars of the act to its brutal, but gripping, conclusion. This is cleverness indeed, but in the service of both music and drama, and the audience teeters on the edge of its seat.

Within a year, Britten had done it again. The score of *The Young Person's Guide to the Orchestra* was intended as an educational venture. It was a nice idea to take the 'timeless' tune from Purcell's *Abdelazer* and write modern variations on it to showcase each family of instruments. But the tour de force was to follow this with a fast (or, rather, quick) and complex fugue for all the different instruments, and then, when the texture was at its most furious and elaborate, to superimpose Purcell's original melody, broad and loud. How it all fits together is a musical miracle, but it is a crowning moment, which never fails to thrill and move an audience. Britten is also reminding us he was still top of the class – and winning every race. The triumph is intellectual, emotional and physical – all three.

Britten has sometimes been called a Peter Pan figure – a boy who never grew up. To my mind, this is quite wrong. He is very much an adult (indeed, perhaps became one prematurely) with a mature understanding of the dark undercurrents in society and in relationships. Most adults are keen to shed their childhood frames of reference as so many milk teeth, whereas Britten rejoiced in them, and never let his boyhood out of his sight – or his memory. He carried it in his knapsack, as it were, all his life, refreshed by the easy friendships with teenage boys which it enabled. He never forgot what it was like to be an adolescent on the cusp of experience, as Imogen Holst makes clear in the daily journal she kept in 1953-4, when she first worked for Britten.

Her diary certainly has its hilarious moments, but offers unparalleled insight into Britten's working methods, as well as astute observations of his skill as a composer. Indeed, it must be one of the most valuable documents ever written about a composer in his prime. During the gestation of *Gloriana*, she told Britten how effective his quaver rests were in the Act III chorus for boys ('Now rouse up all the city'), and how true to life they were for boys of 13. She had been drinking both rum and sherry (alcohol flowed generously in the Britten household), but her comment was spot on. Britten responded with a telltale revelation: 'it's because I'm still 13'. Although he was actually three times that age, he imagined himself as stuck for ever in the golden year when he was head boy at his prep school, and lord of all he surveyed on the sports field. The quaver rests that Holst so perceptively identified give the chorus of marching boys its rhythmic energy and vitality – the *ragazzo* quality that the tenor Adrian Thompson describes from his schoolday service in the Wandsworth Boys' Choir. It's the world of the raucous street urchin, with just a hint of rent-boy – far, far removed from the treble purity of Ernest Lough in O *for the wings of a dove*, which had only briefly caught Britten's imagination as a teenager. The strutting jauntiness of the whistling boys in the *Spring Symphony*'s 'Whenas the rye reach to the chin' was much more to his taste. Britten knew in his head what it was to be one of them, so in the *Gloriana* marching song he notated their breathing patterns on the page, without even thinking about it. Similarly, it is the rests that achieve the boisterous attack in the opening of his children's piece *Psalm 150*, and he expected the same from the LSO in rehearsals of Purcell's *Chacony* in G minor, when his insistence on the semiquaver rests was captured on film.

Even after the heart surgery in 1973 which terminated his tennis, his squash, his conducting and his electricity-laden pianism, the boyhood knapsack remained to be rifled through. He unearthed his early String Quartet in D, as well as his first opera, *Paul Bunyan*. But it also infused the new works he was writing, despite his disability – not just the Jig in the *Welcome Ode*, but 'Cakes and Ale' and 'Hunt the Squirrel' in his *Suite on English Folk Tunes*, and 'Leezie Lindsay' in *A Birthday Hansel*.

Those last years were also flavoured by his final opera *Death in Venice*, which percolated through audiences in Snape, then London and New York, as well as being recorded by Decca. In scoring the 'Games of Apollo', Britten had managed to re-create on the stage the thrill of his own school sports days. These games are often the despair of producers, and indeed his friends tried to advise him that they outstayed their welcome, and needed cutting back or out. He was usually not hostile to revisions of this sort – after all he had re-shaped the four-act *Billy Budd* into two acts a decade after its premiere. But on this occasion, weak and unsure as he was after his heart operation, Britten stood firm. The games were an inseparable part of him – more so because he could no longer participate physically himself. In his mind, however, he was still the gleaming Tadzio, triumphant over his friends in every contest, every race.

Back to the Future: The Work of the Britten-Pears Foundation

Richard Jarman

All composers live on after their death in their own ways. Most, however great their music, suffer a period of obscurity before being re-discovered with the pendulum of fashion. Some are remembered by the houses they lived in, some leave an archive for scholars to mine for new insights and some leave a legacy through the institutions they founded. Benjamin Britten has turned out to be as lucky in death as he was in life. Since his death in 1976, his reputation as a composer has continued to grow and spread and not a day passes when his music is not played somewhere in the world. And while his genius as a composer must be the main reason for this, the physical and musical legacy he left behind in Aldeburgh has helped constantly to remind the world of the enormous contribution he made to cultural life in the twentieth-century.

Visitors to the Red House often say that it still feels very much like the home that Britten and Pears shared from 1957. It is as though they had gone out to take the dogs for a walk but not returned. I sometimes wonder, if they were to return, how they would feel about the way things had turned out since their deaths.

About the state of the world Britten would surely have mixed feelings. Although the Cold War ended without a major conflagration (and now allowing Russian musicians to practise their art freely in a way that was so often denied to his Soviet friends), he would surely be dismayed that wars and violence are still so prevalent in the world. Well over 50 performances of the *War Requiem* will be given in the Centenary year, and this underlines what a powerful message this work still brings to us. But on the other hand, he would find the modern world a more tolerant, accepting place and I trust that if they were alive today Britten and Pears would want to recognize their lifetime relationship by entering into a civil partnership.

On the musical front, I think Britten would be astonished at how his reputation has continued to grow since his death, how year after year some 200 performances of his operas are given all around the world, even if some of the more conceptual productions might puzzle or upset him. He would be delighted to see the role of education in music taken seriously these days, though things have come a long way since his pioneering film, *Instruments of the Orchestra*. But, having been criticized in his lifetime for stylistic conservatism, he would be dismayed to be thought by some to be a difficult, contemporary composer, even more than 35 years after his death.

He would surely also be heartened to see the Maltings at Snape develop as one of the UK's most important centres of music, still promoting the work of new composers and still helping to train and encourage young musicians as they start on their professional careers.

The Centenary is a great opportunity to celebrate Britten's impressive achievements as a composer, performer and man, but also to try to set right some misconceptions and to bring his music to new audiences. This is a worldwide act of celebration with the Britten-Pears Foundation at the centre of it. It is something we have been preparing for over many years and it has been a transformational process for us.

From quite modest beginnings in Britten's lifetime, the Foundation has grown into one of the most important organizations supporting music in the UK and it is certainly unique among composer foundations all around the world. This is because it combines a living house with a comprehensive archive, and because it faces out to the world in supporting not only Britten's music but also new music and the ideals Britten and Pears espoused. The Centenary is an opportunity to increase the Foundation's strength in all these areas.

An important implication of the relationship between Britten and Pears is that they left no direct descendants. As Britten's health began to deteriorate in the 1970s, he and Pears began to think about the eventual use of their priceless collection of music, manuscripts, books, art and artifacts, and they saw the benefit of retaining it at The Red House rather than willing it to an academic institution. The key person in helping them determine what to do was Britten's lawyer Isador Caplan, who was to have a central role in designing the mechanisms to protect Britten's legacy, notably the formation of the Britten-Pears Foundation. As early as the 1950s Caplan had recognized the potential historical interest that Britten's composition sketches might have for future generations. So in 1973 the Britten-Pears Library Trust was set up. Its principal objective was to ensure that in the future the contents of the library could be used by scholars, musicians and general visitors who shared their interests. One of the first tasks was to draw up a list of friends and collaborators to whom Britten might have given some of his working musical sketches, and to see if the Trust could get them back for depositing in the Library either through sale, gift or loan. Thus was established the body and the collection that would eventually become the Britten-Pears Foundation.

Following Britten's death in 1976 the focus of life at The Red House changed. Pears was occupied with his own performing career and the planning of the Festival, but with no new compositions being created his attention turned to the question of Britten's legacy and the part that the collection of manuscripts, papers and books could play in this. So the process of organizing, cataloguing and expanding the archive began. In May 1980 Pears opened the Britten-Pears Library and, with a new reading room, the archive was made available for scholars.

Despite its establishment as a research centre, wider knowledge of the Library was at first relatively limited. Researchers were few and far between and the operation was very much a cottage industry. In 1986, following the death of Peter Pears, the Library Trust became subsumed into the new Britten-Pears Foundation, which had the same duty of care for the collections but as part of a wider educational and promotional remit. The story of the 40 years since its inception has been the development from a private collection in a domestic setting to a busy, public research institution as part of a centre devoted to promoting the legacy of Britten and Pears. Nowadays the Foundation receives between 200 and 300 readers every year, in a wide range of subjects for academic research, for books or films and radio programmes. This research now covers every aspect of Britten's life and music, the work of other composers, as well as the art, the printed books and the sound recordings it holds.

Britten's mother famously stated that she saw her son becoming the fourth B among composers, alongside Bach, Beethoven and Brahms. This sense of destiny must have been transmitted to the young Britten and from an early age he was meticulous in retaining every scrap of his juvenile compositions and other material, such as diaries, photographs and artifacts. One of the most charming is the system he used to take his first steps in learning about music and its notation, which we displayed in an exhibition on his childhood. In later years he kept all the documents and notes involved in the creation of his operas, so that it is often possible to trace the development of the work from its very inception to the finished work on stage. For example, with *Billy Budd* we have not only the original book of Melville's story which Britten read, but the notes taken at his very first meeting with librettists E. M. Forster and Eric Crozier, when Britten was anxious to sketch exactly how an eighteenth-century fighting ship would have been laid out. Further on in the process of composition we have all the musical sketches and letters that flowed as the work was planned. It makes a compelling story!

Britten was an avid letter-writer and his correspondence with colleagues, collaborators and friends gives us great insight into what he was trying to achieve in his works. Britten was one of the central figures in British and international cultural life in the middle of the last century and this brought him into contact and correspondence with many of the major figures of the day, such as E. M. Forster, Dmitri Shostakovich, T. S. Eliot, Yehudi Menuhin, John Piper, Edith Sitwell, W. H. Auden, Aaron Copland, Duncan Grant, Kathleen Ferrier, William Walton, Lennox Berkeley, Sviatoslav Richter and Mstislav Rostropovich. In our collection are some 80,000 letters, which are an invaluable fund of research, not only into Britten's output but also into the cultural life of the twentieth-century.

Since Britten's death the collection has expanded considerably. We have the overwhelming majority of Britten's finished manuscript scores, but there was a big drive to get back many of the composition sketches he gave away, some of which still turn up unexpectedly for sale. The same applies with his letters – only a couple of years ago a letter to fellow composer Alan Bush was discovered and it was a major statement of his musical credo, written in 1936. When we can, we try to acquire these treasures, although Britten is now commanding huge prices in the saleroom. We have also acquired other items such as original costumes, costume designs and programmes, as well as archive collections of some of Britten's contemporaries and colleagues, such as Joan Cross and Lennox Berkeley.

With this expansion has come the problem of housing all the material, some of it, such as costumes and set models, reasonably bulky. In the 1990s the old swimming pool next to the Library was covered over and this became a store room and exhibition gallery,. but by the turn of the century space was again a problem and Britten's old composing studio, which he had abandoned in 1970, was converted into an archive store. While these were reasonable temporary solutions, as we approached the Centenary it was clear that we needed to find a purpose-built space to ensure that the collection could be stored in perfect conditions for the very long term. Thus we set out on a course of decisions that have had a transformational effect on the work of the Foundation.

The key decision was to retain the collection long-term at The Red House site and to build an archive centre in the garden. This has been designed by the Stirling Prize-winning architects Stanton Williams to fit, in style and scale, within the domestic setting of the house and its grounds. The building is not only beautiful, but breaks new ground as a way to store an archive collection. The important thing for long-term conservation of paper is to have not only a cool and dry atmosphere but a stable one. Normally this has been achieved by means of massive, energy-hungry air-conditioning, but this building has hardly any plant and the internal climate is stabilized by purely natural means.

One of the fundamental principles of the Britten-Pears Foundation is that the archive should be very much more than a collection stored away in a closed room, available only for specialist researchers. The Britten-Pears archive is so incredibly rich in objects that illuminate Britten's life that we are keen to use them to tell the world about him. From the start the Foundation has been busy on the publishing front. The major project was the publication of a selection of Britten's correspondence, *Letters from a Life*. This was initiated by the authoritative Britten scholar, and his musical executor, Donald Mitchell, assisted by Philip Reed and also later by Mervyn Cooke. After some 35 years the project was completed in 2012 and stretches to six hefty volumes, full of illuminating footnotes, all of which make this series an invaluable source of information for anyone interested in the minutiae and processes of Britten's life. Another key publication was the Catalogue of Published Works, designed to be a reference tool for performers. It is still an invaluable source of practical information, but as new works were published and there was growing interest in his unpublished juvenilia, it became clear that something more comprehensive was needed. So, in 2006 the Foundation set about compiling the Thematic Catalogue of Britten's works. It details every one of his known works, finished and unfinished, published or unpublished (including full manuscript sources and many musical examples) and is unique of its kind by being published online and not in hard state. This enormous task has taken over six years, under the leadership of Lucy Walker, and becomes fully available in July 2013. In 2009 another fascinating document in our collection was edited by John Evans and published under the title *Journeying Boy*. This is a selection from Britten's diaries, which he kept between 1928 and 1938. It covers his time at school, college and his early years as a composer until the time he met Peter Pears. It is full of insights into his feelings, his reactions to the music of others as well as his own, and to contemporary events.

These publications are all valuable material for research into Britten's life, but the Foundation has also been active in promoting his music to performers and in helping understanding of his work with audiences. We have produced guides to his orchestral music, his choral music, his operas, and in 2011 Paul Kildea produced a general guide to his output, helping programmers with ideas for themes and companion pieces, particularly of Britten's less well-known works. We have also produced short films introducing some of his key works, including *Noye's Fludde*, *War Requiem* and *Billy Budd*, as well as information packs available online. All of these publications have been able to draw on the resources we hold in our collections.

Britten's archive is heavily paper-based, but the Foundation is now firmly rooted in the digital world. Bit by bit we are moving to store all our photographs, sound and video material in digital form. The website allows a visitor to view many documents online, as well as to take an online tour of The Red House. For the Centenary we have developed a new website, dedicated to introducing Britten to new listeners, including a digital sampler containing excerpts from most of his works, searchable by mood, speed, popularity, genre, author and instrument. This website is available in seven different languages, making it accessible to many people all around the world.

One of the most exciting consequences of building a dedicated archive centre is that is frees up considerable space that can be used for other purposes. Thanks to a grant from the Heritage

Lottery Fund, we are expanding into new areas of education and promotion. The refurbishment of the old Library Building incorporates a new exhibition gallery and a permanent display introducing Britten's work to newcomers in a lively, graphic way. For the first time there is a dedicated Education Space, so that groups from local schools can visit The Red House and learn about this Suffolk hero. In the years to come we aim to strengthen our educational activity at all levels, not only as a major research centre, but developing links across the board, from schoolchildren to undergraduates and those in adult learning programmes. The development of digital techniques is likely to change the landscape in this area, facilitating greater access and allowing us to reach out to the world from our quiet corner of Suffolk.

Most exciting of all, we are able to bring back to life the room where Britten composed some of his greatest works, such as *The War Requiem*. Thanks to our comprehensive collection, we were able to consult the original drawings by the architect commissioned by Britten to create the room, and we have countless photographs of Britten working there or playing there with friends such as Rostropovich. So the restoration will be faithful, down to the details of colour and fabric, and we have been able to re-assemble the original furnishings. This will surely become a place of real pilgrimage!

Indeed, the scope and depth of the collection is remarkable, but what makes it unique in the world is that it is held in the place where Britten and Pears lived and worked. The Red House is really central to the mission of the Britten-Pears Foundation. After Pears's death in 1986, the house continued to be lived in by Rita Thompson, Britten's nurse, but in the late nineties she moved out and the house underwent some conversion, mainly modernizing the bedrooms for guests. In the early years of the century the house began to be used for a modest amount of entertaining, mostly for artists and those involved in putting on Britten performances all over the world. For such people to come and stay at The Red House is a powerful experience.

In 2005 we opened the house up for paying visitors for the first time. Numbers are necessarily limited by the scale of the rooms, but this has proved a popular attraction and people enjoy the domestic feeling of the house, its sense of peace and the haunting spirit of place. A particular pleasure is the way the garden has also been restored to something like its previous state (again, the archive threw up the original invoices from the garden centre from which the plants were ordered after Britten and Pears moved into the house in 1957!). In recent years, therefore, the Foundation has become conscious of the heritage value of what it owns and looks after. It is important that this is conserved as far as possible for future generations, but it is also important to preserve the living spirit in the house. Britten and Pears did not want The Red House to become a museum, and I hope that they would be pleased at the balance we have created by making limited use of the house for entertaining but keeping it in its historic condition.

One of the by-products of opening the house up to visitors has been an appreciation of the art collection it contains. Pears was an avid collector and supported the work of a number of contemporary artists by buying their paintings. Many of them became friends or collaborators (notably John Piper) and the house is huge enriched by a collection that is both eclectic and very personal, a remarkable showing of art of the twentieth-century, including John Craxton, Duncan Grant, Sidney Nolan, Mary Potter, Keith Grant, Philip Sutton, F. N. Souza and David Hockney, as well as sculpture by Geoffrey Clarke and George Ehrlich. In 2012 the collection was the subject of a new book entitled *A Musical Eye*, edited by Judith LeGrove.

Britten's huge contribution to British musical life, quite apart from his compositions, came from the support he gave to contemporary composers. One of his enduring legacies is the publishing house Faber Music, which he founded with the encouragement of T. S. Eliot and which continues to publish many of the most important contemporary composers. But it was through the work of the Aldeburgh Festival that he was able to give practical support, often to composers whose style was very far from his own. He famously invited Harrison Birtwistle to give the first performances of his opera *Punch and Judy* in Aldeburgh, and the 1954 Festival included a concert of Musique Concrete! In other ways Britten and Pears were also men of principle. Their strong pacifist views often did not win them friends, and the example of their homosexual relationship brought them moments of great anxiety in the deeply conservative and intolerant society of the time. The Britten-Pears Foundation has tried to follow our founders' principles, most notably in its grant-giving programme.

By way and by far our largest grant goes to Aldeburgh Music.

This grant is now channelled to support the Britten-Pears Young Artist Programme, which has developed out of the Britten-Pears School, a vision of both Britten and Pears. Both men were passionate about encouraging young people to be involved with music-making and to receive expert training if they were studying for a professional life in music. They would, I hope, applaud the breadth and quality of the programme now offered, which allows young people from all around the world to come to Snape and benefit from its facilities, the excellence of the artistic teaching and the special atmosphere of the place.

The rest of the Foundation's grants programme goes to three areas: to contemporary music; to support performances of Britten's music; and to support community projects in and around Aldeburgh. We also used to support a number of other causes close to the hearts of our founders, including gay rights, environment issues and world peace. However, a few years ago we took the decision to focus our work on the actual commissioning of new music, an area where few other bodies were specializing and which lies at the heart of the creation of new music. After the BBC and the PRS Foundation, the Britten-Pears Foundation is the most important source of funding for the commissioning of new scores. In the Centenary we have made a special contribution, combining with the Royal Philharmonic Society to produce six new works from some of the world's best composers, in genres where Britten specialised: Wolfgang Rihm writing for symphony orchestra, Judith Weir for chamber orchestra, Magnus Lindberg for large-scale ensemble, Poul Ruders for string quartet, Harrison Birtwistle for tenor and piano and Thea Musgrave, Sally Beamish, Anna Meredith and Charlotte Bray collaborating on settings of Blake for children to perform. This impressive line-up is a tremendous statement, not only about Britten's historic commitment to new music, but also about the Foundation's continuing work in this area.

Britten's music is played all over the world, but there are still many places where it is unfamiliar and while the *Young Person's Guide*, the *War Requiem* and the *Four Sea Interludes* receive countless performances every year there are many works in his catalogue that deserve wider exposure. So the focus of our grants is to encourage performances in new places or of less familiar works, or performances that involve young people getting to know Britten's music. The Centenary has proved a golden opportunity and we have given grants, big and small, to projects all over the world, including the premieres of *Billy Budd* in Chile, of *A Midsummer Night's Dream* in Brazil, a film of *Noye's Fludde* in the townships of South Africa, a series of choral concerts in Palestine and the first Britten opera in China (*Noye's Fludde* again).

Britten and Pears cared deeply about the community in which they spent most of their time. They were very much involved in many of the local activities, and not just the musical ones. For example, Britten was instrumental in getting a reading library built in Aldeburgh and made a contribution to its construction. The Foundation has helped with a number of capital projects in Aldeburgh, including the construction of a Music Room at the Aldeburgh Primary School and the upgrading of the Jubilee Hall. Our current grant programme allows us to continue this work by supporting activities and it is open to any kind of community effort in the area in and around Aldeburgh. It is good to be able to help projects of all kinds, including local schools, sports clubs, museums and village halls, as well as Aldeburgh Church and Aldeburgh Cinema.

How does the Britten-Pears Foundation finance this activity? The overwhelming majority of our income comes from the royalties on performances of Britten's music, of which we are the sole beneficiary, once the proceeds have been divided with the publishers. This is why we work closely with the publishers to promote Britten's music, because the more performances that are given the more funds we have to give away or use for good causes. Since Britten's death we had built up a fund of reserves to provide for the day when copyright expires, but in 2006 the trustees decided that the Centenary was such a key event that we needed to celebrate it with maximum effect. We therefore decided to spend the reserves and gave Aldeburgh Music £1.5m to secure the future of its base at the Snape Maltings. We undertook to develop the Red House site and to support a range of major projects in the Centenary year that would bring Britten's music to new prominence. Once the party is over, we shall need to start setting money aside so that when copyright ends (broadly speaking in 30 years' time) there will be sufficient funds for the Foundation's work to continue, particularly in maintaining the Red House and the Archive Centre.

The pleasures of working for the Britten-Pears Foundation are manifold, but it is particularly life-enhancing to work with a group of professional colleagues and trustees all so totally dedicated to their task, and inspired. And this is easy, because it is not difficult to be inspired by Britten's music and by his achievements as a man. The other principal pleasure is the sheer diversity of our work – as a leading research and educational body, as a funder of exciting international work, as a heritage body responsible for a very special property and giving support to musical organizations and audiences all over the world, helping to make Britten's music ever more accessible. The Centenary is a transformational event for us, but once it is over it will be evident that the work of bringing Britten's music to the world will be even wider and richer than when we set out. We hope our founders would be pleased with what has been achieved so far and would support our ambitions for the future.

Notes on the Contributors

Janet Baker is an English mezzo-soprano, well known as an opera, concert and lieder performer. During her career, she was closely associated with baroque and early Italian opera, and with the works of Benjamin Britten. She was also famous for her interpretations of works by Gustav Mahler and Edward Elgar. At Aldeburgh in 1962, she sang the role of Polly in Britten's version of *The Beggar's Opera*, and Lucretia in the composer's *The Rape of Lucretia*. She played Kate in a Covent Garden production of Britten's *Owen Wingrave*, and in 1976 premièred Britten's solo cantata *Phaedra*. Janet Baker was created a DBE in 1976. She became a Companion of Honour in 1994.

Alan Bennett has been an actor, director, and broadcaster, and has written for stage, television, radio and film. He has published two prose collections, a novella *The Uncommon Reader* (2007), and *Smut. Two Unseemly Stories* (2011). His plays include *Forty Years On* (1969), *Kafka's Dick* (1987), *The Wind in the Willows* (1991), *The Madness of King George* (1992), *The History Boys* (2004), and, most recently, *People* (2012). His play *The Habit of Art* (2009) centred on a fictional meeting between Britten and W.H. Auden while Britten was composing his opera *Death in Venice*. His work for film includes *A Private Function* (1984), *Prick Up Your Ears* (1987), and *The Madness of King George* (1994), for which he received an Oscar nomination for his screenplay adaptation.

Michael Berkeley was born in 1948, the eldest son of Sir Lennox Berkeley and a godson of Benjamin Britten. He was a chorister at Westminster Cathedral, and then studied at the Royal Academy of Music and later with Richard Rodney Bennett.

While Composer in Association to the BBC National Orchestra of Wales, he wrote three new works including the *Concerto for Orchestra*. In 2008 Berkeley's third opera, *For You*, to a libretto by Ian McEwan, was premiered at the Linbury Theatre, Royal Opera House. Recent works include *Into the Ravine*, written for Nicholas Daniel and the Carducci Quartet, and first performed at the Presteigne Festival in 2012. Berkeley was commissioned to compose the anthem for the Enthronement of the new Archbishop of Canterbury, Justin Welby, on 21st March 2013 in Canterbury Cathedral. In addition to composing, Berkeley presents BBC Radio 3's 'Private Passions'. He was appointed a CBE for services to music in 2012.

Ian Bostridge has appeared at the Salzburg, Edinburgh, Munich, Vienna and Aldeburgh festivals, and had residencies at Het Concertgebouw Amsterdam, the Konzerthaus Vienna, Carnegie Hall New York, the Barbican, Luxembourg Philharmonie and at Wigmore Hall. In opera he has performed the roles of Tamino, Jupiter (*Semele*) and Aschenbach (*Death in Venice*) at ENO, Quint (*The Turn of the Screw*), Don Ottavio (*Don Giovanni*) and Caliban (*The Tempest*) for the Royal Opera, Don Ottavio in Vienna and Tom Rakewell (*The Rake's Progress*) in Munich.

His recordings include Schubert with Graham Johnson, Schumann with Julius Drake (Gramophone Award 1998), *The Turn of the Screw* (Gramophone Award 2003) and *Billy Budd* (Grammy Award 2010). In 2010 he sang the world première of Henze's *Opfergang*. He was created a CBE in the 2004 New Year's Honours.

Philip Brett, who died in 2002, was a conductor and musicologist. He specialised in the study of Tudor music, in particular the work of William Byrd. Brett was the first to observe publicly that the study of Britten's sexuality would provide a significant context for the understanding of Britten's music.

John Bridcut has written *Essential Britten: A Pocket Guide for the Britten Centenary* (Faber & Faber) as well as *Britten's Children* (2006). He has written and directed television documentaries about Elgar, Vaughan Williams and Delius, as well as the film *Britten's Children* and a new film for the Centenary.

Guy Dammann is a music critic for the *Times Literary Supplement* and the *Guardian*. He teaches at the Guildhall School of Music and Drama and is currently editing a volume of essays on music and morality to be published by Oxford University Press in 2014.

Edward Gardner began his tenure as Music Director of English National Opera in May 2007 with a critically acclaimed production of Britten's *Death in Venice*. Under his direction, the ENO has presented a series of stellar productions, including *Damnation of Faust*, *Boris Godunov*, *Der Rosenkavalier*, *Punch and Judy*, *Peter Grimes* and a double bill of *The Rite of Spring* and *Bluebeard's Castle*. In recognition of his talent and commitment, he received the Royal Philharmonic Society Award in 2008 for Best Conductor and in 2009, the Olivier award for Outstanding Achievement in Opera. In June 2012 Gardner was awarded an OBE for Services to Music.

Nicholas Hammond lectures in the French department at the University of Cambridge. He has published widely on seventeenth-century literature, culture and thought. His most recent books include *Gossip, Sexuality and Scandal in France (1610–1715)* (Peter Lang, 2011); as co-editor, *The Cambridge History of French Literature* (Cambridge University Press, 2011); and as editor, Saint-Pavin's *Poésies* (Paris: Classiques Garnier, 2012).

Stephen Hough is one of the most distinctive artists of his generation, Stephen Hough combines a distinguished career as a concert pianist with those of a composer and a writer. A laureate of the MacArthur Fellowship and Royal Philharmonic Society Award, he has played with many of the world greatest orchestras. His catalogue of over fifty CDs has garnered accolades including eight Gramophone Awards and, in 2011, Diapason d'Or de l'Année for his recording of Chopin's Waltzes. As a composer, he has been commissioned by the Wigmore Hall, the Musée du Louvre, musicians of the Berliner Philharmoniker, Westminster Abbey and Westminster Cathedral. He writes a celebrated and widely-read cultural blog for the *Daily Telegraph*

Richard Jarman has had a distinguished career in arts management, with leadership positions at the Edinburgh International Festival, English National Ballet, Scottish Opera and the Royal Opera House. He has also undertaken some high level arts consultancies including for Askonas Holt, The Lowry, The Sage Gateshead and the Cambridge Arts Theatre. In 2002 he became General Director of the Britten-Pears Foundation.

Hans Keller, who died in 1985, was an influential writer on music who became one of Britten's most passionate and insightful advocates. With Donald Mitchell, he edited an important collection of essays about Britten, *Benjamin Britten: A Commentary on His Works from a Group of Specialists* (1952). Keller's other books include *Stravinsky Seen and Heard* (with Milein Cosman, 1982) and *The Great Haydn Quartets: Their Interpretation* (1986).

Nicholas Kenyon has been Managing Director of the Barbican Centre since October 2007. He was a music critic for *The New Yorker*, *The Times* and *Observer*, and editor of *Early Music* between 1983 and 1992. He was appointed Controller of BBC Radio 3 in 1992, and was responsible for the award-winning seasons *Fairest Isle* and *Sounding the Century*. He oversaw the BBC's programming for the Millennium and then ran the BBC's Live Events and TV Classical Music departments. He was Director of the BBC Proms from 1996 to 2007. He has continued to write and lecture on the arts, publishing books on Bach, Mozart, Simon Rattle, the BBC Symphony Orchestra and early music. He is a member of Arts Council England, a board member of Sage Gateshead, and a Trustee of the Dartington Hall Trust. He was knighted in the 2008 New Year Honours; he has been a Visiting Fellow at All Souls College Oxford, and in 2011 he received the British Academy President's Medal for outstanding services to the arts and humanities.

Paul Kildea is a conductor and writer. Born in Australia, he studied piano as an undergraduate at The University of Melbourne and holds a doctorate from Oxford. He was head of music at the Aldeburgh Festival between 1999 and 2002 and subsequently artistic director of the Wigmore Hall in London. His most recent book is *Benjamin Britten: A Life in the Twentieth Century*.

Colin Matthews studied at the Universities of Nottingham and Sussex, and subsequently worked as assistant to Benjamin Britten in the 1970s, and with Imogen Holst. He collaborated with Deryck Cooke for many years on the performing version of Mahler's Tenth Symphony. From 1992–9 he was Associate Composer with the London Symphony Orchestra and from 2001–10 Associate Composer, now Composer Emeritus, with the Hallé. He has in recent years composed works for the Concertgebouw Orchestra, New York Philharmonic, San

Francisco Symphony, City of Birmingham Symphony Orchestra and Leipzig Gewandhaus.

Janette Miller was born in Windsor in 1943. She spent 14 years as a performer in London in ballet, opera and in West End intimate revues and musicals. Her major artistic work was done in Auckland, New Zealand, where she was artistic director of a small serious professional opera/ballet company. The Auckland City Opera and Ballet Company specialized in multi media productions. Her 'Erwartung' Schoenberg and 'Bluebeard's Castle' Bartok were memorable and groundbreaking for the time. Her innovative children's ballet shows, Dance Tales Story Ballets, achieved international theatrical success and were shown on the BBC.

Blake Morrison is a poet, novelist and librettist, probably best known for his two memoirs, *And When Did You Last See Your Father?*, which was made into a film with Jim Broadbent and Colin Firth, and *Things My Mother Never Told Me*. His poetry includes the collection *The Ballad of the Yorkshire Ripper*, and he also published an account of the Bulger murder case, *As If*. He has adapted several plays for the Northern Broadsides theatre company; collaborated with the composer Gavin Bryars on two operas and a song cycle; and published three novels, *The Justification of Johann Gutenberg*, *South of the River* and *The Last Weekend*. He is Professor of Creative Writing at Goldsmiths College.

Peter Parker is the author of *The Old Lie: The Great War and the Public-School Ethos* (1987), biographies of J. R. Ackerley (1989) and Christopher Isherwood (2004), and *The Last Veteran: Harry Patch and the Legacy of War* (2009). He edited (and wrote much of) *A Reader's Guide to the Twentieth-Century Novel* (1995) and *A Reader's Guide to Twentieth-Century Writers* (1996). He was also an associate editor of the *Oxford Dictionary of National Biography* (2004), with responsibility for modern literature, and remains an advisory editor for its regular online updates and the addition of new articles. His edition of G. F. Green's 1952 novel *In the Making* was published as a Penguin Modern Classic in 2012.

Roger Vignoles is one of the foremost piano accompanists of our time, known throughout the musical world for his outstanding interpretations of the song and chamber music repertoire, in company with many of the world's greatest artists, and in a career that has already spanned more than four decades. His lifelong relationship with the music of Britten has included recordings of *The Five Canticles* with Anthony Rolfe Johnson, and of the cycles *Who are these Children?*, *Sechs Hölderlin-Fragmente*, *The Holy Sonnets of John Donne*, and *Winter Words* with Mark Padmore.

Acknowledgements

'The Britten Century' was originally published as 'The Britten Era' in Philip Brett, *Music and Sexuality in Britten: Selected Essays*, ed. George E. Haggerty (University of California Press: California, 2006). Reproduced by permission.

Alan Bennett's introduction to *The Habit of Art* was originally published by Faber and Faber in 2009. Reproduced by kind permission of the author and publisher.

'A Haunting Relationship' was originally published in *The Times* on 10 August 2011. © Hannah Nepil / *The Times* / NI Syndication. Reproduced by permission.

The publishers are grateful to Plumbago Books and the Cosman Keller Art and Music Trust for permission to reproduce '*Gloriana* as Music Drama: a Reaffirmation' and 'Britten's Last Masterpiece', originally published in Hans Keller, *Britten*, ed. Christopher Wintle (Plumbago: London, 2013).